There's Always

the Sea....

Giusy Cecilia Oddo

Translated from the Italian
by Diego Bastianutti
Copyright © 2014

There's Always the Sea...

Originally published as *Il Lungo corridoio*
Longo Editore, Ravenna, Italy
Copyright © 2006 Giusy Cecilia Oddo

All rights reserved.

ISBN-13:
978-1502548948

ISBN-10:
1502548941

To my faithful Sandra, with gratitude Ginny Goldo

february 2015

A Diego, il mio compagno, che mi ha saputo "leggere" così profondamente, e ha curato con tanto amore e impegno questa edizione inglese.

Résistante douceur de cette atmosphère interposée qui a l'étendue de notre vie, et qui est toute la poésie de la mémoire.

M. Proust

The Translator's Notes

In his well-known essay, "Translation: Literature and Literalness," Octavio Paz says that in his opinion no written or spoken text is "original" at all since all language, whatever its form is merely the translation of the non-verbal world: "learning to speak is learning to translate." Thus, to reproduce the original book of Giusy Oddo from Italian into English, I had to mentally recreate whatever non-verbal reality the author had tried to transmute in her original text.

It was a challenge to find a good balance between a readable English text while not straying too far from the original syntax. The style of the author is intentionally impressionistic in her attempt to recreate the sense of a series of emotionally charged still images. The author, however, catches in only apparently static poses the vivid current of reality she has lived. In actual fact she is able to charge each scene, each picture with a degree of energy and emotion which weaves them into the continuity of life. The past, present and future are fused in the existential living instant of the narrator in a bergsonian sense; because life is a matter of time, the bergsonian accretion which imbues and informs each subsequent event, *"the continuous progress of the past which gnaws into the future and which swells as it advances."* And memory is the vehicle of this *"duration."*

I feel honoured to have been the privileged first reader of this work of literature and to have had its translation entrusted to me by its author. Even a superficial first reading of the book will reveal its historical, cultural and psychological depth. Through the emotional intensity which emanates from the reconstruction of a familial and social atmosphere, by interweaving the historical and personal events in a seamless flow, the author is able to give continuity, value and depth to each event, to each experience. Every personal event is in fact a tessera of a larger historical mosaic.

The author does not aspire to encompass the world, nor to explain it. She merely wants to understand the code of the blueprint of her life, so that her ache might become endurable. As the writer herself comments at one point, "it's not the quality of what I have lived, but rather that which I have really felt that gives importance to my memories, to make me what I am now." And yet, the author is often reticent in revealing all the emotions she has really felt over the course of her lifetime, mindful perhaps that everyone is a slave of what one says, and a master of what one leaves unsaid.

  As my translation was taking shape page after page, I felt like a photographer in the red dusk of the darkroom, anxiously awaiting the emergence of the first faint ghosts of images, the slow configuration of a face, of eyes rising up from the developer tray. Ever so slowly I began to distinguish those previously hidden converging lines that tied the work into a meaningful whole. The text has in fact two distinct alternating narrative voices, the growing girl in the past and the woman in the present observing with a degree of detachment, each with her own character; each with her own perspective on the reality described. The girl has the voice and the innocence of her age, while the woman has the voice of the wisdom matured over a long life.

  All is in the backwash of her own memory, and the scenes that line its shores are like markers. Her retracing of moods and emotions is only now possible, now that the pulse is beating more slowly. Midway through the book the reader begins to notice a greater frequency in the alternating voices, until toward the end the two narrative lines converge into a single voice.

  The reader will notice how for well over two thirds of the book the author tends to idealize her reality through romantic literature. By contrast, in the last part the author lives an unfiltered reality whose rough edges are blunted by irony.

  Oddo's prose is exquisitely refined, able to evoke vividly tangible images. It is not merely a generic story of her life, but a pulsating tableau of a period and an ambient, full of insightful observations, and mature and detached judgement. Her intense and compelling emotions are always expressed with reserve. It is a well-balanced work of wisdom, wit and discretion, difficult to put down.

It was a pleasure to translate it and I hope to have done justice to the original Italian.

Diego Bastianutti

There's Always the Sea...

Table of Contents

Chapter One	/ 1
Chapter Two	/ 9
Chapter Three	/ 18
Chapter Four	/ 30
Chapter Five	/ 44
Chapter Six	/ 53
Chapter Seven	/ 70
Chapter Eight	/ 80
Chapter Nine	/ 97
Chapter Ten	/ 108
Chapter Eleven	/ 126
Chapter Twelve	/ 143
Chapter Thirteen	/ 153
Chapter Fourteen	/ 164
Chapter Fifteen	/ 177
Chapter Sixteen	/ 189
Chapter Seventeen	/ 200
Chapter Eighteen	/ 209
Chapter Nineteen	/ 218
Chapter Twenty	/ 226
Chapter Twenty-one	/ 239
Chapter Twenty-two	/ 245
Chapter Twenty-three	/ 256
Chapter Twenty-four	/ 268
Chapter Twenty-five	/ 283
Chapter Twenty-six	/ 296
Epilogue	/ 310

There's Always the Sea...

CHAPTER ONE

The same image keeps reappearing in the warm penumbra of that long corridor that seems to issue from the depths of my memories. The short white piqué skirt, sticking up like a sail, revealing two small bony knees; white booties, their points slightly turned inward, a clear sign of embarrassment; the face of the little girl faintly bent forward, a bit hampered by the dress, a bit by her shyness; a little white purse hangs from her rigidly bent arm, much like Queen Elizabeth.

I search a leitmotiv in the kaleidoscope of images rising up in my conscience, in that blurry dimension between things lived and things imagined.

The shutters, half-closed against the summer sun, kept the hallway darkened. The coolness was added to by the shiny marble tiles of the floor. Perhaps the windows of the villa had been closed in readiness for our return to Milano.

How does one make sense of a life one cannot even remember? Or find justifications behind a hopelessly lost series of events that ebb and flow, following secret impulses of the soul? It just doesn't add up.

The little girl had been dressed up to go and "*visit papà.*" The little purse had been a gift from him. And she was proud to show it off. Inside she had put some candies to bring to him. From what the grownups were saying, papà had been "*in the hospital*" for some time, and she had not seen him anymore. Finally the big event: they would go and visit papà. It was meant to be the last time, as they later explained to me when I became older, but at the last moment he refused to see me. He did not want me to have "*that image*" as a final memory of himself. They told me that they had placed the candies near him. And since I was then already studying the history of Egyptians, secretly happy I imagined him like the pharaohs, comforted by gifts for the long voyage.

How does one grasp the earliest memory, that very first one in which one is conscious of being? The white figure at the end of the darkened hallway? Is this the beginning of the story which has floated to my conscience in the nebula of a life already going on? Or merely the trace of a certain recollection? Our selective memory creates unconsciously the narrative structure of the novel of our life. It discards, conserves, and connects experiences according to an innermost logic. Is it possible to recognize their leitmotif? And the influence of others? The stories of "the grownups" often spurred by the desire to add details to a portrait destined to remain incomplete. Their retelling the events was transformed in me in precise indelible images, even if none of them is part of my own recollection. Crowding in on the stage along with other memories, are words heard spoken, together with period photographs. And the suggestion is so overwhelming that everything merges with the same intensity with the unsolicited recollections I have of life with my father.

It all goes back to my first five years. Memories that might have easily been lost if they could have been overlapped by subsequent ones. My own true memory of papà is that of an exuberant man full of life. I see him as a commanding presence behind the enormous empire style desk in his study of our home in Milano; or marching in the vast anteroom of the apartment in a parody of the Fascist "goose step," as my brother and I amid guffaws attempt to imitate him. He would say that it was a good exercise. I remember how vexed he was by the fact that Ninetto, six years older than me, had been forced to wear the uniform of *il Piccolo Balilla*, the Fascist Party youth group, though his bitterness was assuaged by the fact that I was still too young. Finally I managed to score a point over my brother! The idea made me gloat so much that I didn't really care to understand the real reason behind it. The uniform was so handsome! From then on it became a point of pride to have kept myself *"uncontaminated,"* as my father would say. Such a well-chosen word, as I later understood, must have been dictated by the humiliation he had suffered in being forced to submit to the famous "professors' oath" demanded by the regime in

1931. My uncle, 17-year his senior and for him more a father than a brother, convinced him to think of his family. My brother had just been born, and the price to pay would have been the expulsion from the university.

"*The Sorbonne had offered him a position,*" nonna loved to repeat, drawing out with emphasis that name in which she took pride, in order to dazzle her friends at their five-o'clock tea. But papà didn't think right to abandon Italy in that moment. He had however already left his imprint in France, through the indirect collaboration with Victor Grignard, Nobel Prize for Chemistry in 1912. In his acceptance speech held in Stockholm, Grignard mentioned the name of my father, whose previous discoveries had led Grignard to his own.

The potential alternative to my destiny with a life in France has often whetted my fantasy. Would I have been the same person, or would I have been overwhelmed by the elements that have always made me sensitive not only to the well-known spell of Paris, but to the subtle influences wielded over me by the spirit, the culture, the landscape, simply put by the soul of France? Were there echoes of affinities with my great-great-grandmother, Maman Cécile, *la Baronne* from Aix-en-Provence, or of a previous life? There is no doubt that a fascinating French life appealed much more to my imagination. But everything should have been brought to the more realistic level of how I would have survived the war in France rather than Italy. Supposing that I had been born!

If I think about it, I wonder how I could have gathered so many memories in less than five years, having been conscious for barely two or three. These were also the years when papà had started his long fight against cancer. The psychological perception seems to have stretched the thread of time beyond the possible. Years later, nonna told me that he would open up only with her,

"*I don't know how much longer I'll be able to hold on, Cecilia,*" he would say. "*But don't tell this to Angiola.*"

He was the same age as his mother-in-law, and they were on a first-name basis. My mother was twenty-five years younger than he. They had met in a chemistry class at the university, as professor and student. Her beauty and youth, and the Sicilian origins of papà had been of grave concern for my grandparents when the prospect of marriage was broached. But nonna would tell me all this with a smile, because rather than jealousy he had always shown pride for mamma's success. He wanted her to accompany him to all scientific conventions. She was his assistant.

Coming back from one of these conventions, he had recounted an amusing incident. It seems he had been chatting with a colleague, who had profused himself in praise for the beauty of a certain lady. Papà had let him go on, and then, asked if he knew that lady, deadpan he had replied, "*Certainly, she is my wife,*" enjoying the embarrassment of his colleague.

From every trip he would bring me a gift, one more wonderful than the other. I loved playing with the "Post Office" and the "Grocery Store" that stimulated my natural inclination for order. I would spend hours putting rubber stamps, stamps, and pieces of paper in order, or to distribute a variety of dry beans in tiny drawers. He had also brought me Totò, my inseparable papier-mâché and cloth doll, soft and flexible like a real baby. It was a real drama when, with me always underfoot around papà, it was crushed. It would have been difficult to tell who was more distraught, he or I. It was brought to the "doll hospital," and returned home restored to health.

It seems I caused headaches for my papà even before I was born. Pregnant with me, mamma had developed a craving for *marrons glacés*. Once - so I was told - she had awakened with this terrible craving. I don't know if it was because papà loved to indulge all the whims of mamma's, whom he adored, or so that I would not be born with a nice *marron* on my face, the fact is that he patiently dressed and walked several blocks in the middle of the night to buy them at the famous pastry shop "Miglierina." Apparently even that had not been enough. I was born, in fact, with a strange birthmark in the shape of a *marron glacé*, luckily well out of prying eyes.

My favourite place for building the "doll house" was right under papà's large desk, well enclosed and over the soft

Persian carpet, where I was captivated by the coloured arabesques I traced with my finger. I think it was also a way of making him aware of my presence, while I anxiously waited for when he would take a break from his work and take me up on his knees. This was the moment when I could take possession of the field and explore the vast surface of the desk, grabbing the most curious objects: the little ebony elephants of the inkwell, the bright mineral collection, the scimitar-shaped letter opener. From the filing cabinet next to the desk a stuffed ground hog mesmerized me with its small bright glass eyes. I would beg my papà to tell me once more how he had hunted it in the Russian steppes, where he had been taken during one of his trips for scientific gatherings.

If papà forgot this ritual of ours and made me wait too long, he'd find me sulking; something I easily resorted to, and he would have to *"cut off with the scissors"* my pouting lips. I see myself in a scene with mamma and papà bouncing me across the large matrimonial bed, trying to dispel with laughter my pouting, which was stubbornly going on far too long, perhaps in the hope that the game would last a little longer. And yet I seem to remember more my sulking than the fun, almost as if papà and mamma had hardly noticed my pique.

I don't know when things changed, exactly when the bright lights of receptions, of laughter, of games were turned off; when silence fell in the large apartment, while in the streets the noise of military parades increased. Before I became conscious of it, I was taken away from Milano. The illness must have started to eat into papa's energies. Meanwhile, the world outside was in the grip of another advancing wave of destructive forces. This marked the beginning of the disintegration of my family.

All the more precious to me, then, the fact that I had been able to take part in the way we were "before." To have experienced a "forbidden" era, when the house, alive with an intense social life, had required the presence of maids. I can see again the sombre lions that supported the table and sat majestically at the foot of the sideboards in the dining room. They surely created a striking stage for the games my brother, already engrossed in the adventures of Salgari, dragged me into. Or the austere china cabinet that enchanted me with its delicate figurines and precious porcelains, all the more fascinating because held prisoners and for me inaccessible. Or the dinners beneath the warm light filtering on the table from the fringed red-silk of the wrought-iron chandelier.

Hanging from the centre was the bell my brother and I quarrelled over every time the maid had to be called. I thought there was something magic about the way it made her appear suddenly like a fable elf in white organza pinafore and starched ruffle headband. For her part, mamma's torment was the cook, because she found the songs that reached us from the kitchen worrisome for *"the children's ears."* I found rather funny and bizarre mamma's indignation, usually so kind with the household help. I could not understand why we should have been troubled by songs we found so cheerful. Not even my brother could explain it to me.

For the great occasions, the salon was all a glimmer of crystals and gildings, softened by the velvet of the armchairs and the satin curtains that draped a setting for balls and parties, off limits for me. Still, I could always delight in the tinkling crystal forest of the chandelier that carried me off into Nordic fables, whenever the maid stood on a ladder to clean the hundred teardrops with alcohol-soaked cotton balls. And then there was the mystery of *la camera dei forestieri* (the guests room - 'foreigners') off limits as well for the children. For me it was a scary place I stayed away from because it was always dark, and I imagined it destined for strange visitors from far away countries.

I can still see mamma in her beautiful long gowns, ready for evenings at "La Scala," where papà rented a box for the season. All of mamma's dresses were made to order for her by Mrs. Scappardini (that name filled my mouth), "the best seamstress in Milano." She would come to our house and would unroll to my wide-open eyes cascades of silks and velvets worthy of the princesses I read about. And Mrs. Scappardini was a fairy godmother who wove those fabrics for mamma with her own hands. One day she came and surprised me with a sailor suit for my doll. I was on cloud nine.

Among all others, though, there is one scene that keeps creeping in, like a gash in a beautiful picture book. It has the bronzed sombre colour of the dining room, and of the reddish glows diffused by the chandelier. The high French door is open to the balcony in a dark summer evening, letting in a stifling muggy air. On a leather chair against the wall, I see mamma crying. At the other end of the room stands papà furious. There is an implied menace in his vehement rebuke against mamma. I don't know how I happened to catch them in this situation. Perhaps I had slipped out of bed when the rage of his voice woke me. I can't even remember their reaction upon seeing me there, if they even saw me. Anyway, I would not have cared if I was punished. I recall only my terror and dismay in seeing mamma weeping desperately. It was the first time I had seen mamma sobbing. For several nights afterward I had nightmares of papà, tired of mamma, who wanted to throw her down from the balcony.

For a very long time I racked my mind trying to understand how papà could have gotten so angry to make mamma cry, mamma, so sweet and gentle. Years later something nonna said reminded me of the scene, and helped to put it in a less tragic context,

"Your papà had a fiery character; he was like a match, quick to flare up and just as quick to burn out."

Besides, for many years I was struck by the "adult matters" I could not understand. Words caught without their being aware, and then when they did notice me, they would be embarrassed and refuse to explain anything to me. I was racked by curiosity but, knowing I could not satisfy it, I had found a way to ease it for the time being. I would immediately force myself to memorize the words and facts, certain that the day would come when I'd grow up and they would reveal their secret. I knew how to wait! And I did everything I could to remember, almost with a passion, because it was my secret weapon against the adults who excluded me from their world. Still, I think I forgot all of them

The grown-ups must have gone to great lengths to ensure that even the death of papà would not touch my childhood. The knowledge, nevertheless, came as usual from above, while they were whispering with friends met on the street. They were gathered in a tight circle, in a small town square. I have no idea where. I caught nods made in my direction. As usual, they thought that down there in that forest of legs (I can't remember anything else in fact, not even who they were) I could not hear or understand. In fact, I was not even five at the time. That's how I overheard that papà had died.

I did not ask any questions, as if I wanted to respect their secret. I was not even sure what it really meant. Only a vague sensation that I would not see him anymore. I had not seen him for so long already. He had spent months in the hospital, of which I have no recollection. I understood in a confused way, and so also I accepted it, as if I knew that nothing could have changed the situation. The presence of papà in my life had dissolved just like another magic mystery, and there was no bell that would bring him back. For a long time his disappearance continued to be something vague that had settled in my subconscious. When I became completely conscious of it, it was already an event that had taken place such a long time ago.

Years later I saw some large photos of papa's funeral among our family records. I was long held spellbound by that anachronistic black carriage pulled by six black horses, with absurd black plumes on their heads. These were signs of the important official burial services accorded to him, in spite of the fact that it was wartime, and of his well-known troublesome anti-fascist feelings. But to me that black carriage seemed but a dark parody of Cinderella, where at the crucial moment, everything disappears.

CHAPTER TWO

Ten at most were the "happy" years granted to my parents. They had married in 1930. I shared their last four. I wonder if they knew they were living their best years. Usually we realize that when we look back, but they did not have the time, together, to consider their past. Living as they did in the shadow of Fascism, their happiness had to be darkened by the threat of events of that period. Nonetheless, those were still their glorious years. They were the years of my father's intense scientific activity, of trips around the world, with his heavy leather suitcases covered with labels of Grand Hotels. I fantasized over those labels, whose palms, columns, and exotic architectures stirred in me images of fabulous lands.

These were the years when they vacationed in Sicily, home of my paternal ancestors. Our family name tells us we originated in Germany, probably coming to Sicily with the retinue of Frederick II, and settling in the rocky terrain of the Madonie Mountains. The Germanic etymology of the name is in fact *audha*, "wealth and power", such as for the names "Otto" and "Ottone".

In old photos, the vast terrace of the house is outlined against the Rock which, like a mythical bird, stretches out its beak and wings over the town below bearing its name - Caltavuturo, the Vulture's Castle. Against this background of rocks and prickly pears, appears the gentle and somewhat out of place face of my mother.

I have never been able to fit this delicate image of her as wife and mother with that of her as a young girl in Piemonte, appearing in older photos equipped with ice axe and boots with crampons, together with her older sister, for me "zia Mariuccia," better known as *zia Mariù,* and their daredevil brother, zio Marco, who would lead them in climbs over alpine glaciers. There is a story told of zia Mariuccia always ready to liven up the group of friends with her dash of madness. It seems that, while the roped party had been climbing, she had mentioned how much fun it would be to feel the thrill of falling in a crevasse. She had barely laughed a daring, "*A la sarìa pròpi bela!*" (It'd be really something!), when, turning to warn her not to joke about such things, zio Marco did not see her anywhere. From deep in the cavern where she had fallen, her last words were still echoing. Dangling in the void, she was yelling, "*Tireme sù!*" (Pull me up*!*), while, true to form, her brother made her beg for a while.

The family album shows other photos of fun picnics, groups of carefree friends, in which mamma stands out for her reserved beauty, and where zia Mariù dominates the scene with her playful antics, winking from beneath a funny parasol. One can just guess the jokes and laughter around the tablecloths spread out on the grass. In more recent photos taken amid the harsh beauty of their beloved Gaby, a most favoured mountain resort, my father can be seen among the group of their usual friends. Mamma's face reveals a sense of new awareness. More reserved and aloof, she appears to accept already the new life that awaits her. Her life will in fact take a turn that will make her the mother I remember.

From then on, with papà around, the setting for their vacations would become the great hotels at Gressoney or at Mules. I appear in Tyrolean dresses. I remember Mules as a fairy tale. Nestled among fir trees and ferns, I still see little houses of burnt honey-coloured wood, with red geranium-potted balconies. I imagined elves and gnomes living there. There was even a witch in the castle-like hotel where we were staying - the old marchioness, who was the dread of the staff. Her haughty presence, her imposing bulk that swayed amid black velvets, plus the Teutonic accent radiated a mysterious power that seemed to intimidate everyone.

I remember the first time I saw her vast form on the threshold of the wide glass doors that opened unto the garden. On a long leash she held an equally annoying and equally black lapdog, which ran riot around her. Just then, I dropped my red ball and I froze, watching both fascinated and frightened. With a sudden tug, the lapdog broke loose from the marchioness's claws to chase my ball, and in an instant a pandemonium broke out. The hysterical cries of the owner launched the entire staff after the dog, while I sought refuge in the arms of my governess. From that day, no shelter could protect me from that frightening being; when her cane swung to the rhythm of her ponderous tread, I thought it pointed at me, and I felt immediately guilty.

Up until that day, I had taken my meals with the adults in the large dining salon. The evening after, I found myself confined to the kitchen with my governess: the marchioness had expressed her disapproval of children in the dining salon. Yet in spite of her, my exile did not last long. My presence was missed, and the announcement of my banishment provoked the indignant reaction of the other guests. In short, it seems that I was re-admitted in the company of adults, *vox populi*.

Our stays in the mountains alternated with those by the seashore, which for us meant Loano, on the Ligurian Riviera. In those days it was a sophisticated summer resort town, set between the sea and the rare villas on the facing hills. The tone of seaside strolls was set by the pretentious Liberty-style Lidos in characteristically ochre-yellow colour, and the beautiful palmed boulevard, among which stood in stark contrast, the regional pride: two bare lanky palms, the tallest in Italy. To me they looked like they were touching the sky, and I imagined them as two whimsical sisters sharing secrets as they swayed their heads in the wind. Just like *le ziette* (the aunties), who once in a while would join the social set of Loano, dragging even me in a lively whirlwind of fun and play. *Le ziette* were two unmarried sisters who lived together and were just the opposite of what adults defined as "spinsters": always cheerful and smiling, ready to help others, they especially loved to look after their friends' children, gathering them under their wings to the parents' great joy. And so they became the quintessential *"ziette."*

Their sudden appearance in Loano constituted a major event for me. It was as if the ring of parental control and discipline that surrounded me was loosened, and I could feel a rare sense of freedom. Suddenly, I was allowed even things usually forbidden. The noisy chatter of the adults on the beach of the Doria Lido was enlivened by the *ziette*'s gaiety, and my attention was now riveted on them.

Our friends, gathered around the deckchairs and folding chairs, were spilling beyond the boundaries marked by the two beach umbrellas we usually occupied. The photos of that period will be the last ones to show my mother luminous and blossoming in the shade of wide-brim hats. She appears on the beach or on a rowboat, with me tethered close to her. She was beautiful even in the large bathing suits of the 1930s that covered half her legs and rose up the neckline, finishing in two wide straps that looked like a prizefighter tee-shirt.

The *ziette* were the sisters of Mrs. Baldoni, mamma's best friend. In fact, the Baldonis had always been great friends of our family. We even spent our vacations in Loano together with them. My father and Professor Baldoni, his friend and university colleague, would join us on weekends. Mrs. Baldoni was older than mamma, and her children were already grown. The youngest and my brother were the same age, and were inseparable playmates and school friends. The other two children were some ten-years older, and I considered them clearly part of that mysterious world of adults which intimidated me most of the time. They would bend down to my level to amuse themselves with me, well aware of my confusion. In fact, I'm still not able to explain that indefinable something I felt setting them off from me. Even the passing of time has not allowed me to break it down.

And yet, throughout my life the Baldonis have remained an invaluable presence, more like an "institution." They represented a solid continuity in the void and instability felt when my brother and I were orphaned. Theirs and ours were definitely two different worlds, separated by the ever increasing gap in our respective economic conditions. Nonetheless, they watched and protected us from afar, ever aware of our needs.

With the passage of time, Mrs. Baldoni became a very special image for me; a soft full-bodied presence that cushioned the blows in our lives, almost as if that warm body of hers would absorb them. I remember her leaden forceful stride that created a strange sighing of thighs. Her vigour was later reduced by the advancing years. I still remember with tenderness the soft folds of her flaccid face, in contrast with the youthful milky freshness of her skin, unblemished even in old age. Her violet-veined lips stood out on her face. She was indeed a rare presence for me, an object of feelings mixed with awe and hearty fondness, that in time became an ever more deeply felt admiration.

Oddly full purple lips, protruding between hanging cheeks, distinguished her husband as well, in a strange twinning with his wife. He was older than her and not handsome. In my childish imagination, he was King Toad and she Beauty united to him by love. *"Professor Baldoni"* - as he was always referred to - disappeared from my life shortly after my parents died. *"La Signora Baldoni,"* with her firm, strong, heavy footstep, remained to follow my progress, with that typical bold efficiency, that decisive approach that expressed her Milanese roots.

As a child, it was probably that brisk practical sense of hers, conceding no dilly-dallying, which intimidated me, and made me unable to accept that motherly love which I would later desperately seek. And so for years she remained only "Mrs. Baldoni" for me, incapable as I was to feel and to transform her into *"zia Maria,"* as she would have so wanted.

Meanwhile, the photos of those long-gone summers at the Doria Lido show me among the Baldonis as a frisky lamb. At times in these photos I can be seen sitting high up in the arms of the eldest son Vanni. Raised over his lanky body, I still remember the strange effect of finding myself face to face with two impenetrable thick dark lenses, as round as owlish eyes. I look like a scared sparrow perched on top of a crane. The grownups never understood my shyness. And yet I know I was not a child easily scared. In fact, I was never happier than when I could escape everyone's attention and slip quietly in the sea, lying on a cork lifesaver, floating up and down on waves that carried me far. Inevitable was the panic of the grownups when they could not find me anymore. And so, I was given a "body guard" - Pedro, the Baldonis' factotum:

There's Always the Sea...

lifeguard at the seaside resort and chauffeur in the city. One day though, I managed to escape even his guard, and I watched amused and relieved how the grownups meted out their anxiety and rebuke on him instead of me.

Maybe it was that "something" extra in the Baldonis' entourage which gave them a different status with respect to my family, and made me feel ill at ease. As the presence of Pedro, who had literally become my shadow, a dour man of few words, almost always incomprehensible to me. Only years later, when I was old enough, his story of political refugee from the civil war in Spain explained what I had not understood before. For now, in Milano he was just a dark figure, a worthy pair with the black sedan, which swallowed me up whenever I went to the Baldonis. I can still feel the shivering cold touch of the stiff leather seats. I was at the mercy of Pedro, more stiff and dark than ever in his uniform and cap. After settling me in the rear seat, he would grasp the steering wheel and whisk me away.

At four years of age, I couldn't yet appreciate this personal door-to-door service. It felt more worthy of a postal package than of a great lady. I had much more fun in Milano's rattling trams which seemed like toys to me, or in the green and black taxis that darted to you at a mere wave of the hand. I couldn't for the life of me understand why Pedro would suddenly lose his name to take on that strange nickname of *chauffeur*. It seemed to be a habit of the Baldonis to tag everyone with the most unpredictable names. Even their own children had been transformed in the very original trio of Vanni, Lalla, and Mirko. They were unusual and affected sounds for my then elementary sensibility. Later, as I grew up, I discovered that it was part of the artificiality typical of the Milanese onomasticon. I never stopped being irritated by the effect of this custom, except for those three who became among the dearest persons for me. The sound of their names became ever more familiar and bound in my love.

What bothered me however was that I became victim of it as well. I don't know how, I don't know when, but one day I woke up and I was *Dudi*. That sound jarred in my ears. It was as if the name had changed me into a strange little animal.   Not that I particularly cared for the name Giuseppina, in fact I've always hated it. I couldn't identify with it. One day I decided to rebel and to stop answering when they called me. The battle was lost and I paid dearly. Afterward, in vain I begged mamma to call me Nicoletta. After all it was my saint's day. I felt that with such a name I could be whimsical and a bit naughty. Just as, as an adolescent, I had wanted to have curly hair. Instead I was stuck with strong straight Southern hair that fell on either side of my face, emphasizing that boring oval like a "*little pierced Madonna,*" according to the then popular expression. I dreamed of being a femme fatale with an intense look, but how could I, branded as I was by that pet name of Dudi?

Merely snobberies of the time! I wasn't then yet aware of them, although there was already something discordant to my ears, because I remember feeling all the possible indignation of my four years of age, when this type of language tampered even with words for me already linguistically well codified.

It happens that from birth I was so afflicted by a particular physiological condition that I remember myself sitting on the potty for a long part of my childhood. The one advantage of this condition was that the remedy I was given was *mannite,* which I found delicious. Just thinking about it, I can still feel the sweet velvety sensation of those white rectangles of frothy stuff. When later I learned of the biblical tale of the Jews saved from starvation in the desert by a rain of delicious manna, I immediately saw it as my *mannite*, and with my mouth watering, I imagined the lucky Jews, their noses up in the air as soft flakes of *mannite* are falling. Strangely enough though, I never asked myself how they dealt with the effects of a *mannite* feast in the desert.

Needless to say, this condition of mine forced me to spend a great deal of "sitting time" at the Baldonis, where I was a regular guest. On those sad occasions, I was cloistered in the washrooms area, at the end of a long series of dark hallways in their huge apartment in Milano. Feeling pity for my distress, they'd let the various doors open, so they could really check on me.   In fact, every few minutes Mrs. Baldoni's voice would reach me, "*Dudi, have you gone 'pupù'?"* This was too much. It was like the scraping of a nail on a blackboard. As far as I was concerned, one had to call a spade a spade. What in the world were these ridiculous fancy words? And when I got back home, I would pour out my indignation to mamma: "*Why does Mrs. Baldoni always say 'pu-pù'?*" - I would burst out, pronouncing the word with contempt while turning up my nose , "*It's supposed to be 'popò.*" And so my first democratic battle was fought in defence of *popò*, against *pupù*. I felt like the ugly duckling not allowed to freely splash in the world of swans.

I was a young rebel with a lot to learn. Time would teach me why my parents considered the Baldonis their best friends, in spite of some fundamental differences of values. Their rather innocent snobbishness was a charming gloss that masked the much healthier and honest nature of Lombards, full of kindness and generosity. But then, even my family suffered a kind of snobbism, the intellectual kind. My father approved only money earned with the sweat of one's own intellectual and professional brow. We were raised to disdain any form of commerce and speculation. The innate practical sense of the Baldonis clashed therefore with the speculative tendencies of my father, typical of his southern mind frame. He was bewildered to note that Professor Baldoni had given up his scientific research in favour of profitable investments in his pharmaceutical discoveries, which he produced in homemade laboratories. Profits that had already made him owner of an entire city block of apartment buildings in the centre of Milano.

They were *Signori Baldoni*, not simply *the Baldonis*, and that's the way they would always remain for me, with the eccentric names for their children; with the huge apartment with a never-ending series of hallways which intimidated and fascinated me with its mysterious treasures, always kept in the shadows of the half-drawn shutters; with the annex for the domestic help, at whose entrance hung a small chalkboard with the duties for each day of the week clearly written: "Wednesday, the young master's bedroom." Ostentations of upper-class breeding that were underlined by a "u". Most probably the difference between them and us consisted precisely in the difference between *popò* and *pupù!*

In Loano the Baldonis stayed at the Hotel Vittoria overlooking the sea, with its tall neoclassical columns. Inside, the pomp of the enormous chandeliers descended from stucco ceilings in fresco-decorated salons.

The days were spent between the beach and the gaming rooms of the luxurious Doria Lido. At sunset, we strolled along the promenade in the refreshing evening breeze. For me it meant walking in a forest of grownups' legs, with their chatting taking place above my head. I trotted alongside them with an ice-cream cone in hand. I had developed an expert licking technique which allowed the ice-cream to last me for almost the entire promenade. After having licked it to the last drop, I had to throw the cone away, because papà considered it heavy on the digestion. I obeyed, though I thought it was a great injustice. At times I got tired and bored, and my feet reacted by turning inward. Without fail, a slap, meant to straighten them up, would be quickly delivered. And finally, even this part of the day would come to an end, and I could go back to "my" Loano.

CHAPTER THREE

Right after the last lidos along the sea walk, the road turned away from the coast, reaching beyond the picturesque houses and narrow lanes of the historical centre, and started uphill losing itself in the verdant woods. There, out of nowhere, you'd come across the arched Roman bridge over the stream, inevitably marked midway through by a Christian shrine. Beyond the bridge, blending with the green woods and the sound of fresh water coursing over stones, stood the aged ochre of the Doria Family Tower, whose typical shape, replicated in all the modern villas, gives Liguria its traditional trait, last trace of the glorious past of the Dorias.

On this side of the bridge stands the squarish rose-coloured Villa Perelli, partly hidden by a stone-based black wrought-iron railing surrounding it. Little by little Loano's other face, the sunny and noisy marine, dies away and Villa Perelli becomes the centre of my life. It was the "*seaside villa*" papà had rented for us all year round. Yet few are my memories of him there, and even mamma soon disappeared to be with him, already ill in Milano. Both were pulled away from me by forces that were then still a mystery for me, that suddenly changed everything, and to which I had to submit without appeal.

It marked the end of our halcyon days in Loano. Ninetto and I remained there with nonni, our grandparents, who had come on purpose from Milan to take care of us. Hushed voices and homey smells from nonna's cooking surrounded me in a world made more to my measure, in which I felt a protagonist once more. Villa Perelli is the theatre of the most vivid memories of my first years of life. I still see that green-hued postcard in which the Villa was immortalized with a bed sheet spread out in the sun on a window sill. I was so proud that it had been chosen to represent Loano. But I remember how disappointed mamma was to notice that the picture card showed that homey and private touch. *"They could have warned us,"* she would complain with a note of regret. Yet for me, that bed sheet remained forever emblematic of that childhood nest, the last one to see all my family together. All sensations and memories which remained associated for me together with the perfume of the Ligurian yellow peaches, growing large and velvety in the orchard behind the villa. I would spend hours on end playing alone among the rows of peach trees, making up stories and adventures for my inanimate friends.

My favourite corner, however, was that of the stone vats for the laundry, where I would splash in the water and where the mishap of the goldfish occurred. He was a nicely plump, bright red and smooth plastic fish. I just loved squeezing him under water and seeing him dart as if alive. As far as I was concerned, he definitely had a soul, and I talked to him and took him everywhere with me. It so happened that one day the plug at the bottom of the vat came loose and in a flash my fish was caught in the whirlpool and sucked down the drain. As usual my tears and drama found their way to nonna's bosom - strong, experienced, and full of resources, she could fix anything and solve any problem. Taken stock of the situation, with the skill of a hydraulic engineer she found the outlet of the water drainage in the moat behind the house. We could still save the day.

We reached the drainage pipe coming out of the garden's retaining wall, and there, flashing among the green grass, exultantly I spied a shining bit of red. While focusing on the green, however, it slowly took the shape of two huge stock-still toads staring at us with their bulging eyes. We stared back with our eyes popping out at these ungainly slimy twins of ugly oozing forms blocking the drainage pipe; not only, but my goldfish had landed smack against their backs. Our undertaking had come to an end, it was indeed hopeless. Against those repulsive monsters, surely even my nonna would be helpless. Instead, I saw her gather her wits, bend down and pluck the little fish off the horrid barrier. From that day on, she was my absolute heroine during my entire childhood. Her heroism was confirmed under the harshest realities when, already in her sixties and after having lost in a brief span of time her daughter and her own husband, she raised my brother and me throughout the dangerous war years and the poverty of the postwar period.

Loano was not without some fears for me. A few villas away from ours was the residence of the "enemy" - Villa Zanoni. My brother always took me there with him because he was friends with the four rascals who lived in it. I could never convince anyone what holy terror they were for me. I can still see myself in fear of that wild Zanoni foursome chasing me, as I try to hide amid the junk of the garage to escape their pranks. My brother would finally appear as if a knight errant to save me. Had they planned the whole thing? They never really did anything to me; just the same my fear was very real. The grownups never could understand these things.

With fall approaching, Nino had to go back to Milano to start school, and I was in peace. The summer outings were over as well, too tiring for my small legs. Outings like the one to the Shrine of Santa Libera destined to go down in the family annals because of something I did.

We had started off in the early morning hours to avoid the heat of the day. We were supposed to reach this famous Shrine in time for the midday lunch. The sun was already overhead and we were still struggling up a dusty mountain trail, curving this way and that with no end in sight. Perspiring, exhausted, and hungry the grownups began to think they had taken the wrong path when, right around a curve, a small chapel appeared. The sense of relief was very short-lived because it obviously was not the anticipated Shrine. Nonetheless, we sought shelter in the coolness of its walls. A short while later, everyone but I was ready to continue the climb. My strength was completely drained, and I couldn't for the life of me understand why they should want to leave that welcomed oasis, even if of little interest, for a place that maybe didn't even exist. My dismay and my hunger made me blurt out, "*Let's make this Santa Libera!*" A rather simple and natural solution to my way of thinking, but my proposal fell among the general laughter. This confirmed my opinion that adults are generally absurd and without any imagination.

I have no recollection of the Shrine of Santa Libera, if we ever found it, but my remark went down in history, and became part of the "family lexicon" as an invitation to give up impossible dreams and settle for what life has to offer.

I had the most wonderful time when I remained alone with my grandparents in Loano. The three of us would play card games at the large round dining table in the evenings. I can still feel the rough touch of the dark flowered cover that reflected the warm light of the chandelier, a cocoon of light in the penumbra of the room. We would play *Omino Nero*. After three Jacks had been taken out, leaving only the Jack of spades, the *Omino Nero,* the deck of cards was distributed. Everyone in turn had to fish a covered card from his neighbour; if one achieved a pair, these were discarded. Whoever reached the end of the game holding only the Jack of spades had to submit to some form of penance. We would urge each other to choose the O*mino Nero* rather than another card, sometimes bluffing, and relishing their indecision; and then enjoying seeing our victim fall into the trap. The nonni never failed to make me cheer their wrong choices. It was probably this exciting introduction of the world of cards to a four-year old that explains why they fascinated me all my life.

Then there were the rides on the crossbar of nonno's bicycle. Tall, wiry, and retiring nonno's contemplative calm contrasted the energetic and chatty character of nonna. Besides his passion for horses, which led him to the Pinerolo Cavalry Academy, nonno loved fishing. I think this was an excuse to withdraw from the distractions of the world and indulge in his interior monologue and meditation.

With his "toothbrush" moustache and a thick mop of silvery hair clipped short in "King Umberto" style, he cut a fascinating figure of times gone by, who had not lost his aristocratic dignity as he passed from the saddle on his horse to that on his bicycle. We'd run precariously on stony paths, and our only safety measure was a weird backpedalling to slow down our ride. I can't remember the effect of that type of mechanism in case we had to brake suddenly. But it must have worked well enough, because I don't recall ever having been thrown. We'd often ride on the road to Pietraligure, famous then for its factory of quince marmalade, called *cotognata*, made into small prune-colour cubes of sweet rubbery gelatine. For us the area was instead infamous for the unbelievably foul smell the factory produced which polluted the entire area. *"Get ready to hold your breath! Hold on tight!"* Shouted nonno, as he pressed hard on the pedals taking us to safety, both of us holding our noses. By the time we were out of danger, we couldn't even laugh, we were so out of breath.

Together the two of us spent glorious days in secluded areas in the woods, along a stream where nonno would initiate his elaborate fishing ritual. Many years later, in preparing for my university examination during the summer in nonna's country house, I loved going through the woods looking for the ideal spot where to read and study - an out of the way grassy clearing, along a stream. Perhaps I was merely following the deep trace left in me by my experiences with nonno.

When nonno finally cast the fishing line in the middle of the stream and settled down to the waiting game, I set myself to listen to his fascinating stories. My imagination ran riot around the adventures of Zebri, the beloved horse that had accompanied nonno throughout his military career as a cavalry officer, up to and including the battle of Caporetto in World War I, where even this faithful companion that had saved his life on several occasions could do nothing to stave off the general defeat. With a bullet in his lung, nonno fell prisoner to the Austrians.

The exploits of Zebri alternated with the bungling of his orderly. During the war he, *l'attendente,* had to attend to nonno's personal needs, such as mending his socks. Having no practical knowledge of homemaking, when faced with a large hole, he would pass the thread all around its perimeter and then pull tight. This resulted not only in a shortening of the sock, but also in a number of knots around the heel which, according to nonno, created a rather unfortunate sensation inside his boots.

His passion for horses and his love for Zebri led him to take a degree in veterinary medicine. Nevertheless, he hardly made use of it in peacetime, pharmacy being his real profession. Still, he always practiced it more than a certain colleague of his who, in the centre of Milano, had a sign on the door of his veterinary clinic claiming: "Specialized in Camel Diseases." He had taken his degree during Italy's Africa campaign.

Nonna was usually quite frustrated with nonno because he was a total loss when it came to helping around the house, inclined as he was to philosophy and abstract dreaming. The poor woman would complain that whenever anything broke in the house, nonno had only one way of fixing it, putting a sticking plaster on it. In fact, I seem to recall a lampshade showing off its beautiful shape of green glass decorated with small pink patches. It survived nonno, and nonna would later show it off with ill-concealed quiet pleasure, filled with regret. To tell the truth, they were two diametrically opposed characters, who clashed quite frequently. In the last years of his life nonno had become a venerated figure in the town where we had evacuated from Milano during the war. They called him "the Saint." As I grew older, I've often asked myself if that was due to his religious devotion, to that mystical aura that surrounded him, or to the patient kindness with which he endured the authoritarian, critical, and quarrelsome character of nonna. And yet, I know they loved each other.

I can still see him in his white lab coat, behind the counter of the town's pharmacy, where he had taken over for the young pharmacists drafted in time of war. His calm erect bearing inspired a type of otherworldly serenity. I could hardly reconcile that image with the tales of his being tormented his entire life by nonna's distressing jealousy. But it was easy to understand it if you saw photos of him as a young man in his officer uniform on horseback, so handsome and compelling for that subtle contrast between the military guise and the hint of melancholy in his large grey eyes, fixed on a far-off invisible horizon.

As an adult, I began to understand the drama of nonna as well, a victim of her own character that alienated the affection of her family, which she desperately cried out for. And yet she always gave generously of herself to others, ready to do anything, even when not asked, unfortunately. Her extraordinary drive enabled her to face any challenge or adversity. One such challenge was when, amid the difficulties of raising three children during the World War I, compounded with having her husband prisoner of war, she took a basic training course to enable her to keep her husband's pharmacy operating. She was one of thousands of women who rolled up their sleeves in the absence of men, and showed themselves capable of keeping the ship afloat.

However, the nonna of my childhood memories was the one of Loano, always willing to spoil me, and I quite eager to take advantage of her, as she would later recount. She would tell me how at night, just when I should have gone to bed, I always managed to appeal to her for one final whim:

"I bet you are so good that you'll make me a glass of lemon water and sugar."

It was my favourite drink, but I think that what was at stake, more than thirst or yen for it, was my need to prevail one last time on her love. This unforgettable ritual started at the beginning of my life and concluded at the end of hers, when from Milano I would go and visit her in her countryside retreat in Cunardo. In the evening, before retiring, she loved taking a camomile tea. And so, with a knowing smile she would say,

"And I bet you are so good that you'll make me a camomile tea with a lemon peel."

The interiors of Villa Perelli seemed to acquire a soul especially in the evening. During the day it was kept in the silent penumbra of rooms with shuttered windows against the fierceness of the sun. As evening shadows fell upon our day outdoors, it seemed to come alive. The electric lights brought to life the dining table as we busied ourselves for dinner. The mild long summer evenings were drawn out with the nonni taking their coffee as they sat on the kitchen steps facing the garden. Much to my regret, this sometimes was followed by a stroll around the house, while I impatiently waited for the last ritual, a game of *Omino Nero*.

My day ended before the grownups', but I didn't mind. I liked to tuck myself away in the comfort of my bed, over which, just like the curtain at the end of a play, the pure white gauze netting was dropped to wrap me as if in a magic cocoon. Then, for my last and very personal ritual, out of habit, I would automatically bring my left thumb to my mouth, while my right hand reached the lace of the pillow case, delicately rubbing it between two fingers, enjoying its coarse touch. I would then fall into a safe and untroubled sleep. The dreams I had then were not yet scary. These were the years of innocence, in which we accept everything with absolute naturalness, pleasures and pains, just like animals petted and beaten. Just so, until we learn the tragic possibility of asking ourselves, "Why?" It's then that we too bite into the poisoned apple. That's when the monsters are given a face - illness, death - and we learn to fear them.

They had shaved my hair off, and every night before tucking me into bed, nonna would put an ointment over the rash which had spread over my head and face. She then would wrap me in a tight nightcap, with only eyes, nose, and little else visible. Finally, to prevent the urge to scratch myself during the night, she'd encase my hands in a pair of thick white cotton gloves. I had been attacked by a form of eczema, and every night I had to submit to this uncomfortable ritual. Nevertheless, I had quickly accepted it as a necessary part of my daily routine, thanks also to the loving care nonna showered me with. Only much later, discovering myself grown with a small bald spot in my otherwise thick mane, I became conscious of having been a victim of sort in my childhood. That strange word - "eczema," remained impressed in my childish imagination with a sense of dismay; it became one of the obscure threats that imperil our life.

The kitchen was the only room bustling with light, noise, and movement throughout the day. You could hear the cheerful clashing of saucepans and dishes as nonna went about producing her delicious meals. I learned to appreciate the Piedmontese cuisine even before I could pronounce the names of the various dishes. Whenever nonna would ask me what I wanted for lunch, my immediate answer was *"otto e ella,"* which stood for *risotto e cervella* - risotto and calf's brain. I continued to call it *otto e ella* even after I had learned to talk. Piedmont's famous variety of croquettes, *fritto misto*, has remained for me the all-time favourite, blissfully unaware of such a thing as cholesterol. The golden aroma of calf's brain, artichokes, potatoes, cauliflowers, all manner of rice, and even sweet croquettes was imprinted on my subconscious. That aroma was to re-emerge in me my whole life long to awaken Proustian-like, warm childhood memories.

The cheerfulness of the kitchen drew even nonno. He usually insisted on putting to the test his scarce mechanical aptitude by busying himself with contraptions of his own devise. I moved between the two of them, watching their goings-on. On one particular day, nonna was nimbly turning out a whole series of small potatoes croquettes, piling a golden fragrant mountain of them on the serving dish, which I was devouring with my eyes. In spite of this, my attention was also drawn to a strange gadget taking shape in nonno's hands: he was struggling to attach something like prongs to a stick. I waited for the most opportune moment to ask him what it was, and he promptly answered,

"Why, it's a double fork to serve myself potatoes croquettes. With this I can take two or three at a time."

The dismay of my four years must have been clearly painted on my face, as I considered I could never win against such a massive assault. Nonna didn't let me agonize for too long before revealing that the object was of course one of those impossible contraptions nonno invented for his fishing.

As the season came to an end, so did the days we spent outdoors. Always fewer were the bicycle rides nonno would take me on. Before going out for his errands, he would pad himself with newspapers under his shirt. We spent a cold winter, huddled in our insufficiently heated empty villa. It was the winter of 1940. Even my grandparents' conversations seemed more subdued, with mysterious undertones which left me disquieted. We would sit on the balcony to watch the sunset and the fading autumn colours on the hills. Every time our eyes would fall upon a distant outline, a shapeless bluish mass emerging among the vegetation: "Villa Morfeo." For a long time, mamma had referred to it as *"The villa that Bernardo wants to buy."* As the trees became bare now, the villa revealed its round turreted façade, which seemed to have a sly smile. The bitter and melancholic voice of nonna now mentioned it as *"the villa that Bernardo <u>wanted</u> to buy."* I never saw it up close. It became for everyone part of the world of myths and dreams, as its very name seemed to suggest. The ever sleepier face lost in the enchantment of Morpheus.

Unexpectedly, the pall of our days was shattered by the arrival of zio Marco. He had come to introduce his new bride. It was a hurried war-time wedding, before he left for the Albanian campaign. And that's how zia Ida came into my life. I immediately loved her youthful sweet maternal presence. As for my uncle, I always had ambivalent feelings towards him. Like everyone, I too fell under the spell of his extraordinary *élan vital*. I would buzz around him like a moth around a flame, however intimidated by his reckless and exciting impetuousness. And he did indeed constantly tease me, as if I were an amusing toy of which he never grew tired.

Once more, we started to go on outings and picnics in meadows. Now we saw the sunset from Monte Carmelo, where the great baroque bulk of the Shrine with its imposing ochre cupola dominated Loano down below. We'd take our daily evening stroll, picking wild blackberries or enjoying an ice cream, cone and all. When I was with my uncle, I was constantly picked up and set in the most dangerous places: on the top of a rock or a dizzy narrow column. Once he had me in a satisfactory pose, he would take a photo or have me recite some nursery rhyme. My aunt tried to shield me, but she rarely managed to dissuade him from his wild ideas, the riskier they were the more they amused him. They were according to him a necessary training for life, and maybe he was right. There is a photo he took of me perched on a tall pedestal barely wide enough for my feet. In the photo I appear to be swaying dangerously, like a frightened bird about to fly off, and stretched toward me the protective arm of zia Ida can be seen, like that of God in the fresco by Michelangelo.

According to the best Piedmontese tradition, both my grandparents and my uncle never shied from giving me a bit

There's Always the Sea...

of red wine, because *"il vino fa buon sangue"* (it makes good blood). I welcomed the idea with such enthusiasm that I earned the sobriquet of *Madame Barbera* from my favourite wine. When I least expected, I was picked up by my uncle who would tease me, *"So, Madame Barbera, what did little Rita do this morning?"* There was no way to avoid it; blushing and confused, I would reel off the nursery rhyme,

> *Stamattina la piccola Rita*
> *nel bell'orto di mele è finita,*
> *ma le mele non eran mature,*
> *eran verdi, amarognole e dure,*
> *e la Rita per sua punizione*
> *finì a letto con "lindi-gestione."*

(In the nice apple orchard this morning, little Rita landed. But the apples weren't ripe; they were green, bitter, and hard. And for punishment Rita landed in bed with *"anindigestion."*)

Zio Marco went to war and zia Ida went back to her family in Milano. At the end of the summer of 1941, my grandparents and I also left Loano and Villa Perelli never to return. In Milano, papà had died in May.

Even before the war, it was that year's winter storm to lay flat the Loano waterfront, destroying the Lidos, among them Lido Doria, and washing away the famous sea walk. The two tallest twin palms were uprooted, and the sand beaches were reduced to ribbons of stones. Loano never recovered, and nothing was left of the seaside resort's luxurious social life before the war.

The unregulated real estate speculation in the '60s, would transform it into a forest of cement. Passing through it in those years, I could not recognize at all the forms and outlines once so familiar. I hardly noticed the signs indicating the city limits, so gobbled up by a continuous barrier of apartment buildings that ran all along the coast without interruption. I was with my husband and my little eight-year old daughter. He soon lost his patience, even when Angiola begged him to try again to find the places of her mamma's childhood.

One day I returned by myself. I was visiting my brother who, already ill, had chosen Loano as his refuge - a return to the cocoon of his childhood. Though he was six years older than me, I saw him again as a little boy and vulnerable. I suffered to see his joy for life brought so low. He had loved to travel so much. But seeing me so troubled, he would quip:

"Don't worry, Dudina. There's always the sea."

He took me to the old pastry shop in the centre of town. Already on the doorway, I was engulfed by an aroma swell of vanilla and emotions that made me giddy; delicate and friable emotions, just like the S-shaped shortbread pastries of our childhood. They melted in me in a symphony of flavours and memories. Later on, I went walking alone in the cramped lanes of Loano's historical centre, passing under the narrow medieval arch. I was now far from the modern wall of cement, and suddenly I found the road leading to the hill. I forced myself to face with indifference what I thought might be another bitter let-down. And then suddenly, everything reappeared almost picture-postcard perfect: the stream, the little Roman bridge, all a bit more bare and lacklustre; the Tower of the Dorias, somewhat diminished by the presence of a mini-golf that wound its way along the park surrounding it. Incredibly, Villa Perelli was still standing, only slightly worn by age. The shutters were closed and there was no bed sheet on the window sill. No human presence to disturb it. Inert and silent. Gently, without touching it, I slowly left it behind.

CHAPTER FOUR

The apartment seemed to have entered into a state of permanent and colourless penumbra. My life had taken on the look of those wartime black and white movies - I now lived in a grey and frightened Milano. Even words could not breach the silence in which mamma had immersed herself: a silence of her very soul that was palpable, that isolated her in that impenetrable world of adults.

Ninetto was going to school, so I tried to expand my world through my imagination, talking with my dolls and moving things around their little wooden house in the space set aside for my games. But when my brother was home and free from his studies, we'd create an elaborate bond made up of games and plots, always carried out quietly, in whispers.

The vast marble-floor reception room provided us with unlimited space for our battles, races, and chases. We had to keep the noise down to a bare minimum, and so we had thought up the use of the flat square cushions of the raffia armchairs sitting against the walls of the anteroom. They had a thick weave of red, orange, and black threads depicting abstract figures of women and amphorae. Papà had brought them from Sardinia. One cushion under each knee and one under each hand, we would silently slide on all fours over the shiny waxed floor. Hands and knees would propel us in a headlong race to the finish line. With his long and faster arms and legs, my brother had always the advantage, but I loved these special moments when I could let loose. In case of trouble, it would be my older brother who would be scolded.

The cushion train was our favourite mode of transportation. It allowed us to glide unnoticed along the dark hallways that branched off from the anteroom, in opposite directions across the entire house. The ladies visiting mamma were the favourite object of our explorations. These visits were a great distraction from the loneliness of our days, and subjects of no small interest to us.

We found mamma's friends very bizarre creatures, as curious as those Ninetto and I would look at in the great zoological encyclopedia, as we laid on the carpet of the study with our noses buried in the rust-coloured illustrations. Nino would teach me to recognize all the exotic animals, and seemed to enjoy insisting that we look at the page of the *"popotamus and its little popotamuses."*

In that other type of scouting expedition instead, our noses protruded from the doorframe, almost at floor level, as we peered in the room where mamma was entertaining her guests. It was no longer the large salon, now always closed and not utilized. Mamma preferred to receive in papà's studio, sitting with her friends in the comfortable dark studded leather armchairs. I too loved those heavy armchairs, and whenever I could escape everyone's attention, I would snuggle in one of them, in the darkened empty study. Its horseshoe shape hugged my curled-up body. Its intense leather smell brought me back to a time when I used to sit on papà's knees. I had felt warm and safe in his arms.

Clara Menegatti and Maria Carbone would regularly thrust themselves upon our world, the first with her firm and ponderous tread, the other moving in a shyly hesitant slither. One came wearing feathered hats, the other wrapped in long dark mantles. With the naïveté of a five-year old, I still lacked any critical sense, but the extra six years of experience made Ninetto more able to appreciate the exotic character of these figures, and to indicate the points in common with the fauna in our book: the ostrich feathers, the elephant trunks, the owl's eyes.

We couldn't really understand what mamma had in common with those strange creatures, and we told her so. She looked at us with her sad eyes, *"They are good persons, those poor women. They are so alone!"* As usual mamma forgot herself to reach out to those she felt even more in need.

Menegatti was a painter, she loved painting roosters. For a long time, a proud broad-chested specimen, brazen in his glory of colourful plumage, would come at me from a black frame hanging in the dining room. I would look at it and see Menegatti; it looked like her self-portrait.

More than the curiosity of listening to the grownups' conversations and the relish of spying on them, what drove us to these transgressions was the thrill of getting away with it. And success pushed us to be ever more carelessly daring, until one day mamma caught us in *flagrante delicto*. Her outrage was great indeed, but the reprimand was not enough to discourage us. I can't really say what my contribution was to all this derring-do; I merely followed my brother's schemes slavishly, feeling safe in his shadow. And we were caught other times as well.

Ninetto of course took the brunt of the final punishment; he was confined to his room for a whole day. Mamma was very strict, and her forgiveness did not come even when we went to bed. This was very serious, because mamma always came to tuck us in, and in giving us a goodnight kiss, she'd wish us "*sweet dreams*." They were the magic words that kept away all bad dreams during the night. That evening, she came only to me, and the thought of my brother abandoned by mamma, without her sweet voice to bring peacefulness to his sleep, filled me with anguish. In vain I called mamma again and again, crying and begging her to go and say "*sweet dreams*" to Nino. Without that protection, I knew very well how scary dreams could be!

Every night I'd go to bed afraid to see that recurring vast and dark water surface, always that same black lake, motionless, that filled my eyes. It felt like I was in a terrifying fable, in a mysterious spellbound place. I was lured by it, drawn in; I felt the terror of silently sinking, as if within a suspended silence. As I grew older, the dream vanished as it had come. But one day, when I was already thirteen, zio Marco found out that because of the war I had not learned to swim yet. He decided to promptly put a remedy to my deficiency.

Since at that time we were vacationing in the mountains, he took me rowing on a dark lake full of shadows. As soon as we reached the middle of the lake, he suddenly grabbed me and, in fascist-like harshness, threw me overboard. I sank in darkness, deeper and deeper, pulled under as if into an endless funnel. I surfaced, floundering and breathless, and to this day I have an absolute fear of water. My childhood nightmare, in a strange premonition of my subconscious, had become a reality.

And then there was that other nightmare, where the darkness within my eyes took on the form of a wall that started leaning toward me, threatening to crush me, in a never-ending fall which prolonged my agony.

The bombing raids had begun, and our apartment building was a mere two blocks from a primary objective: Milano Central Station. Now real nightmares disrupted our sleep, periodically broken by air-raid sirens. I soon learned to distinguish the signals that ripped through the silence of the night. It made me think of the howling of a mysterious monster that wrenched us from our sleep with a start. Where was the sound coming from? Who was warning us of the danger? The first siren warned us to be ready for an air raid. A crescendo of brief alarm sounds meant immediate danger. Finally, a protracted sound, matching our long sigh of relief, signalled the cease alarm, the danger was over.

On the first warning signal, mamma would get us ready to go down to the bomb shelter. The so-called "shelter" was nothing more than the basement of the apartment building, built at the start of the century. Those basements were not meant to provide the tenants any real protection against bombs. Nevertheless, these deep underground cellars had been promoted to the role of shelters. After all, it was proclaimed by a sign in white chalk, underscored by a thick arrow, hastily scribbled on the stairway wall leading to the cellars. It all seemed done at the last moment by the hand of an illiterate. It was still visible many years after the war ended. Perhaps no one dared to tempt fate by erasing it.

The main purpose of the cellars was really the collection of garbage from the tenants of the entire building. The landing on each floor had a chute where refuse would be dropped. Everything ended up in a large refuse collection room. The chute was as high as the building itself, and going down the stairs you could hear every now and then the headlong crashing of things within the wall. Or at least we

There's Always the Sea...

kids heard it, because we avoided the slow and stately elevator, enclosed in its cast-iron and shiny brass cage going up and down within the marble stairwell.

Besides the refuse, the cellars were also used to keep the mountains of coal - already scarce in those days - to fuel the gigantic furnace that furnished heat to all the apartments in the building. Then, there was the room with the electrical system, the rooms for various control panels, pipes, and mechanisms necessary to guarantee the comfort of the prestigious tenants of an elegant turn-of-the-century apartment building. The cellars were a kind of grimy belly with corresponding innards, whose perfect operation was essential to the maintenance of the beautiful and dignified façade.

Along some of these dark and dusty dens, benches and chairs had been provided for the tenants seeking safety. I felt like Jonah in the belly of the whale, in the dim light of a few smoky light bulbs and the occasional hand-held flashlight. Wrapped in our blankets, my brother and I hugged each other next to mamma. We listened in silence to the talk of grownups which, if anything, made our fears loom larger in our minds.

"Are we really going to be safe down here?"

"Of course! The cement foundations make this as strong as a bunker."

People talked to cover up their fear. Sometimes, the scurrying of a mouse in the corner would create a break in the conversation.

"Who knows what all these pipes are for?"

"They are water pipes and gas pipes."

"A lot of good then these cement walls would do us! If a pipe blows up down here, we'll either drown like rats or asphyxiate!"

After the first few nights, mamma decided we would not go down there anymore. Whenever the air-raid sounded, we'd gather our blankets and mattresses, and we'd line up along the "bearing wall." Mamma explained that that was the strongest wall in the apartment, because it was part of the bearing wall that supported the entire building, and would withstand the bombing. I wondered if that was the wall in my dreams. Crouched against it, I hoped the wall would never fall on us, as in the dream.

It was not only at night that fears were visited upon us. An air-raid could catch us just as easily during the day, and if we were on the street, we'd have to run for the nearest public shelter, in other words bury ourselves in the basements of someone else's building. Running, fleeing, hiding, breathlessly; eyes scanning the sky, mutterings of anxiety, sighs of relief; a stifled furtive life of curfews, of shutters tightly closed from sunset on. What in the beginning had seemed to me a game was fast turning everything into the colour of fear. And unlike the fables, there was no safe way back to the comfort of our home when we came out of the dark forest.

The threats were everywhere; evil forces had permeated everything. Grownups had to be careful of their words and behaviour, because they could be seized and taken away. Every building had its spy, and we had "Mr. Livi." And so, whenever he would appear with his thin, livid figure, as keen-edged as his name, quick glances were exchanged, conversations interrupted. He seemed to slither and appear everywhere with his syrupy smile.

"Be careful of Livi!", *"Livi's coming!"*, *"Be quiet, there's Livi!"*

Everyone feared him and felt somehow guilty in front of him.

My grandparents, however, seemed to escape all this. Their dark-red brick house, almost covered by a cascade of wisteria, among the tree-lined boulevards of Città degli Studi, appeared as if isolated in a world all of its own. At least that's how it looked to me.

I can still see them waiting for me at the gate: nonno's tall figure, so unconsciously elegant in his familiar garnet-coloured velvet smoking jacket, trimmed by a braid of the same colour that matched the tress-like belt. The image was completed by his short-cropped hair and his moustache reflecting the grey of his large eyes, always fixed on a distant invisible horizon. Smaller, standing next to him, nonna, in whose maternally prosperous body I loved to run, feeling enfolded and protected. Her inviting hazel eyes, so intense and anxious; her thick hair, softly done up in a fin-de-siècle style. And then Milly, with her grey curly fur, always at their feet, held back with difficulty by nonna's hand on her collar. I joyfully broke away even from mamma to run to my nonni. Days with them were like a party. And yet even Milly had risked going to war at one point.

Milly was the professional name of the most famous soubrette and chanteuse of the times who, as zia Mariù confided with a touch of cattiness, *"had been the mistress of Prince Umberto of Savoy. His favourite among the many! A real passion!"* And there was a hint of pride in her voice when she would remind us that she had gone to school with Milly, and that they had been great friends, as if she felt thus included in the aura of that royal scandal. *"Eh....Milly!"* she'd sigh with a vague look and a sublimated smile full of allusions. That name seemed to carry her off to a mysterious world of thrilling memories, or dreams.

One day Milly disappeared, our own Milly that is, and it was a tragedy, because that dog was a faithful and inseparable part of the family, as expressive as a human being. *"If she could only talk!"* Nonna would declare. We all knew that the real reason for her great love for Milly was the fact that the little dog had developed an incredible attachment to zio Marco. Anything having to do with her favourite son held a special place in nonna's heart. She'd tell us that, in spite of all the traffic of Milano, Milly was still able to recognize the noise of his motorcycle miles away,

"When she starts barking and runs to the gate, we know Marco will be here in five minutes. I can count on it, and put the pasta in the pot."

And now, Milly was gone. She had already been gone for days when, walking downtown with mamma, I stopped to watch a regiment of soldiers marching by. And that's when I saw her, her curly little snout barely peeping out of the rucksack of one of the soldiers. There and then, I was flabbergasted, speechless. When I finally managed to catch mamma's attention, it was too late.

Later, no one would believe me, there were too many chances that it was just a case of mistaken identity. But, seeing my insistence, nonno decided to look into the matter, and that was my moment of great triumph. The search was not easy, but in the end Milly was found. She had become the regiment's mascot. Nonno told us that when he called her name, she went crazy with joy. *"She was jumping like a small kangaroo."*

I remember thinking then that it was only right for the soldier to be punished. Now I see only a boy leaving his family to go to war and, at the last moment, taking with him the teddy bear to keep him company and conquer his fear. I can just imagine those young men laughing and playing with their new mascot, for a brief moment forgetting everything and finding the hope to live.

When winter came, our life was engulfed in a constant night. The sun set very early, and the tall window shutters, folded into the side recesses, would be shut tight in view of the impending curfew. The vast apartment felt even larger with its long hallways fading into the darkness, while the various rooms and the salon existed in their own mystery behind closed doors. Life was nestled in few, faintly lit corners of the house. Who took possession of those empty dark spaces we no longer dwelt in?

How difficult it is to see myself in that reality dating back more than half a century, to realize that I myself was in the darkness of our home in Milano! As part of a scene in which the actors have all disappeared, isn't that someone I used to be also someone who no longer exists, in a drama which ended a long time ago? I look at it as an old movie with no sequel, and only a few stills remaining. I'm merely an eye that watches, not a presence. And yet, I do identify myself with those scenes, and from my eyes they trickle into my very soul. In effect, they issued from my own soul.

Mamma is sitting at her dressing table; the tilted long oval mirror reflects her face, framed by the lock of loose black hair that covers her shoulders down to her waist. The oval face, the large black eyes with a melancholic softness call more to mind certain classic southern features than her Piedmontese origins. With a rhythmic motion, the comb flows through the entire length of her hair. Then the scene takes on a more romantic quality, as she takes up the brush with its fine silver-chiselled handle and starts to stroke her hair in long leisurely movements. Unexpectedly, I see the image of papà begin to take shape in the mirror behind mamma. It is he now who blends the silver of the brush with her raven-black hair. The following morning mamma's long hair will be gathered in a braid coiled in a crown around her head, and her image in the mirror will be immersed in the light pouring in from the French windows that open onto the two balconies.

My parent's bedroom was set at the very end of our apartment, at the corner of the building. As a result, it faced two different streets and it was spacious and full of light. Next to it was Ninetto's room. These bedrooms were closed off by a door at the entrance of the hallway leading to them. From the day I was born, I slept along the wall next to mamma and papa's bed, in a small rose-coloured metal bed, whose rope-web siding could be raised and lowered. I still slept there when papà was no longer with us. During the day *Pupa* would sit on my bed, the blonde doll that mysteriously had taken her place there one Christmas night. She had replaced old *Totò* in my heart because she was more sophisticated, more "adult."

She was the doll whose dress had been made by mamma's seamstress. I had yearned for it for so long. "*A doll with blond hair,*" that's what I wanted for Christmas, nothing else. I was given to hope that if I had been a good girl, baby Jesus would bring it; but it didn't look like a sure thing at all. That night my sleep was quite restless. I was trying to stay awake to hear baby Jesus arrive, but my eyelids were heavy with sleep, and I just could not manage to keep them open. At a certain point I thought I heard a slight sound. Before my half-closed eyes, a fleeting shadow was moving at the foot of my bed. In the darkness of the room my eyes couldn't distinguish, and in the fog of sleep my mind couldn't grasp.

In the morning, the most beautiful blond doll with rosy cheeks and red lips was staring at me from the foot of my bed, her blue eyes veiled by long black eyelashes. I was happy, and I recalled the fleeting scene during the night. I wasn't sure what I had seen, but the shadow was too big to be baby Jesus. I confided with my brother who insisted that I must have had a dream. I didn't insist, preferring not to verify the doubt that had been troubling me for some time already. If the question of baby Jesus was a fairy-tale, I wanted to continue enjoying it.

I recall so many other Christmases, not marked by gifts but by aromas of the wonderful pastries mamma baked. To tell the truth, mamma was good at so many things. Although the everyday running of the house was in the hands of the household staff, she knew how to do everything.

"Pick up a skill; you never know when you might need it." "Before you give orders, you better know how to do it yourself," were the mottos in my family.

Over the years, I remember opening the drawer in the dining room where mamma kept the beautiful tablecloths she embroidered. I would caress the delicate multi-coloured threads woven in perfect designs, as if reaching to touch her. I was so proud to have had such a talented mamma, while I was totally hopeless. It was on these elegant tablecloths that she would lay out the Christmas baked goods: Sicilian and Piedmontese sweets. The *pignolata* with its pyramid of small golden balls drenched by a cascade of honey rose next to *Monte Bianco*, a delicious mound of *marrons glacés* covered in whipped cream. But, because it was so hard to achieve, the masterpiece was the *crème Chantilly*. It deserved applause only when it reached a silky-smooth and velvety consistency. The light and foamy *îles flottantes* were set to sail on this golden creamy lake.

I wonder why back then I didn't look on with pride at mamma's academic achievements. Her publications in chemistry brought for years an income from the Vallardi Publishing House, yet no one had encouraged me to consider its importance. The image handed down to me of my mother was first of all of a very beautiful, elegant, and refined woman, whose duty was to be "the lady of the house." Had she been overshadowed by the fact that my father was the "great chemist?" Or regardless, as a married woman, was she expected to adorn herself with her professional qualifications as if with a pearl necklace that you keep locked away in a drawer?

If flavours and aromas can bring back distant images, these in turn can recall perfumes that the senses associate with the emotions of those distant times. And so aromas, flavours, and sounds become the very soul of that world that once was mine, and give immediate substance to my fading evermore distant memories.

For many years, we associated Easter with a wave of intense and sensuous fragrance of almonds and sugar violets emanating from the gift box that would arrive from Sicily. It was like a fruit crate, made of strips of light wood, nailed together. Kneeling on the dining room carpet, I followed anxiously the un-nailing operation carried out by my brother. One nail after the other, one strip after another and there, we could begin to see the straw. The cover falls off, and we are overwhelmed by the intoxicating perfume. I can still feel in my fingers the tangle of straw which we pull out by the handful to reach the treasure we know so well. But already from the straw sugar violets spill out, filling our nostrils with that unique perfume of violets and vanilla. Finally, the Pasqual lamb of almond paste appears in all its realistic beauty. It has curly wool; its head is turned sideways, looking at us with its great big innocent eyes. It's lying down, with its forelegs folded underneath, as if to better hold the festive banner rising from them; its hind legs hidden under chubby flanks. Only our incorrigible sweet tooth would give us the nerve to demolish it piece by piece and wolf it down.

I also recall certain hard candy that defined a period and evoke a person in my childhood. It could well be that in the effort to retain the memory of those I loved and lost along the way, my subconscious held on to them by associating them to objects, and to the most powerful physical childhood sensations: tastes.

Whenever I was a good girl, mamma would get me the smooth and colourful *sassolini* (pebbles). I delighted in looking at them, rolling them between my fingers, just as years later, for some sort of emotional association, I would pick up and stroke the pebbles on the seashore, so similar to the sweet "pebbles" of my childhood. How long I wavered between playing with mamma's "pebbles" and eating them, tempted by their unmistakeable sweet taste. Nonna, on the other hand, preferred the *Moretto* hard candy, chocolate coated small balls wrapped in transparent yellow paper. Deliciously crunchy, they had a taste somewhere between chocolate and coffee. As for nonno, being a pharmacist, he always carried with him metal tins with serious medicinal-looking, green rubbery sugar pills. In my mouth they would release a taste of exotic mountain herbs. On the cover there was the picture of an *edelweiss*, which was also its brand name. Whenever he felt a bit frivolous, nonno would instead buy liquorice lozenges, called *Golia*. *"Golia! For your voice, for your throat!"* As proclaimed by its publicity.

I also remember the *enfant terrible* that my brother Ninetto was in those years, so much so that pepper became his symbolic attribute. One evening, when mamma and papà were going to the theatre, Nino promised them that when they came back, he would have *"cured"* Dudi from the habit of sucking her thumb. His brilliant idea was to ground my wet thumb into pepper. Perhaps it was my fault if the experiment failed, because before putting it in my mouth I touched my eyes. I especially remember my nanny's reaction to my cries and howls, and the reaction of my parents to her outcries.

My memory continues to roll out frame after frame, ill-assorted at times, as if they belonged to different movies. Now Nino has grown, he's eleven years old, and I see him in front of a large map hanging on one of the walls in his room. It's covered with red-headed and blue-headed pins. He moves them from one side to the other, explaining that the red ones indicate the movements of the German armies, and the blue ones those of the Allies. I see his eyes flash a joy of triumph whenever the blue area spreads out.

Nino was no longer attending the German school on Via Boscovich. Perhaps, the real reason had nothing to do with mamma's concern about the school demanding that the children swim in the pool as soon as they returned to school after lunch. She had considered it dangerous for the digestion, but while papà was alive, mamma had been forced to accept this. Papà claimed that it was good for Ninetto, that *"it would make him grow strong."* But maybe he stopped going because he had completed the elementary grades and had learned German quite well. He had even learned to play the flute. I so liked to hear him play *"Oh Vienna, Vienna tu...."* He didn't seem to know anything else.

Lili Marleen was in vogue then, and Rina, the only help mamma could afford during the war, was constantly singing it. It was a sad song, not like the ones that our cook had sung and that had scandalized mamma. But mamma didn't appreciate it just the same, and she would reprove Rina, as if reproaching her, that she had learned it from the German soldiers. She also warned her that she'd do better to forget the song, because one day it could prove dangerous to know it. This constant incompatibility of mamma with the maids' songs was something I could not understand.

There are other sounds that still come to me, forming the sombre and ominous sound-track of an otherwise silent movie: **"tum-tum-tum-tum"**, the four drum-tap signal of the BBC Radio that echoed dull and gloomy in the darkened dining room, where mamma and my brother would sit in the evening after dinner listening to *Radio Londra*. They seemed to be doing something dangerous and forbidden, like some conspirators. I was caught by fear too, as those drum taps became the beats of my own heart in alarm. The sounds issued from the speakers of our *Marelli* radio, which had the shape of the stained glass windows of Milano's Duomo, seemed to come from a distant cathedral like a divine warning. But when I'd see mamma rejoicing at the news, I was as happy as I could be.

One morning, while shopping with mamma, I heard in the stores two words pass in whispers from mouth to mouth, as if by wireless: *Gorla* and *Precotto*. They were uttered in horror, but I found them funny, with that sound that rhymed with a bread soup, *pancotto*. I imagined them like two characters, one short and plump, the other tall and thin, a bit ungainly, something like the fox and the cat in "Pinocchio," but good natured all in all. Instead, they were two areas in the suburbs of Milano. Bombs had fallen on some schools; hundreds of children had been killed.

From deeper still in my memory come the sounds of voices, hardly human: coral laments, like moans of wounded animals. I think we were about to take the train at the station to go to see mamma's sister, zia Mariuccia in Vigevano. In the midst of the confusion, the general disorder, the uncertainty of departures, I noticed a train completely sealed, with no windows at all, and with high sliding doors, which one day I'll identify as cattle cars. I shuddered at the unrecognizable sounds that were coming from within. They had to be human voices, because outstretched arms, as if in offer, could be seen protruding from some openings - they were gripping small pieces of paper. Mamma was trying to divert my attention, but I saw a piece of paper fall down and, breaking away from her, I ran to pick it up. Mamma quickly took it from me and made it disappear in her purse, snapping it shut with a metallic click. I think a short time after that, the Rosenthals came into our lives.

The scenes follow on the heels of each other, conveying different and often contradictory tales; but all of them carry one clear message: the best of that period had passed by then, and I'm left with the sensation of having arrived too late. The flavours of those early days dissolve in a bitter-sweet aftertaste. I'm gripped by a sense of nausea, as if for a physical void in my stomach. But it's a void of the soul, a void made up of losses.

"Mamma, I feel 'nasua'!" I would cry as a child, when I was recurrently attacked by a sudden retch. Now it's a spiritual nausea, a counterpoint to that of my childhood, which looking back seems to have been a metaphorical premonition. And it too grips at the pit of my stomach.

CHAPTER FIVE

The provincial road reached the top of the hill among fields of flowers that stretched to the horizon. At the very top, a large grassy, sun-beaten clearing, scattered with groves overlooked the deep valley below. Isolated among the trees, our house. This was Ponzone, the village which rested on a big *poggio* (hillock), as the name declares. We all went there for the first time in the summer of '42. Mamma, however, had been there already the year before, alone, after the death of my father. Family friends, the Gentas, who had a villa up there, had convinced mamma to leave the city and join them for a short rest.

"I was welcomed with so much love when I reached Ponzone," she wrote to her sister. *"The Gentas are going out of their way to make me forget how alone I am."*

She immediately fell in love with the place. It was her beloved Piemonte, and it reminded her of the places she had known as a girl, her grandfather's property in Ozzano, where she had spent her carefree years.

"Ponzone is one of the enchanting villages of the Monferrato, very much like our Ozzano, but with a more sweeping panorama. The walks are more beautiful, because being higher up, there are many more trees. Luckily, all of them are walks that I can manage, even weakened as I am."

She went back there with us two children for another two summers, in search of peace, in a Pavese-like flight to the hills. In the same way as the troubled poet, more than from the actual war, pressing and threatening on all sides, and reaching even the very top of those hills, she was running away from her personal struggle, from an enemy within herself.

July 18, 1943. In a letter to her sister, mindful of the censorship, *"I would be quite happy if it weren't for...the*

English. The latest events, however, are worrying me, afraid of not being able to get back home. I'm ready to be on my way when it will be necessary, and if it won't be too late. Of course I'll miss it because I feel at peace here, and I'd be quite happy to remain until the end of the war if all my things weren't in Cunardo."

July 30, 1943.

"I'm still in Ponzone but I'm getting ready to return to Cunardo. The war still goes on and, in view of the measures being taken in Acqui in the event of a landing on the Liguria coast, I think it prudent to return home. I'm sure we wouldn't be in any danger here, but I can't leave in Cunardo everything which is now, in effect, my sole means of survival. Today the government's affixed posters make it quite clear that, should the need arise, no one will be allowed to leave the place where they are currently residing. So I must leave while I still can. I think I'll come back here if the war will ever end or if it should move elsewhere."

She was never to go back there again.

But for two years I enjoyed "my summer" with mamma, and I lived in a magic spell. For the first time I felt that I was living the intimacy of a family life to the fullest with mamma and Ninetto. We were, the three of us, inseparable, living time in complete unison, mostly outdoors, up in those hills, isolated from everything and everyone, communing with nature.

Boschetto Paradiso, (Paradise Grove) - only the mystery of it lingers in my memory. The grove opened up like a vast funnel as we descended into the valley. The wide path wound in a spiral series of curves in ever darker shadows under a canopy of leafy fronds. I can still see the first curves with patches of sun filtering through the trees, and the stone benches along the path where mamma would rest while pulling out delicious local fruit from her straw bag. The leaves of the elms flickered patches of sunlight and shadows on her face. It was a veritable paradise for me. The footpath ends there, in that last curve that fades away in the shadows of my memory. I can no longer see the mystery it led to, and yet it still holds a magic spell for me.

There's Always the Sea...

I can still see Ninetto and me, at night before going to bed, snuggled next to mamma, our heads resting on her arms as we listen to fairy tales. I always asked to hear the story of the hunter who did not have the courage to kill the fawn whose heart he was to take, and was of course rewarded by the love of the girl he had saved.

Mamma would visit with her friends the Gentas, and I didn't mind sharing her for a while in the beautiful garden where they'd invite us: the ladies stretched out on lawn chairs under the trees in their white linen dresses, the small tables with the tea set, or the bright tablecloths spread on the grass for a lunch *al fresco*. I was pleased to see mamma smiling among those people, always the prettiest. Mrs. Genta fell into the bizarre human zoo my brother and I loved to observe: a long horse-face with her hair flattened by a thick hairnet, which turned her head even more into a stiff rectangular shape; that's how she's remained in my memory. She was kind with us children and she even let us explore her house garage, which for us turned out to be a veritable treasure trove. One day we dug out an old little red bicycle on which I learned to ride, first with training wheels and then with my brother pushing me until I'd find my balance and would take off by myself. Of course it was much easier to go than to stop, and my wildest rides ended up in some rather crazy tumbles. Nonetheless, I've never lost my love for the bicycle.

This idyllic life was soon upset, however, at least for me, by the arrival of Mrs. Baldoni visiting mamma with her son Mirko, Nino's friend. I felt then excluded by the bond which was immediately recreated between the two boys. To be fair, mamma had insisted that the boys include me in their games, and I did my best to be accepted and be useful. But their games were mostly building forts and fighting battles. They would roll big stones into place, and between those two Hercules I would try my best to push as well. And then, on one of these occasions, a big stone slipped from their hands and rolled right over my ankle. The scene which presented itself to the adults was like a strategic withdrawal from the front - I, flanked and held up by the two "men" dragging me on one leg, stifling my sobs with a huge handkerchief, all red!

The bucolic peace of the ladies was shattered and they rushed to me, thinking I was stanching a flow of blood. There was no blood, but the ankle really hurt and, unfortunately, most of the town's doctors were posted at the front taking care of real soldiers. And thus began my misadventures with the only doctor available, a dentist. The ankle was bandaged as best he could, with a traditional splint which made me look like a hobbling puppy. In time the ankle was set, but years later when I began to take some interest in my legs, I realized that the ankle had developed two distinct bumps. Too late to do anything about it.

There was another heaven-sent intervention of the tooth-pulling doctor that left a mark on me. The occasion: the smallpox vaccination. For *"aesthetic reasons,"* as he defined them, he chose to "scar" me on the curve of the shoulder in order to avoid - as he said - *"to disfigure my arm,"* as if the arm were the only part ever to be exposed in public, and not the shoulder. Nor was it clear why he should in any event *"disfigure"* me. Yet he managed to do just that. I had a violent reaction to the vaccination, and I responded to the itching the only way a five year-old girl could - scratching it away, which was easy because the protective gauze, of course, kept slipping off my bony shoulder. The result was a quite deep infection. Thanks to my further contribution, my right eye was promptly infected as well, and I ran the serious risk of losing it.

In his rightful role as a dentist, however, the good doctor would redeem himself, acting out and enjoying his professional authority to the fullest. He made an odd couple with his nurse, both of them tall and wiry, with a foreign look about them. Silent and efficient, she moved to his every command, her face reflecting a severe sense of responsibility tinged with a slight look of contempt for the rest of the world. For his part, dignified as well in a supercilious manner, the doctor would address her from time to time with a stentorian voice, *"Mar-ta, the ce-ment!"* The solemn command was synchronized with the raising of the left eyebrow, and underscored with a swift authoritative wave of the hand.

Their "diversity," the obscure accent, perhaps north European, the aura of mystery generated by their aloofness

There's Always the Sea...

had inevitably attracted everyone's malicious curiosity tinged with gossip. It was whispered that they were wild lovers who had escaped from their country because of their illicit liaison. My brother's imagination, on the contrary, fed by his adolescent readings, had seized upon the dark side of that unusual form of address, "*Marta, the cement!*" and he liked to associate it to crime scenes and felonious burials. From then on "*Marta, the cement!*" became another expression in our "family lexicon." Such is the power of the word! What's important is to pronounce it with the right tone and inflection for it to leave its mark on the world.

And that's exactly how my brother had his own moment of glory as well; a moment that became part of our family's history. He had been invited to take part in a children's play in town. For weeks on end he disappeared every day for the rehearsals. Though I missed him, I nonetheless followed with trepidation this unusual event bringing a degree of excitement in our family. The fateful evening finally arrived. Being myself always extremely reluctant to appear in public, I was indeed proud of my brother for what seemed to me to be a very courageous act on his part. The play seemed to be quite tedious, perhaps because I kept waiting anxiously for my brother to appear on the scene. Finally, there he was on stage, together with a group of "dignitaries," all in dark suits, white shirts, and ties.

To tell the truth, Ninetto was looking more like a funeral director with his thin shoulders lost inside the large jacket. The minutes go by, and still he continues to stand there speechless, while other actors exchange the occasional dialogue. I become impatient and begin to worry when, in the total silence, I hear my brother's voice declaim, "*It's nine o'clock, and still no mayor!*" With that, the curtains fell on the first act as well as on my brother's future stage career. Years later, when I teasingly reminded him of the episode, he swore that his role had been much more noteworthy than that, but I could not honestly recall seeing anything else. Still, I never forgot that phrase, and even now, whenever I hear "*It's nine o'clock,*" I can't help completing the phrase in my mind:

"*...and still no mayor!*" It certainly gave me occasion to tease my brother for a long time.

Rainy days would see the three of us together in the cozy half-light of the house. In my childhood memories, those are the moments that come closest to the feeling of home life and family togetherness. In one corner mamma would read or embroider in her armchair, in the cone of light of the lamp. At the table Ninetto is bent over his school books to keep up with his studies during the summer; and I would pull out from the bottom of an old chest its precious treasure. I would lay it on the carpet and carefully open its heavy cover of embossed leather. It was like raising the curtains to a kaleidoscopic world of colours and images exploding before my eyes. It was a collection of several years of the *Corriere dei Piccoli*, a monthly magazine for children. I happily lost myself with those outlandish characters as they invaded my eager imagination: Arcibaldo, Petronilla, Popeye. I couldn't yet understand the meaning of every word, but I could recite by memory,

"Re Giorgetto d'Inghilterra ha paura della guerra, e chiede aiuto e protezione al suo amico Ciurcillone." (Little King George of England is afraid of the war and seeks the help and protection of his big fat friend Churchill.)

I was, of course, happily unaware of the satirical allusions motivated by the Fascist regime. Or I would endlessly repeat the rhyming start of a story, *"Qui comincia l'avventura del Signor Bonaventura,"* (Here begins the adventure of Mr. Lucky) which always ended at the bottom of the page with the drawing of the main character bent over a huge 1,000 liras bill, luckily gained as a reward for his candid good heart. After the war, those "1000 *lire*" would be appropriately updated to "one million!"

Then there was my fascination with the ancient mirror in mamma's bedroom, a strong attraction for my precocious vanity. In reality, it was more like a game in which I tried to imitate mamma. Her dressing table full of small bottles, perfumes, and shiny objects had fascinated me for a long time, as I watched her go through her mysterious rituals. So I too built up my own set from the vials and small bottles she had discarded. I filled them with water, got hold of some wads of cotton and, putting on the airs of an expert, I'd proceed to dab my face with what for me were precious scents. I spent so much time in front of the mirror that mamma began to worry and told me that one day I would see the devil appear in it. The thought didn't bother me too much, but every now and then I would peer more deeply into the darkness of that glass blackened by time. I never saw the devil, as I had imagined, but in time I understood the metaphor my mamma had used to warn me against the little devil of my vanity.

It was in Ponzone that I realized for the first time that mamma was not well. She was increasingly reluctant to take our usual evening walks at sunset, one of our most cherished rituals of the day. The field of flowers on the hillside was one of our favourite places. I would lose myself in that vast carpet of daisies which we'd gather by the armful to brighten the house with. I've always loved yellow flowers with the colour of the sun, *"frenzied with light,"* as the poet Montale would say. When mamma hesitated, my brother and I would beg her to come at least *"up to the Cross,"* where her favourite wild carnations grew. But a veil of weariness hampered every movement of her delicate figure. Her bright eyes misted with melancholy at our every childish entreaty. Her whole being was somehow shadowed by something mysterious within her, a personal secret she was unwilling to share, and which often confined her in her own particular loneliness. And I was even more fascinated by her elusive gentleness, that fleeting something in her, which drew her increasingly away from me, while my whole being reached desperately out to her. I still see her in her flowered dress merging with the orange blotches of the daisies, as in an Impressionist painting. But her silhouette bent over the flowers slowly dissolves, and fades away.

The next thing I remember is the beginning of my life at school when we returned to Milano. It was the autumn of '42, a few months before my sixth birthday. I recall the enclosed courtyard of the Sacro Cuore Convent, with its columns and walls shaded by ivy, creating an intense feeling of mystery; the ink-black shadows of the nuns darting about like birds among grey stones; the high heavy gate that every morning was shut behind me, cutting me off from my mamma. I can recall, in fact, only the moment I walked in the school and the moment I left; between those two moments, a total blank. It was a short experience which left no trace in me. A few months later my entire life would change.

At noon the cheerful flock of little girls swarmed towards the throng of waiting mothers, and they merged, searching each other in a skylark of voices and arms. That one time, amid the crowd of parents, I saw the flash of the red fox, and I could hardly believe my eyes when I spotted nonna. I was overjoyed. It would be the last time I would see her so richly elegant and urbane, and consequently I never forgot that image. The fox looked almost alive the way it wrapped itself around the rust-coloured suit, embracing and rounding off even more those prosperous curves. In crude realism that went unnoticed back then, the fox's sharp snout with its restless glass eyes rested on nonna's shoulder, biting its own luxuriant tail with a masochistic grin. The dead paws softly fell here and there, in a flashy dance. Under the veil of a whimsical little hat, nonna's smile softened some of the thin sharp lines of her face, which vaguely echoed the small animal near it. Nonna had been beautiful in her youth. Under the marks of age, I could still see the fine features of the old darkened photos I so loved, its sulky look reflecting the romantic melancholy that held sway in that period.

I was very proud of my grandmother, and I joyfully ran towards her trying to attract the attention of my schoolmates, *"My nonna's here! My nonna's here!"* I had not seen her for such a long time, nor had I expected to see her. It had been months since my grandparents had left the city, and had closed and abandoned forever their small villa on Via Tiepolo. The bombing raids over Milano had become more frequent, and they had gone to find a house in the countryside where we could be evacuated. Nonna had now come to urge our departure. Cunardo was waiting for us, nestled in the humid valleys of the Varesotto.

We kept hearing threatening rumours of that terrible bombing raid that was to eventually strike Milano in October

There's Always the Sea...

1942. Mamma had been talking of leaving for quite some time, but Ninetto was begging her to postpone it, taken seriously as he was by his studies in the second year of *Scuole Medie* and by the challenges of Latin. He had an important test he just could not miss. And so the bombing raid came, and the Central Station was its main target. Our building was hit by a great many bomb fragments, one of which broke through the roof and tore apart an apartment on the last floor. We felt the walls of our house shake like in a violent earthquake: the doors were ripped off their hinges, the windows were shattered, a partition wall moved half a meter, but the weight-bearing wall held firm for us.

The following day we found out that the *ziette* had died. They had been about to join the Baldoni family evacuated in the Valsassina area, but they too had put off the departure, and ended up buried in the rubble of their apartment.

In the end, we too left Milano, and with it all the flavours associated with my early childhood, and I lost for ever the perfume of the wisteria on Via Tiepolo.

CHAPTER SIX

Just like the "city mouse" in the fable, I had to suddenly change into a country mouse, and fit into a setting and a life completely alien to me. No longer would I have black limousines to carry me around, no more familiar smiles to walk me to school and pick me up. Every day I was pushed out the door at dawn, like a cat that has to go for a pee. All bundled up to withstand the bitter winter, I had to walk the long road that stretched along two kilometres till it reached the imposing building of "Scuola Elementare Rosina Vaccarossi." The frigid wind of the night was still whipping and reddening my cheeks. The thin city ankle boots were not meant for the mud and stones of the road often covered with snow.

I would start out from the centre of town, still wrapped in the warmth of the houses, and the comforting cozy scents pouring out from the first stores already open. In the tiny square, the fragrance of freshly-baked bread; in front of the bread store, the bar with its pungent coffee aroma; the butcher raising the rolling shutter; then the last store of the village, the grocery store, still closed at that hour. I would reach the larger square with its Post Office and the gardens. I would pass by the dentist's house, and after the last narrow part of the street, the cluster of old houses became more sparse and the street stretched itself out among the villas away from the town, shut behind high walls, iron railings and gates; steep narrow stairs, some tree-tops poking above it all. By now I'd reached Villa Molteni, with its small snarling dogs - two fox terriers, known in town for their hysterics. At that point my heart was in my mouth. As I drew nearer, they would invariably burst in furious barking and hysterical convulsions. Those two hairy raucous mouths jabbing at me through the gate bars, alternating in a grotesque dance of leaps and convulsions were my first direct experience of savagery and violence, and I was terrorized. Then there was the villa of the Mandelli sisters, who would soon enter my life.

The last stretch of my walk passed through fields as white as laid-out sheets, and some poor isolated farmhouses. The cold that had slowly penetrated through every opening in my clothes was now seeping down into my very bones. Nonna had tried to compensate for the problem; she gave me an old hot-water bottle of bronzed metal which, just before I stepped out of the house, she would slip boiling hot into a muff she had sewn from an army blanket. It stayed warm almost till I reached the school.

The road was always deserted, and only towards the end I would meet up with some classmates, but they were usually the big farm boys that frightened me with their taunts. *Cecchin* was the only nice one. He would smile at me with his big horse teeth, and I was happy when I'd see him and be escorted by him.

Finally, the fork where the road divided would come into view, climbing either up the hill or going down to the valley, where you could catch a glimpse of the grey ribbon of the provincial road. In the middle, the anachronistic palatial façade of the new Fascist school, pride of the town, built a few years before with the bequest of the oldest and richest family of the area, to commemorate an ancestress.

In vain the large classrooms flaunted imposing radiators, invariably turned off. If a hopeful hand rested on it, the contact with the ice-cold metal hurt, even more so because unexpected. They had installed a temporary wood-burning stove, with the pipe passing through a hole in the window. But it was stoked only with whatever wood we children were able to bring.

And that was not easy, not only because wood was sought after by everybody, but because whatever we were able to pick up in the woods was fresh and wet. The little bit of smoky heat was lost drifting up to the high ceilings. We would sit at our desks wearing our coats, numbed with cold, writing with our gloves on.

At home, however, all the talk and worry centered on Ninetto. In Cunardo, they had not yet started the *Scuole*

Medie, though the classrooms were ready. Therefore, every morning my brother had to ride ten kilometres on his bicycle to reach the town of Marchirolo, up and down the hills, in the freezing mountain valleys. When I heard these talks, I imagined him riding a bicycle track along the crest of the hills - like the marble races we used to have on the beach dunes in Loano - with him outlined against the sky, bent over the bicycle, fighting the cold. In fact, he must have looked like a forerunner of Bartali or Coppi, who ten years later would thrill me as they passed through *Le Tre Valli Varesine* in the *Giro d'Italia*.

In fact, the one who suffered the most was mamma. Cunardo did not agree with her, she hated it from the very start, frowning at my grandparents' choice, so cold and melancholy, deep down among the narrow foggy valleys of the Varesotto. She missed her beloved Ponzone, high, sunny, "*Piedmontese*." Mamma was failing. Day by day she was finding it more difficult to travel back and forth to Milano, to take care of private matters and keep a check on the apartment we'd had to leave empty.

On her returns, even our shows of affection and concern exhausted her: *"...and the house? Is the house still standing?"* She would immediately collapse on the sofa, her opossum fur coat still on, her evermore spare figure lost in it. She looked like a frightened little animal with shaggy fur.

The question of Nino's schooling was settled thanks to the Baldonis, who took him with them to Maggio, in their beautiful villa in Valsassina, where they had evacuated. Nino was happy to join his friend Mirko and go to school with him. Their long daily trek through the fields was a treat for the two boys, almost an adventure in the middle of the partisan war spreading in the north. Their excitement reached its peak when they felt the thrill of being rounded up by the Germans, or rather when they were able to tell all about it at the end of the adventure. They had been suspected of being messengers for the partisans. They had been stopped by a German patrol jeep and questioned. When Ninetto naively thought of getting round them showing off his German, they had no more doubts - they were loaded up and taken to Headquarters. It took a lot for the Baldonis to persuade them of the boys' innocence and bring them back home.

Mamma went away as well, caught as she was in the grip of the unrelenting force that was taking her away for ever. With a melancholic uneasiness, she followed in the footsteps of the Crepuscular poet who travelled *"to elude another journey."* She went off to mend at "Villa Quies" near Bergamo, which meant far from Cunardo and from the days galvanized by nonna's irrepressible energy, as she demurely said to her sister.

Now, from the silk-lined leather box I take in my hands a bunch of old postcards, the colours still fresh, and with them the illustrations emerge, the short notes, the memories of that period, all that mamma would send me regularly to lighten the weight of her absence.

I look at the images of chubby little girls depicted in the postcards, which tickled my fantasy back then. They are portrayed as if taken by surprise while they awkwardly carry out the various tasks of a homemaker: one washing the dishes, barely reaching the sink as she stands on top of a stool; one who's cooking; another doing the ironing; and so on. There is also one who's playing the piano, while little swallows are flying around her... I can't help smiling at that starry-eyed bid to be the "good little housewife." Yet I still feel the echo of the appeal I had felt then. There is a flash of poetry in those shapes and colours, and they still carry to me a note of my mother's tenderness.

On folded sheets of onion skin appear then the caricatures of *"Stalin"* and *"Chamberlain," "the two ladies"* heroines of the many funny stories mamma would write to me. At the clinic, she had met these two sisters who also came, by an odd chance, from Cunardo, from one of the town's prominent families. One was strong and bewhiskered, the other tall and lanky. Mamma had dubbed them Stalin and Chamberlain. They appeared, to say the least, somewhat eccentric and absent-minded. Chamberlain was obsessed by the cold, and she constantly went around with seven caps on her head; but at least she seemed to be in control of her faculties compared to the foggy mental state of the other.

I read again one of the stories mamma used to write me. One day she had gone to visit the two ladies in their room, and she'd found only Stalin. While chatting, mamma asked if she had any news of her grandson Gigi.

"*Gigi?*" replied Stalin. "*Yes, Gigi has been enlisted. He is captain of a submarine; he's the one who shoots torpedoes.*"

"*You don't say?*"

"*Of course! He's captain of a submarine and shoots torpedoes.*" And she repeated it five or six times. Just when she was repeating "*Gigi is in a submarine...*" Chamberlain walked in and blurted,

"*Go on, he's in Milan, at the Precinct, in the Office of the exempted!*"

I look at the last postcard, a black and white photo with an aerial view of the clinic lost in its vast park, where "*mamma strolls every day,*" it reads on the back in the small handwriting of mamma. In the photo, the vast grassy spaces of the gardens, with geometrically trimmed and well groomed small trees, appear crossed by a vast tangle of promenades, perfectly intersecting at right angles.

My mind's eye is lost in that desolate artificial chessboard. I imagine mamma there, walking, ephemeral, almost an abstraction in that emptiness, along the ribbon of asphalt going nowhere. I shiver seeing her imprisoned in a surrealistic geometry, like the protagonist of *L'année derniére à Marien Bad*. What were her thoughts? What exit could she glimpse from within that labyrinth?

Towards the end of winter, when the *Scuole Medie* were finally opened in Cunardo, Ninetto came back home, and soon after mamma joined us as well.

"*If I could have the children with me,*" she had written to her sister from "Villa Quies," "*I would stay here till the war ended. Valganna is lethal for me.*"

She managed to get in Cunardo a few rooms separate from my grandparents' apartment, on the same floor of the villa, and there our small family nucleus was recomposed.

The yellow-ochre bulk of "Villa Contegni" rose high at the junction of two roads climbing the steep slope at the entrance to Cunardo. It dominated the part of town that became sparse as it dropped toward Val Cuvia. Three L-shaped floors formed a corner for a small garden. A rock wall and a flower-covered fence formed the other two sides. In the very centre, rose the huge ancient magnolia, almost as tall as the house, surrounded by full bushes of hydrangeas of the most intense indigo. It was reached through a romantic steep series of steps carved in the rock.

I saw it in its multi-coloured look only months after we arrived. In the beginning everything was whitened by the snow, which was meters high in the garden; so high that Ninetto and I would dig tunnels and trenches to wage war games. In its heyday, the various apartments in the wings of the villa must have accommodated, besides the owners, also the servants and guests. Of these bygone days of glory, only three melancholic survivors remained: two old spinster sisters, who hated each other, and an ancient uncle over whose favours they quarrelled while they waited to squabble over the inheritance. The villa was therefore available to be subdivided into small units and offered for rent to evacuees, with solutions naturally inadequate.

We had the top floor. Nonna had a magnificent view of the valley below, which made up for the limited living quarters. At one time, they must have been the servants' living quarters, made up of a square area of four rooms that gave onto the central vestibule, from which a large internal staircase led down to the other apartments, making us feel we were intruding in other people's home. A so-called toilet on the landing of the staircase provided the bare essentials. In the vestibule, which nonna had managed to transform in a small sitting room, there was a mysterious tiny green door. Behind it was a small wooden ladder that led to a large utility room in the attic, a source of nightly fear for me. One façade of the villa, overlooking the garden, opened on every floor into a vast vault-covered terrace. We entered our living quarters from the terrace on the last floor, which I made into a playing area.

The two sisters lived apart. Having taken an immediate liking to Miss Olimpia, nonna promptly addressed her with the familiar Piedmontese *Tota Olimpia*. Tota Olimpia lived on the ground floor, in the most beautiful part of the villa, because she shared it with her uncle who was still sole owner of the entire property. He was old and in poor health and, as an ex nurse, she took care of him. The town gossip claimed they had been lovers. Good hearted, a bit of a ninny and slightly humped, she was always running around like a little mouse.

Snobbish Annetta lived alone on the second floor in the other wing, the so-called *piano nobile*. Still fresh, with traces of a recent beauty in her blonde hair and the oval face, she moved with maidenly reserve in her immaculate world, where the eye was drawn from the starched lace on the end tables and armchairs to those that veiled her neckline. She focused all of life's virtues and duties in the pious reverence toward the priests and the Church, where she spent most of her time, earning herself the title of "churchy." She was quite capable of masking her envious and prickly nature with her honeysweet manners. She became incensed only if someone called her "Mrs." by mistake. With pursed lips, she would then hiss that she was a "Miss." The beauty of it was that in actual fact she had been married. We heard all the juicy details from Paolina.

Paolina was a pretty blond girl from town that mamma had been delighted to take on to help her manage the household. It had not been easy to find someone to fit the bill, after losing the very efficient Rina in Milano, who refused to follow us in the evacuation in order not to abandon her own family. There had been a number of failed attempts. I remember the Bulgarian woman: gloomy and silent, mysterious and dark, like the long Mother Hubbard type garments she wore. She frightened me, yet she had one virtue for me irresistible: I'll never forget the most fantastic cornflour cookies she used to make.

It wasn't easy for mamma to find help, because the poor women had to put up with the criticism and harassment from nonna, in whose eyes no one was ever good enough - evidence of her morbid jealousy, for mamma in this case. But Paolina grew so attached to my mother that she came through all the acid tests, and never left her. For years she and I

There's Always the Sea...

remained friends as well, until life took me away to the far corners of the world.

To go back to the story of Annetta, Paolina told us that at the start of the First World War, a young officer had fallen madly in love with her. To his every passionate proposal, however, the young Anna would shy away, wanting to protect her maiden virtue. It so happened that the young soldier fell victim of a fatal fever which brought him close to death. To his pleas that she grant him his dying wish, Annetta was moved to pity and married him.

The official version provided by *Signorina Anna* was that, given the groom's conditions, *"the marriage was not consummated,"* and therefore she could rightly consider herself free of the stigma and a *"Signorina"* to all effects. With a sarcastic smile, Paolina concluded: *"But there must have been a moment when the temperature dropped to 37°!"* All this I would learn much later from nonna, as I matured. At six, I was certainly not privy to "life's secrets." Still, my horizon was slowly widening.

The exodus from the city was swelling daily. The owners of country villas, once used only for vacations, arrived now to take refuge in them. My classroom filled up with new classmates from the city. In that class, I forged my first friendships, some of which would follow me into adulthood. But not Lucio's, whose face I still see only as a child, slight and bright like a Peter Pan. My classmates would taunt me because he would always hover around me. He made me discover natural liquorice, which I didn't even know existed in a form different from the black gummy strips available in drugstores. These were wood sticks, black under the bark. I was flattered that Lucio would go in the woods and find them for me. And what a strange sensation to chew on that fibrous twig and feel the taste of liquorice!

Then there was Carla Belloni, who became my first very best friend. Carla was beautiful, with soft blonde curls. I felt privileged when she'd invite me; I was delighted to walk the long road to her beautiful villa, protected by a high gate that opened as if by magic at the ring of a bell. I would then enter a fairy-tale world, wrapped in the intense perfume of an entire wall of jasmine that made me giddy. Tuffi, the poodle, would immediately run towards me, jumping like a ball. He really was a ball of dense, soft white curls covering even his eyes. As I walked on, I'd discover other treasures, like the red and green currant bushes which I had never seen. Not only did I stuff myself, picking them straight from the bushes, but they also turned up in the sweet jelly served on crispy croutons with hot chocolate that the maid would bring us for the four o'clock snack.

It certainly did not feel like wartime, but I had heard the adults say that Dott. Belloni was the director of the Chamber of Commerce and therefore, *"his home was full of all sorts of goodies."* And sure enough, I discovered other secret caches. Carla had a new baby brother, and one day she secretly took me into a walk-in cupboard with a heap of stuff. Amid everything, I noticed a pyramid of cans stacked high. Carla told me it was powdered milk for the baby and that it was delicious. *"You want to taste it?"* I thought it was something both forbidden and risky, which in fact it was. But Carla insisted that there was no danger because her parents were out. And so I was introduced to orgies of powdered milk and the thrilling experience of the forbidden. We would eat it by the spoonful, filling our mouths with a sweet milky paste. It reminded me of my delicious manna-based laxative of back when... Milano was just a memory now.

The real mystifying secret, however, was Carla's mother. Unlike Carla, who was tall and strong like her father, she was tiny, with a delicate kind of beauty. Slender, with large periwinkle eyes, dark hair against a fair-skin complexion. Her fragile body plagued by incessant tremors. The explanations grownups gave never went beyond a terminology meaningless for me: *delirium tremens, tremor post-partum.* It all started with the birth of the baby, disproportionately large compared to the mother, a real giant. I could not grasp the sense of all this however; and I was dismayed by those senile palsied arms, and hands reaching out to me from the armchair to embrace me, in horrible contrast with that youthful woman. She seemed to be the victim of an evil spell.

Then the Martinotti family arrived - father and mother with three children, who were introduced as my third cousins. Giacomo Martinotti was the son of one of my grandmother's sisters. They settled in an apartment of the house across the street from ours. The oldest girl shared both my age and my odious name. We were destined to become inseparable, though Giuseppina Martinotti's presence in my life brought me no joy. A mischief-maker, and as saucy as her turned-up nose, she caused strains, new to me till then in my dealings with others. I did not like to argue, but somehow she would always draw me into it, and apparently she relished needling me. Mamma was not happy with my new friend either, whom she considered not well behaved; but we had to accept her because we were relatives.

In the warmer weather, we would go together twice a week to get milk at the Bulgheroni's farm, skipping and singing some two kilometres down the Val Cuvia road. We'd stop at the laundry house to drink from the fresh running water, among the chattering gossips bent over the shiny stones of the basins scrubbing their wash. We'd stop and chat until we'd realize the time we'd wasted and the work still to be done. Sometimes the women would ask us to help to spread the white sheets on the fields. They would lay them down like swelling sails in the sun, and collect them freshly perfumed at sunset. Going back was instead slow and difficult, all uphill, with the weight of the large metal pitchers full of milk, which we held by a ring that cut into our fingers. Occasionally, we were lucky enough to meet with an ox cart slowly climbing up the hill. The farmers would pick us up and we'd finish our trip tossed about in the hay. We'd get home late, smelling of hay and manure, and mamma would scold us.

Giuseppina would always come to play at my house, because it was impossible in hers. Her house was all sparkling with tiles, mirrors, and furniture. One could always find her mother, Giulia, with a cleaning cloth and a wax jar in hand, wiping and shining. She would shine even the apples that stood out red and dazzling on the fruit bowl in the centre of the table, as if made of wax. They were so beautiful that I felt like taking one, though I would have hesitated biting into it because they looked so much like the poisoned apple of Snow White.

The only fun was the slippers used to slide on the waxed floors to avoid marring their shine. But the moment we let ourselves go into a long slide, we were chased away. Nonna said that Giulia had fallen victim to this obsession for cleanliness because of her insane jealousy for her husband, quite a bit younger. She had started by burnishing the brass door handles at home, to check if anyone suspicious had left their fingerprints. Mamma laughed at these tales, and nonna thought it silly that one could be jealous of Giacomo, a putty of a man, patient, humble, and entirely submissive to his wife.

It was Giuseppina Martinotti who tried in vain to pique my sexual curiosity, with me barely seven, by exploring our anatomy. The attempt failed because of my naive indifference and total lack of curiosity. So it all stopped there for many years until, having reached the needed maturity and not knowing where to turn for guidance, I ended up seeking the help of those scientific manuals, made precisely for simple souls like me.

During those same years, after we had both taken different paths, I was kept informed by nonna's "newsletter" of the *"scandalous life"* of that distant cousin of mine. Disapprovingly, nonna would burst out,

"*She ended up marrying - just imagine! - a young man who gave her an obscene book for their engagement. A real piece of filth!*"

And I would ask her, "*But how do you know about all this?*"

"*That poor Giulia tells me everything, she is desperate.*"

I never found out what the book was. It would have been too much to ask my poor nonna. Who knows, perhaps it was a beautiful "leather" edition of "the Kamasutra."

The most exciting event was the arrival of zia Ida with her newborn Pinuccio. Nonna put them up in a large room that opened out to the terrace; still, they spent the daytime at my grandparents' home. I felt quite important to have a baby cousin in the house and to be asked by my aunt to

There's Always the Sea...

share in the care of a live doll. Nevertheless, the baby's presence tended to tire out mamma, increasingly unable to tolerate anything that interfered with her absolute need for peace and quiet. As a result, whenever the baby cried, I was in charge of rocking him. With a great sense of responsibility, I would spend hours next to his little bed trying to make him sleep. Now and then, a girl from the village would come to help out zia Ida but, according to her, I was much better, and that pleased me no end.

One day zia Ida had put the baby food to heat in a pan, and she called out to the girl to *"give the pan a stir."* I could not believe my eyes when I saw Luigina tap the handle of the pan, and the pan..."stirred!"

I soon realized that not all the duties and tasks shaping my life in different ways were always pleasant. Mamma must not have been very pleased with my school work, and she made me work at home as well, on dictations, which I detested. I don't know why, but I just couldn't remember which words needed an accent. Mamma would not give up, and she'd make me do the same dictation over until I had learned every single one. But after the third or fourth time, she'd get angry, and the more she scolded me the more confused I got. Mamma would say that, unlike my brother who was very bright, I would not achieve much in life. Ninetto, however, managed to upset mamma as well, and even more than I. At times he would end up getting spanked with the carpet beater.

Frequently, planes would crash on the hills around the town, at times we'd see them come down in flames. In spite of being severely forbidden by mamma, Nino would travel to the site to pick up fragments. I was supposed to cover up his disappearances when he went on one of these "missions," but lying didn't come easily to me, and my brother would get in trouble. Among his many pranks that caused a great fuss, I remember the tale of Lietta's bicycle.

Lietta was a young woman, a friend of the family, perhaps a distant relative. She would bicycle in from a nearby town to see us now and then. Granted, she was a bit pushy and moody, but she was also kind and pretty. My brother found her frankly disagreeable. It happened that Lietta always left her bicycle under the portico of the garden, at the foot of the stairs leading to the apartments. One day, I don't know how or why, Nino decided to amuse himself by taking it apart like a toy to see how it was made. Pleased with himself, he called on me to wait together and see the reaction of his victim. I was sure that it wouldn't be funny, but I'll never forget Lietta's face when she discovered the prank.

I don't remember what followed, but I know that for Ninetto it was a case of carpet beater and confinement in his room, and maybe going to bed without supper as well. In spite of this, he seemed to still be quite pleased and proud of this exploit of his whenever the matter was brought up again. I, on the other hand, was at a loss, unable to judge. Was it perhaps a first act of defiance to rules, a way of asserting himself on the threshold of adolescence? Or was it part of the even more incoherent behaviour of a twelve year-old boy eager to attract the attention of a beautiful girl, "hated" of course? It wasn't always easy for me to understand my brother, nor for that matter, with the passing years, men in general.

In the meantime, however, mamma, not too convinced of my ability to make my own way in the world, decided to prepare me in the *"feminine arts"* necessary in the inevitable homemaker's role I was destined to fill. And so, once a week, I was confined and abandoned in the courtyard of the nuns' convent, struggling with those hated needles, and threads, and knitting. At sunset, with the nuns having withdrawn to pray, I would be waiting for my release, sitting on a little chair among grey stones and columns - the narrow red scarf growing slowly in my hands, until it covered my lap.

Together with sewing and knitting, I had piano lessons as well after school, which meant I had to go up to Villa Mandelli, to one of the sisters, the terrible Giovanna. Dark, wiry, as sinewy as a man, she ill-treated me and would strike my hands with a ruler. Thanks to this method, I was never able to realize how much I really loved the piano. A long time after that, Giovanna disappeared into the mountains to join the partisans. She was to return a heroine.

Having reached the age for my First Communion, catechism was added to my studies. I can't say I loved it or hated it, I simply didn't understand it, and so it seemed to be a useless exercise. Nevertheless, I did what I was told because I was intimidated by certain mysterious reasons that had something to do with God. I also liked the big bulky priest who taught me. Whenever he hugged me, I would feel lost against his large black cassock, so paternal, as inviting as the lap of a big cuddly bear.

He was Don Attilio, the town's new young parish priest who had become a family friend. He would often come to give spiritual comfort to mamma, causing the insane jealousy of Miss Anna, alias *Tota Anna*, as more familiarly nonna now called her, having lost in her eyes the respect necessary to be called "Miss." Once a week I went to the rectory for my catechism lessons and, when he would come to our home, Don Attilio would examine me. Just like a parrot, I had to reproduce the answers in the exact words. Those times I faltered, Don Attilio showed himself far more forgiving than my mother.

One day mamma had me put on my best dress, telling me we were going to see the Vanvitelli; "Stalin" and "Chamberlain" had come back from the clinic. I was so looking forward to seeing them! Mamma rehearsed me on how I had to behave. "Villa Vanvitelli" was a real palace on top of a hill, at the far end of town. All around the hill ran a tall fence because that was all their property, the park of the villa. A chauffeured car came for us. It would in fact have been impossible for mamma to have walked all that distance.

That's how I met "Seven-Cap" Lina. When I first saw her, the head atop of her lanky body was in fact entirely and thickly covered. While the ladies were chatting, I tried my best to count, without being seen, if she really wore seven caps, but to no avail. The most interesting discovery was that Lina had a husband, and that he was young, lively, and attractive. At home we immediately dubbed him *Il bell'Andrea*, and he became the object of lively and titillating conversations, while nonna, mamma, and Paolina speculated on the motives and the success of such a lopsided marriage.

The fact is that, being an avid explorer and hunter, Andrea was almost always travelling around the world. I promptly fell under the spell of his charm when he kidnapped me from the boredom of the easy chair where I was fidgeting ill at ease, and took me to see his collection of mounted exotic animals. We were introduced also to the third Vanvitelli sister, Luisa, who seemed to be the only really normal member in the family, married to the engineer Riccardo Sala. Quiet and reserved, the engineer preferred to stay by himself, smoking his cigar and looking at everyone with a forbidding and critical scowl that intimidated me.

Tea time came, served on silver trays by a white-gloved waiter. I was appropriately served a soft drink in a tall glass, in which dense syrup gave out a crimson glow. They called it *tamarindo*, a word unknown to me then, and never more forgotten. It slid down my throat, leaving a thick sweet aftertaste, which all at once made me feel like a goblet filled to the brim and spilling over. Immediately, I burst out with the desperate cry of years before, "*Mamma, 'nasua', 'nasua'.*" I can't say why, but of all those present, the engineer Riccardo was the first one at my side, and the *tamarindo* was spewed all over his impeccable pants.

Every day, the conversations of the grownups inevitably led to the progress of the war. The **tum-tum-tum-tum** of Radio-London continued to pound out our evenings, creating an atmosphere of conspiracy and trepidation in our home. With the arrival of the warm weather, we spent our evenings on the terrace. The dark sky on the horizon was often lit up with flashes, like fireworks. "*It's the flares; they're bombing Milan, or Turin,*" the grownups would confirm. For me it had become something of a spectacle, watching it every night after dinner, sitting comfortably on wicker chairs. If the luminous trails flashed on the left of the sky, they were bombing Milano; if they were on the right of our horizon, it was Torino. I would look fascinated, only vaguely taking in the reality that filtered through the conversations of the grownups. Swayed as I was by my imagination, I left the mystery untouched.

There's Always the Sea...

My first memory of him is when he came to see mamma in Milano, during his paratrooper's training course for *La Folgore*. The bell rang and there he was, all preened in a fancy, heavy military uniform. I peeked at him fascinated and fearful from behind mamma's skirt. But I was happy whenever he came. He brought good cheer in our home, even to mamma's melancholic face. He was my cousin Antonino, son of my father's brother. He was sixteen years older than me. Later, I would see him as my hero, making him the object of my admiration and adolescent emotions. I would also find out about his dramatic fight against the polio that had struck him down at eighteen.

Neither he nor his dauntless mother had lost heart. Zia Cornelia was a handsome, stark woman with a noble face, something like an ancient Roman matron. My brother had dubbed her with the historic name of *"Cornelia, mother of the Gracchi brothers,"* and he claimed she looked like Charlton Heston.

When her son was diagnosed with the disease, she decided that she would teach him to walk again; and so she did, with perseverance, patience, and great will power, supporting him in her arms and dragging him from one end of the house to the other. Antonino was left only with a barely noticeable scuffing of his right foot that seemed to add a touch of elegance to his step.

As a challenge and validation of his hard earned physical courage, he enlisted as a volunteer in that battalion of paratroopers, famous for its daredevil feats, *La Folgore,* and ended up fighting in North Africa. We had no word from him after the battle of El Alamein, until one day mamma received a message from Sicily that Nino was an English prisoner in Egypt. The relief was barely registered that a new shadow came over mamma's face.

I had just started second grade; it was the end of summer of 1943. I was returning home on a day imbued with the first golden shades of autumn. When I reached the small square in the centre of town, I found a great commotion. The whole town was in a tumult. The square was full of people yelling something like *"Mirstice! Mirstice!"* *"There is a mirstice!"* *"They have signed a mirstice!"* I didn't understand anything, but I was sure that something nice had happened, and I was gripped by the general euphoria. I couldn't wait to see mamma and tell her the good news, which would make her happy as well. Maybe it meant the end of the war, as she had been hoping. I ran home, climbed up the four flights of stairs, rushed to her, and out of breath I burst out,

"Mamma, mamma there is a mirstice. They've signed a mirstice! Are you happy?" And then, I finally asked, *"But what is a 'mirstice'?"*

CHAPTER SEVEN

I never understood what the armistice was or why everyone in town was so overjoyed. Maybe they were all happy because they had understood as much as I had. What became very clear to everyone, me included, was that life was harsher than before. Cunardo was gripped by hunger and fear. The shops were shutting down one after the other. Even bread became scarce, as there was no flour.

In the early days, Paolina would come in the morning with a small piece of butter or two fresh eggs she had managed to steal from the farm for mamma; then, even that came to an end. Undaunted as usual, nonna managed to find some rice flour, and started making bread. Ninetto and I would laugh when we were given those shapeless grey buns, as heavy as stones. Still, our ravenous teeth would avidly bite into them swallowing even our disappointment. We used as well to walk through the fields, zia Ida and I, to pick chicory, bitter leaves growing in the grass. We'd eat them as salad or we'd boil them; but raw or cooked, they provided nothing more than a few bitter mouthfuls.

One day, I went to the rectory for my usual catechism lesson, but Don Attilio was not there. No one knew anything. Days went by and even mamma could not understand his mysterious disappearance. She was worried, well aware of the impetuous and aggressive temperament of our strapping priest. And then, finally, what we had feared was confirmed - Don Attilio had rounded up the group of parish boys with whom he used to organize soccer games, and had joined the partisans fighting the Germans in the hills around the town.

We knew he was on San Michele, the mountain we could see from our windows. The partisans had set up their base there, utilizing for shelter the trenches still in place from the First World War. Nonno took out his war-time field glasses, and we were able to identify the war zone and a chapel where we thought Don Attilio and his boys had taken their position. Every day we checked at the window for hours, trying to make out what was happening; and every time we heard airplanes flying over that area, we'd anxiously rush to the field glasses. That's where we were that evening at twilight when we heard the roar of the planes and the whistling of a dropping bomb. I actually saw it fall, I heard mamma's scream, and saw the flames rising and ravage the forest. *"Don Attilio's shelter! They have hit Don Attilio's shelter!"* We were left in the dark.

Days later, there was a knock at the door. There was Don Attilio, ragged, muddied, and done in. He had been taken prisoner by the Germans, and had managed to escape. A doctor was called immediately. From my grandparents' exchanges, I pieced together a vaguely disturbing picture, *"He's been tortured ... a red-hot iron bed ... he didn't talk."* All at once, I felt involved in a dangerous conspiracy, a really serious "grownup" matter, in which I shared a terrible secret.

Don Attilio would remain hidden in our house for a few days, and it was vital that no one should know. I could tell no one, really no one, not even Giuseppina; in fact, I had to be careful that especially Giuseppina should not find out. I was very proud of this complicity with the grownups. I could feel the weight of the secret inside me, a real physical weight, and it made me feel filled to the brim as if it were about to spill out from some part of me. I felt very important in front of Giuseppina, but that was enough, I felt no need to reveal it to her. Besides, I had a secret even from mamma, I had discovered a big pistol in the lingerie drawer.

But one day, Giuseppina confronted me. With that sly smile of hers, she asked me if it was true that Don Attilio was hiding in our house. I denied it vehemently, but she kept pressing me, saying that it was useless to deny it because she already knew. I had to swear up and down, with tears in my eyes to convince mamma that it was not I who had told Giuseppina anything. In any event, Don Attilio had to leave, and I felt wretched. Mamma comforted me, telling me that he would not be in danger any more.

There's Always the Sea...

Dr. Agostoni arrived at last. He was coming from the hospital in Varese. Mamma had been waiting for him for months, because in her condition she could no longer make even the half hour train trip to go to Varese for a visit. The doctor ordered mamma to take to her bed. From then on, she endured in the semi-darkness of her *"damp and squalid"* room, as she writes in a letter to zia Mariuccia, trying to shield herself *"from the screams of the baby"* and the perpetual to and fro of nonna, *"always first to rise and last to go to bed."* Her dream was to spend the following winter in Ponzone, well aware of how everything was so uncertain.

"Just intentions, of course, because before then... it's in God's hands!" And she concluded resigned: *"I no longer feel an attachment to any one place now: the home scattered, alone with my children, one solution is as good as another; and I live like this, day by day, surprised to be alive and in this kind of world."*

Every day the nurse would come to give mamma an injection. I would hear her say that mamma was all riddled with punctures, and she didn't know where to give her a shot any more. This created a continuous abscess, another cross for mamma to bear. There was a constant coming and going in her room, with bowls of hot water, cloths and poultice for the compresses. For days on end she would suffer until finally *"the abscess would come to a head and burst,"* and then ... another one would form. In the midst of all this, I moved as if off stage, silent spectator of a drama acted out by the grownups, which seemed to unfold inexorably toward an absurd conclusion. I kept staring at mamma in that bed, in darkness, and I didn't understand. I would squat on the edge of the bed and I would look at her and I could not understand.

"Who can tell me for sure that you are not the wolf in disguise?" I asked her one day.

I then heard her laugh as she had not for such a long time. But I was serious. Whom or what should I believe in order to understand? How could I know what dying meant? Nino often kept mamma company. He'd spend hours by her bed, reading to her, playing the flute, or even singing in German. Mamma would say to me,

"You don't stay here with me like Ninetto. You don't keep me company like he does. You always run off."

Yet I loved her desperately, and I felt, at a level I could not express, unconsciously perhaps, that I was about to lose her. She had pricked her finger, small round drops of blood were trickling. I took her hand and I sucked for a long time. Mamma looked at me surprised. *"So your blood will be in me even after you are dead."* I explained.

One of the last images I have of her is in a beautiful room in the Martinotti's home, lying on a high antique bed, under embroidered sheets and blankets. I still see the little wooden columns shining in the semidarkness, waxed brightly, and the marble floor glittering like a mirror. Giulia had won the argument with nonna, insisting that it would be a more dignified setting to receive visits. In fact, the Baldonis were due to arrive. I now know these were the farewell visits. With the fact that mamma was there, I too spent all day at Giuseppina's home. We would play at the end of a long hallway, along which were all the bedrooms.

I had heard her voice calling me, but I had run to her other times already, and now I was too involved in a game. She could wait just a tiny bit; I would have gone to her in a short while. After all, I might not have heard her right away. But the voice kept calling and I, I cannot say why, I didn't want to hear it. When I finally ran to a more urgent plea and I approached her bed, mamma's hand rose from the bed sheet and struck me hard on the cheek. In a tired and disappointed voice she said,

"When I call, you'd do well to come right away. Later might be too late."

I was stunned by what happened. It was the first time mamma had struck me. Tears rolled down my cheeks, more for the mortification than for the physical pain. I knew I had been wrong, but that reaction seemed excessive to me. Only now do I understand all the anguish behind it. The mark on my face faded away, but what never left me was the burning sensation of that gesture in my soul. With the passing years, it took on a vaguely sad, symbolic sense, perhaps further influenced by the Freudian connotation that same gesture had in Italo Svevo's work. In the end, for me it remained the last gesture of my mother.

I was in school when they came to call me. I was to go home. They asked my cousin, Giuseppina Martinotti, to accompany me. I was surprised and curious to know the reason for that strange request, and yet strangely calm and unwitting. My cousin was instead on pins and needles, as if she could barely keep from blurting out something. We are walking along the deserted street, in the grey-colour shades of February. Just before reaching home, I notice a shadow, also grey and shabby, struggling to drag itself along the opposite wall. It's the town's idiot. He comes towards us stooped, swaying and lolling his head. We can't help laughing at his grotesque grimaces. As he draws nearer, he addresses us with wild gestures and gibberish, then, bit by bit, he moves away. With insensible cruelty we burst out in irrepressible laughter. A short time after, we reach the door of the Martinotti's home. Giuseppina stops me and tells me we must go up, then pauses, as if she wanted to say something. I question her. Yes, there is indeed something she'd like to tell me, but she can't. Her mamma has forbidden her to say anything. It's something very sad, it would make me cry.
"*Nothing could make me cry after laughing so much,*" I insist. "*All I have to do is think of those faces made by the idiot!*"
And I turn to look at him; he looks back at me with one last grin. In that instant the words of my cousin reach me: "*Your mamma is dead.*" I stare at her blankly, as I feel a black abyss open inside me down to the pit of my stomach, then rise to cloud my eyes. As soon as I come into the house, zia Giulia gathers me in her arms. She sharply reprimands Giuseppina, then she speaks and speaks to me, but in my sobbing I don't hear anything any longer. Only one thought slashes my mind like a knife: "*Mamma is no more.*"- Giulia's voice drones on and on.
The small living room in my home is crowded. I'm curled up in zia Mariuccia's lap. I only see and hear what is inside me: a dark lake like that of my dreams, filled with

anguish and fear; a dark aching that takes hold of my whole body as it shakes with sobs. They say I cried for eight hours straight, until, as night fell, exhausted, I fell asleep. But as usual, it's Nino who raises concern in the family. It is twelve hours since he has locked himself in his room, and he refuses to come out.

Only a long time after, I found out that the grownups had had a big discussion about it, particularly because nonna was opposed to it. But in the end zio Piero had been able to impose his opinion. Was the experience positive or not for me? To this day I cannot tell. Only much later, as I grew up, that vision enriched me profoundly.

Barely across the doorway I saw her like that, in gentle sleep, her body moulded down to her ankles by the folds of a dark dress, her long black braids emphasizing her slender figure and accentuating the adolescent freshness of her face. With the grey and taut mask of her illness gone, she was in fact quite young. I became aware of this as the years were passing for me. For so long I had thought of my mamma as an adult, the protective figure, the wise guide I had lost. Now she could be my daughter. In fact, when she died she had my own daughter's age. A young woman then, not allowed to live all the years that instead were granted to me; still unaware of so many things. I find myself thinking of her with the ache of a mother, understanding with horror her suffering. I find myself now between my mother and my daughter, older and wiser than both of them. It is my lot to understand and forgive them both.

The void that was created in my life at that point followed me day and night. But one cannot accept emptiness, and I filled it with dreams. I remember the little girl whose imagination played with a shadow. When at night I'd close my eyes to sleep, I'd go to meet my mother. I would find her in a chestnut grove, where the sunlight filtered through the boughs. It was not easy to see her; I had to move through the trees and then in the thickest part of the grove. But she would finally appear at the end of a path; she would smile and speak to me, I would tell her all about my fears and the day's misadventures. As the years went by, the dream slowly faded away. Yet, as an adolescent, I still found myself seeking her out, asking her advice and approval. At times I would wake up crying, still calling out to her.

A mere ten days after mamma's death, I was told that nonno had gone as well. *"He had followed his beloved daughter."* I felt my heart leap into my mouth, but I could not understand what had happened or what it would mean for me. I had been told he was ill and I had not seen him for days, yet I had not been allowed to go into his room. I could not grasp, unlike for mamma, that absence, that total sudden erasure of his presence. I had not seen any warning signs; I could not accept that he would not ever return to take his place next to us. I would cross the dining room in semi-darkness and the long white curtains seemed to shiver. I imagined nonno hiding behind those filmy screens. More than once, in fact, I saw him standing there, like in the wings of a surrealistic stage, a quiet rigid form locked in an impotent silence. For many days I saw him, and I felt him physically, until he disappeared. I never told this to anyone. I would later find out that he had died of pneumonia in a very few days for having kept vigil a whole night over mamma in a freezing room, praying. He was a Great War invalid, with a punctured lung. Maybe it was true that he had wanted to follow her.

February 1944, and the war showed no signs of ending. Nino and I were now left alone with nonna already in her sixties who, without the slightest hesitation, took on the task of raising the two of us, left orphans at thirteen and seven. And so began my contradictory relationship with nonna Cecilia, a big enigma in my life. Though I spent a lifetime with her, I never understood how she managed to overcome the tragedies that pummelled her within a few days, the death of a daughter and of the husband she adored. Where had she found the strength to think about us two? And yet the answer is perhaps simple: it was precisely that commitment to raise us that helped her to overcome her despair, to forget herself, giving her life one more final purpose. Or as Somerset Maugham says, *"A woman will always sacrifice herself if you give her the opportunity."*

When I was finally able to appreciate her courage and understand what she had done for us, I harboured all the admiration and gratitude due to her. Yet, during the thirteen years I lived with her, I did not always find it easy to love her, and certain sharp character traits plus her obsessive jealousy caused no small degree of suffering for me. After all, hadn't she already harassed nonno, driving him in the last years of his life to "*sainthood,*" as people would say with a smile? And mamma had foreseen all this.

"*Your mamma didn't want you to be entrusted in the care of nonna after her death,*" my aunt told me one day. I was deeply troubled, not only because I really loved nonna, but because of the painful intuitions being unveiled about the life of my family, which until then I had idealized. What painful experiences must have driven mamma to reach such a terrible opinion! And yet she had been the favourite daughter, while my aunt had deeply felt the lack of her mother's affection even as a little girl. She had felt excluded, she told me, when she had been sent to live with "*Màgna Madlinìn and Bàrba Carlo,*" aunt Maddalena and uncle Carlo. It had been in war time, and with her husband far away, it could very well be that nonna had not been able to cope with three children and the pharmacy, where she had to take the place of grandfather. But it was also quite obvious that she favoured her son. I've never been able to understand how one could love one child more than another. A shadow had tinged the people I loved, whom I now saw divided by resentments and jealousies. Yet, was it not thanks to my grandmother's strong character that my brother and I were rescued? After what had happened, who else would have had the strength and the capacity to face what was still to come, to protect us from the dangers and the suffering of the war and post-war period? Mamma had not been able to do it, and she had succumbed to the grief and the harshness of life. As for zia Mariuccia, she was struggling to the breaking point already for her own three children and an unemployed husband.

I often went back in my mind to the scene generated by my aunt's words,

"*The morning your mamma was dying, that wretched mother of mine had gotten into her head to move the furniture in the room next door. 'Tell her to stop,' Angiola would plead in her agony.*"

As I try to see and to judge what had happened with the benefit of hindsight and maturity, my resentment dissolves into infinite sorrow that includes nonna as well, that very *"wretched woman."* Helpless in the face of suffering, unable to express her pain, her only defence was to do, to act. She grasped at anything she felt she could control - concrete reality. Thus rejecting the reality she could not comprehend, that she refused to accept.

I returned to school, I played again with my friends, but nothing was the same again. Something had tainted my world; a kind of poison had seeped into me. It was as if an external force had taken possession of me and, unknown to me, was changing me into another being.

It happened right in Carla Belloni's garden, which from then on lost all its magic allure. I can't explain why I began to hate Tuffi, Carla's little dog. Suddenly his frisky ways of rubbing against me began to irritate me. I see myself again as if in a silent movie, a scene without any words to justify the absurdity of my actions. Yes, it is I whom I see. I can still feel the sensation of that soft thick layer of curly wool, just like the back of a lamb, which my small hand struck with fury. I kept striking, striking with rage, and it was a bitter-sweet sensation in a frenzy of frustrated violence. The tiny dog seemed in fact to be unaffected by my deep-seated need to hurt him. Perhaps protected by the thick coat of hair, he carried on his merry dance of love, as hopeless as mine, that immense love, cut off, wounded. And the more he showed his love the more I kept hitting him, growing more frustrated in my wish to hurt him. Then, the painful scene would be interrupted by the arrival of Carla. Yet it was repeated every time I came to see her. I took advantage of every absence of my friend to carry out my ritual of violence.

I'm still bothered by that memory, as I dig among the myriad interpretations of a Freudian *transfert*. Was I punishing myself out of a sense of guilt? Or did I want another innocent being to suffer like me? Was I exorcising painful experiences? The slap by my mother... her leaving me.... Was I striking out of anger, frustration or vengeance?

Whatever the answer, Tuffi, the little dog, offered me, luckily with no harm to him, a cathartic experience which allowed me to later grow into a human being who abhors violence.

The leitmotif of the slap continued nonetheless to haunt me, reliving it for a long time in my dreams. I see myself in front of an unknown face, whose features are vague, and with a tremendous effort I try to strike it with my hand. But my arm moves in a surrealistically slow movement with no driving force, and falls inert. A slap left incomplete, impotent, that once more comes back to express repressed feelings of rebellion and anger. Restrained violence against a life that offends me, or inability to impose myself in an aggressive world? In its constant resurfacing, the slap of my childhood assumes an emblematic value.

CHAPTER EIGHT

The daily news bulletins of victories and disasters, which were now reaching us uncensored straight from the front, kept us in a state of constant excitement, yet for us life was not getting any better. Nonna refused to give up, and kept up the struggle for our survival. Thanks to her inexhaustible resourcefulness, she moved from one scheme to another.

A huge darkened pot was boiling on the stove, giving off a sickening stench. Brandishing a gnarled stick, nonna kept stirring a gelatinous swill with gruesome bones on the surface. "*Bubbles... Bubbles...*"! But it was neither a witch's brew nor the "divorce Italian style" of Marcello Mastroianni in the famous movie. It was merely the poor desperate attempt of nonna to provide us some soap.

I can still see the spread of hard-boiled eggs covered by a disgusting sulphuric coating, meant to keep them fresh for longer periods of time, but instead turning them into suspicious greenish-looking lumps. Where did those eggs come from? From chickens of course, for whom nonna had set up a nice chicken coop right in the kitchen with great nonchalance. Not that they looked out of place down there in the corner, behind the wire netting. After all, the kitchen was somewhat archaic, with an uneven floor of unfinished brick that gave up a cloud of red dust every time it was swept. In fact, the chickens added colour and coziness, and they certainly were good company. In any event, any unpleasantness was promptly washed off with buckets of water poured out on the dusty floor, which rewarded our efforts by turning into a beautiful shiny blood-red surface ... for at least ten minutes.

Everything was primitive in that kitchen, from the sink carved out of a dark corner wall, lined with a porous granite that tended to retain water in slimy pools, to the bulky stove with large pipes bent in a web of elbows - an engineering feat of zio Marco that was meant to control the draft in the short distance between the stove and the window. The resourcefulness of zio Marco, however, was put to the test by the doubtful kind of fuel used for lack of wood - damp sheets of newspaper pressed into balls. The inevitable result was a constant smoke spread all around and a barrage of "s*acripante!*" uttered by nonna amid coughs. "*Marcooo….!*"

Yet the huge kitchen was the heart of the house, not least because it was the only heated room. And so, especially in winter, we'd all gather in the kitchen with the chickens: we kids doing our homework, zia Ida bathing the baby in the wooden tub (with no harm to the floor), nonna fiercely fighting against the stove's famous elbows that created either "*too much or too little draft*" and had to be continuously taken apart and cleaned of the soot. So that in the end nonna had to finish her day in the wooden tub as well.

But there was also a secret side to the kitchen, hidden behind the doors of the imposing, antique time-scarred wardrobe, and of the massive *credenza*. They were for me like the doors that opened "Wonderland" for Alice, an incongruous and anachronistic world. Piles of immaculate sheets, pillow cases, tablecloths perfectly stacked by size, giving off a smell of lavender, sunshine, and starched freshness. Nonna showed off their intricate embroidered designs, the fringes, the refined hemstitches, the delicacy of Flanders weaving, which, when brushed by the light, would reveal filigrees of silver-grey designs. I felt I was looking at fabrics richly woven for the dowry of a princess described in fables.

Fairy-like indeed were the stories nonna was proud to tell me, tales of her youth in my great-grandfather's estate: "Villa Calleri" in Ozzano, on the hills of Monferrato, as it was identified in the old yellowed postcard she still kept. Ozzano sounded like a magic word in nonna's mouth, lighting up her eyes and carrying her off in a dream world. Perched on a hill, the large villa was overlooking the valley below and surrounded by gardens and wooded areas that went down gentle slopes, as she would illustrate pointing to that green-tinted image, an early photographic effort of the period.

My interest was piqued when the stories were enriched by references to subjects I read about in my school books: Giovanni Lanza, Giolitti, who, she'd stress, had been great friends with great-grandfather Enrico when they were Members of Parliament in one of the first Parliaments of a united Italy. All three hailed from Piedmont. Giovanni Giolitti came from Mondovì, near Cuneo, my great-grandfather's town; while Giovanni Lanza was from Casale Monferrato, where my great-grandfather had his office as a Notary Public. The three friends would travel to Rome together. It was from Giovanni Lanza himself that my great-grandfather had purchased the Ozzano estate in Monferrato. It seems that Lanza had incurred large debts because of the expenditures connected to his political-diplomatic activities. Unlike today, being in politics then was a burden and ...an expensive honour, rather than an opportunity to grow rich! Could that be the reason, I thought, why in Parliament Giovanni Lanza had adopted the policy of *"pare-down-to-the-bone budgets?!"*

These stories were usually inspired by the porcelains and crystals sets jealously kept under lock and key in the *credenza*. The narrating voice of nonna would unlock in my imagination the great halls of the villa that toward the end of the previous century were decorated for banquets and balls attended even by members of the Royal Family.

I could just see nonna, young and beautiful as she played the piano surrounded by elegant officers, courting her and inviting her to dance. Swaying silks and velvets would cross with stiff military uniforms in twirls of waltzes. Scenes of an ancient decorum suggested perhaps by nonna to my childhood imagination to offset the degradation of the present. In time I would come to understand the lesson of moral strength that nonna was able to impart to us children. By nurturing in us the spirit of our ancestors, she was able to raise us with dignity amid hardships.

"*Nostalgia is a positive emotion,* someone said, *if it acquires the value of a memory, useful to understand who one is, and who one will be.*"

Any form of sentimentalism was on the other hand filtered in her by a healthy dose of irony. With only a slight tinge of pride in her voice, she would tell how "*at the home of the Deputy of Parliament Calleri,*" the king felt at ease because he could freely use his beloved Piedmontese dialect. He did not in fact appreciate the Italian language, which he spoke with considerable difficulty, preferring French, if anything. Then, there was the tale of the asparagus, which the guests were sadly prepared to eat with knife and fork when they noticed that the king had calmly picked them up with two fingers. With a general sigh of relief, the banquet proceeded with good cheer for the rest of the evening.

The family emblem was the famous set of dishes *Le farfalle*, so called because of the image of butterflies in breezy colours embossed in the porcelain.

"*Great-grandfather,* nonna would say with emphasis, *given the large family, had placed an order with the renown "Ginori" for hundreds of plates. There were ten children and the plates had to withstand the assaults of the young and of the domestic help. That's why they are so heavy, made of practically indestructible porcelain.*"

In fact, thanks to the quantity and their unique toughness, they had survived more than a century, and when great-grandfather passed away, each of his three daughters and their families had received a share of them. Going to the home of any of the Calleri sisters meant eating off the "*butterfly plates.*" From generation to generation, they have now reached my daughter, and now I tell her their history.

I also tell her about the day - the war already ended - nonna organized a party for my friends. For her these were joyful occasions to recreate on a small scale a few echoes of those long-ago splendours, and so she would launch into making a number of delicacies, and laying out sumptuously decorated tables, where she could finally bring to light and show off her linens and antique porcelains. And, although somewhat overawed, my friends loved the delicate dishes that nonna would produce. That day, however, my best friend's little sister was not able to swallow but a few bites, though she usually had a hearty appetite. She didn't seem ill, and she liked the food. It continued to be a mystery until, sometime later, Antonia had the courage to confess that her sister had a phobia for butterflies, *"and those seemed so real!"*

But those days were still in the future. For the moment my life revolved around raising chickens, which meant as well taking the chickens out *"to pasture."* I don't think there is a better way of saying it, since the chickens had to be brought down from the second floor to scratch about in an open field. The task naturally fell to the two "Giuseppine girl-Fridays." Armed with a stick, my cousin and I had to guide seven or eight chickens down four flights of stairs, and that was the easy part. Somehow we managed to reach the open field. But afterwards, to find and retrieve the chickens scattered and hidden in the bushes and lead them towards the house was an altogether different matter, all the more so because we had to deal with the usual "black chicken" of the bunch.

Nerina, alias *"the American chick,"* was by nature a rebel, small but aggressive and mean; she would challenge us, or rather she imposed her will on us by dint of furious pecking. To our great satisfaction, she dared to challenge even nonna, yet that was the very reason Nerina was her favourite. Nothing gave nonna more pleasure than having a good row, and be able to gloat in victory later by proudly showing her battle scars. Nerina's good fortune, however, began to decline when she started picking fights with her fellow "cellmates." We'd always find one of them half plucked. Rumours began going around that we had to get rid of Nerina, but nonna kept refusing. Nevertheless, the morning we found one of the chickens dead, nonna pronounced sentence. We all felt bad seeing Nerina with her dangling neck, nonna muttering as she plucked the feathers. But nobody complained about the rare rich meal.

We next embarked on "the silk worms" adventure. Somebody convinced nonna that the idea was very profitable. Private breeding was encouraged for the production of parachute silk. And so, there we were with another set rigged up in the kitchen - a long wooden table leaning against the wall, artistically wrapped in mulberry vine leaves, like in a Caravaggio painting. Nonna had bought some silkworm eggs just before they were due to hatch, and microscopic larvae barely a few millimetres had come out in spring. At this point we had to act quickly, because they were voracious little monsters; as usual my cousin and I were unleashed on a new mission - get more mulberry leaves. That's when I got the bug for nature, and its fascination never left me. The search for the mulberry-tree groves took on an almost mystic aura. They were such a rare thing for us girls, so hidden and mysterious, deep in the woods. Often we found ourselves lost and scared. But we were amply repaid, because hanging from those emerald-leaf plants were the most incredibly tasty berries. Before we learned the trick of breaking off the little branch with berries and bringing them to our mouth, like Bacchus with his grape vines, we would come back home with bloodied hands and clothes, as if we had taken part in some desecrating pagan ritual.

Under my very eyes, the magic went on as those yellowish dots that devoured the leaves like woodworms rapidly were turning into so many *"brucaliffi,"* though not as charming as the caterpillar in "Alice in Wonderland." Spellbound and at the same time repelled, I followed them as they humped their way up the mulberry twigs, and enshrouded themselves in their silk cocoon. It was the most glorious moment, when our little grove would light up with drops of gold, the chrysalis. And that's when nonna would come to plunder the spoils. Only a few would be left after her ruthless foray; she kept them to produce other eggs and begin the cycle all over again. And so I could witness the most exciting moment - their metamorphosis into butterflies. Every time, I hoped that from at least one of those cocoons would issue a marvellous butterfly with brilliant colours, the most beautiful creature, the queen of butterflies. But I was always disappointed. The golden pix shattered and a whitish ungainly, squat ugly little thing would bring me back to the real world.

Nonna would have said, *"Not all that glitters is gold"* or maybe *"Clothes don't make the man"*- whose truth would be contradicted by my future life experiences. As a matter of fact, I had much more satisfaction from the prosaic and dirty egg shells of our chickens. Those, following the services of a

There's Always the Sea...

rooster that nonna managed to get, as I was to discover much later, would hatch, and out came golden chicks, sometimes black, which I would gently gather from nonna's hands, thrilled by their delicate heartbeat. The surprise was always intense and I was never disappointed.

Long cold winters, immersed in the mists of the valleys. Ancient crumbling walls seeping humidity. Beyond the heavy green door of the kitchen, were the freezing cold and the gloom of the forsaken rooms, not lived in. Come night, however, we had to move into our bedrooms, whose doors, as the kitchen's, gave onto a common entrance hall turned into a little living room, but they seemed so far and isolated - I together with nonna in the master bedroom, and Ninetto in his own.

That was the time we would carry out the ritual of "*il prete*," "the priest," that we took with us to bed. "The priest," so called for the irreverent reference to its potbellied shape, was a wooden structure formed by four curved long slats, two above and two below, with a small square platform in the middle. It looked like a baby whale. We slipped it under the covers to keep them lifted, then nonna would place in its belly the terracotta brazier filled with burning embers picked from the dying fire in the stove, to warm the sheets. Only then would I slip in the bed that "*il prete*" had warmed for me, blissfully seeking the warmest spots. No electric blanket would ever give me in the years that followed the same sense of comfort as that funny-looking gadget with its human personality.

But it wasn't only the cold that kept me from venturing beyond the warm and cozy confines of the kitchen. That heavy green door was for me a protection from an uncertain and frightening world. In the vestibule behind it, there was as well a tiny door that led to the dark area of the attic. Out of it a storage place had been carved, which had some mysterious hidden niches. After having read "Il Cuore" by De Amicis, a classic for children in those years, certain images imbedded in my mind found their way into that nook. Whenever I passed in front of it, I imagined two ominous thieves hiding between the beams, ready to unleash violence and terror. Nonna kept sending me to get firewood stored there so that I would get used to it. It was useless; I would come back down every time with my heart pounding madly.

Just like a melody that is stuck in our mind, and keeps returning obsessively even days later, so for me is the effect of things seen or read that have upset me. A persistent memory of certain visions has haunted me all my life. Scenes of horror, of morbid violence seen in a movie or on television remain forever embedded in my mind's eye. I carry them with me for days on end; they return with a physical presence even many years later, when I least expect it, calling forth the same sense of anguish and horror. Like the war reprisals that took place in the streets of Cunardo.

If the thieves were only a product of my imagination, the traces discovered in the living room were those of very real enemies. While the kitchen had its happy colourful cackle of chickens, and yes, even something less attractive but picturesque nonetheless - like the twisted sticky fly-catcher tape hanging from the ceiling, covered with its victims - the living room, on the other hand, hosted a fauna all its own, typical of the environment. Another opportunity for nonna to go immediately on the war path. But this battle turned out to be much more challenging than the one against the black chicken or the stove pipes. She refused to give up, and her defeats seemed, if anything, to harden her resolve. There was no doubt about the presence of the enemy in the attic. We could hear them running back and forth over our heads, and in the morning there were signs of their raids in the very living room. Nonna set the traps. The first few days, a couple of sad-looking little mice got caught. But after that, no trace was found of either mice or cheese. With renewed vigour and determination, nonna brushed up on her knowledge of the deadliest pharmaceutical poisons known to man; she dug up the supplies left over from nonno's time, bought the best trap, and she was ready. Come evening, just before going to bed the trap was set full of mouth-watering cheese. A few other victims got caught, but soon they all stayed clear of the trap, and the brazen raids continued unabated.

Then summer came, and even the maligned living room took on a new look. It was enlivened by our more fluid movements, not stiffened by the cold, and by fear in my case. Perhaps, as I grew I changed, and with me the reality did as well. In the sunlight the little living room revealed its capacity for warmth, even emotionally. Just like individuals, so too places and settings can possess their own personality, immutable through the years, though covered by a thick patina of time. The shape of objects, surfaces to caress with the eye - features that become familiar, that we grow fond of, to which it's so nice to return.

I recall the terracotta tile floor glamorized by the large blood-red Persian carpet. In the middle stood the small table at which nonna sweated blood over the bills. From the drawer she'd pull out reams of papers, bills, ledgers, receipts, using all her wits to feed us and keep a roof over our heads. Against the opposite wall was the antique *secrétaire,* nonna's pride, one of the symbols of her lost world, out of which she would pull even more pieces of papers and mysterious letters. The *secrétaire* was a work of extraordinary craftsmanship; nonna had revealed to me its secret compartments which only she knew how to find. In fact, though I had seen them several times, I was not able to find them myself.

There was also the weather-beaten dark red leather armchair. I have always associated it immediately with nonna, since it was her favourite armchair. I can see her stretching out for her afternoon nap. I remember how she insisted I sleep with her, on her lap. But I'd rebel against that forced rest, and if I wasn't able to avoid it, I would submit to it with a long face. Now I understand that it wasn't merely youthful liveliness.

Though needing tenderness, I tended to rebuff nonna's shows of affection, which I found wanting. I could not really say when or why I became alienated from my grandmother. What had happened to our nice understanding? Perhaps instinctively I was starting to feel the rough-edges of her character, or was I becoming bitter myself? As yet unaware of the suffering of grownups, and unable to understand the void that had occurred in nonna's life too, her need for affection, I tended to be more withdrawn, in an unconscious effort to offset the tender love of my mother I had lost. I still feel a sense of guilt.

The curvy enigmatic porcelain mermaid, sitting on the radiator along the wall, stares at me with piercing eyes, while the heavy brass globe of the ancient pendulum beats its slow, ponderous, and seemingly relentless rhythm. And yet, nonna would repeat convinced,

"The day nonno died, the pendulum stopped. It had never happened before."

In the summer my playground expanded to include the large terrace that overlooked the garden. Following mamma's death, our apartment had been taken over by the family of one of zia Ida's sisters. They were from Trieste. There were two daughters; Adele, nicknamed Cicci, was the eldest, while Teresita was my age. For me this now meant having always a playmate. Both our apartments opened on to the terrace, which was of course where we met whenever we had some free time. Unfortunately, I didn't have the nice games left back home in Milano. Maybe mamma had them taken away together with all the furniture to avoid the danger of bombing raids. The fact is that I was never to see them again, like so many other things that had disappeared in that strange town where mamma had had them stored: Usmate in Brianza. Frequently in those years, that name resonated a chord in me, with weird associations. I would imagine my toys taken by the townspeople, walking around the streets *usmaying* - "sniffing."

Cicci, six years older than Teresita and me, encouraged us to compensate the lack of games and toys with our imagination. How rewarded we felt when the instrument, made out of a small cardboard box and many elastics stretched over it, actually produced fascinating sounds. We even managed to make stuffed dolls, because rags were certainly not lacking in the house, and the lack of thread to sew was solved by Cicci who, with great nonchalance, used her own long hair.

My world, however, up to then fairly untroubled, was soon marred by the not wholly positive presence of Teresita.

There's Always the Sea...

The red hair braids and the freckled face of the same colour confirmed what town children used to say, *"Red hair, nasty character."* By comparison, even Giuseppina Martinotti was an angel. For the first time I became the object of meanness and injustice till then not experienced, and I didn't know how to deal with it. I had not been taught to be violent or aggressive. I couldn't think of anything else than to break out in tears, and vexed seek the protection of grownups. But they would only mildly admonish my foe, and I was left feeling inexplicably even more ill at ease.

"Don't make Giuseppina cry! You know she's just lost her mother."

It sounded like asking for special treatment, which had nothing to do with the situation at hand. What I wanted was justice! The villain put on trial and her harassment unmasked. And so, bit by bit the world in all its facets began, or better continued, to reveal itself; and I discovered a new truth as well - the essential need to defend myself and the ability to do so.

The acid test came one day when I went with Teresita to the farm of Paolina, the maid who had remained attached to our family even after mamma had passed away. I was supposed to go and get something for nonna, and Teresita wanted to tag along. There, I met Cecchin, Paolina's brother and my classmate since first grade. He had been my first friend; he defended me from the pranks and teasing of other classmates. I found him playing with a hoop. I had never seen a hoop as a toy. I was captivated, and I too started running around the farmyard, pushing it with a stick and chasing that thin object that rolled ahead of me, as I tried to learn to guide it. Teresita tried it as well. Seeing how enthusiastic I was, Cecchin gave it to me as a gift before we left.

As soon as we were on the road home, Teresita grabbed it and refused to return it. I protested, demanding my turn. This having no results, I pointed out that after all it was mine. Unmoved, Teresita replied that the hoop was hers, that Cecchin had given it to her. After a series of futile charges and counter charges aimed at obtaining justice, my indignation turned to fury. I found myself in the worst fight of my young life. I chased Teresita and ripped the hoop from her. This went on all the way home, screaming, chasing each other, fiercely wresting the toy from each other's hands, but for the first time I did not let go. I reached home upset and dishevelled, but with the trophy of my victory firmly in hand. The next day after school, I dragged Teresita in front of Cecchin, who confirmed that he had given the hoop to me. I had won.

Not long after that, however, I came face to face with other forms of violence which I suffered and witnessed without any chance to resist them. Once I was called to the front of the class by the teacher and given the duty of keeping order, while she left the classroom for a few minutes.

In class there were many unruly boys, they were *i ripetenti*, the ones who had to repeat the grade over and over again, and so they were two or three years older than their classmates. They were rough farm boys who were there *"to warm the benches,"* as they say, until they reached the legal age to leave school and return to work in the fields, abandoning the impossible task of getting even a minimum education. They were difficult to control even with the teacher in class. Besides jabbering on and making noises, as soon as she turned her back, they would leave their seats - naturally in the last rows - and would make all sorts of mischief, while jumping and making faces to provoke her.

Well, now the teacher had asked me to write on the blackboard the names of those who would move from their seats while she was gone. She was barely out of the door, when two or three had already jumped up starting a racket. With my little piece of chalk in hand, I kept looking bewildered first the three bullies, then despairingly the blackboard, feeling not quite up to the task. I tried to warn them, calling them out by name, saying that if they didn't stop, I would have to write down their names. After a while, two of them grew tired and went back to their seats. Not Battista, nicknamed *"Batistun"* because he was built big and square like an ox with his tight swollen skin. He was the biggest bully and the one I most feared. And there he was, out of spite still sitting on the radiator and challenging me,

There's Always the Sea...

"Come on; let's see if you've got the guts to write my name!"

After a bit of a squabble, I felt it my duty to write his name on the board, and there it stayed until the teacher returned.

When school was over, I started to walk home. But after the rest of my classmates had gone off in various directions, I noticed Battista had kept walking behind me. It was soon clear that he was following me. I was surprised; I didn't know what to think. But after a while, when his presence behind me became more pressing, I started to feel uneasy. As I hurried, I noticed that there was no one around at that mid-day hour, the street was deserted. And suddenly Battista was all over me, pushing me under an arcade to our left, pressing me against the stone wall, and giving me two hard slaps on the face, as he hissed *"Snitch!"* I was completely stunned by this unexpected burst of violence, I don't know whether more distressed by the physical pain or by the sense of humiliation.

My memory stops here. I don't recall what happened afterward, whether I talked to anyone, or if any grownup did something about the incident. I only know that the idea of not having understood kept gnawing at me. Had I done something wrong? What should I have done? Disobey the teacher? Of course, I knew that being a telltale was something bad, very bad. Our teacher, Ms. Casali herself, had ended up ... And ....the duty to obey does not always justify our actions....

Now that I think back, I never did like Ms. Casali. Poor old lady! I see the blurry image of a heavy-set woman, a pair of thick lenses on a face with a fixed frown. A perfectly insignificant personality for me, one that left no trace at all in the memories I have of those years except, of course, the last time I saw her.... Maybe that's why I didn't like going to school then, or why I didn't do well in those dictations that upset mamma so, until that is Antonella Mandelli came as our new teacher.

The only thing I remember of those early years of school was my enthusiastic discovery of the art of drawing, a skill which, sadly, would be denied me all my life. But in those first years, I spent hours sitting at my grandfather's desk, that marvellous desk, with a black leather top, surrounded by shelves with the entire collection of the Italian Touring Club Guides. They were full of illustrations of the many beautiful places I wanted to visit when I grew up. Perhaps nonno had collected them precisely for that reason - he too loved to travel. I still keep those guides of the 30's and 40's, with their slightly faded bluish covers, the thick laminated shiny pages, one volume per region - Lombardia, Piemonte, Toscana..., and two for Roma, all so different from present-day Italy!

I especially liked to create what the teacher called *"harmony of colours,"* one colour fading into another until the entire colour wheel was finished. One had to have the *"sense of colour,"* as she explained, to know how to match them harmoniously, and I have always been sensitive to colours. I love colours, they give me joy, and I find it physically painful if they clash. Who knows, perhaps I owe this to my teacher Casali.

Drawing brings me back to the way each season was marked in those days; at Easter and Christmas, I can still see myself bent over the big desk, intent in preparing cards of best wishes. I would copy from real cards, but I also wanted to put my own touch. There was the little shepherd carrying on his shoulder a wicker basket full of coloured eggs, or chicks breaking out of their shells. But my favourites were the Christmas ones; the most evocative were the scenes of brooks running between banks of snow, with sparrows resting on holly tree branches. Still now, whenever I run across similar scenes on Christmas cards, it warms my heart with echoes of the intense emotions felt back then, of Christmases lived merely with my imagination.

In my fantasy I would enter those inviting far away worlds, with enchanting chalets hidden in the woods. Horse-drawn carriages stopping in front of them, and young women alighting wrapped in cloaks and fur muffs. They passed from the cold of the snow to the warmth promised by the glowing windows. What pleasant surprises awaited them within? The warmth of a large joyous family, a festive table set, a crackling fire, gifts under the sparkling tree. All things denied to me and no Dickensian Scrooge to perform the miracle. But just so long as I lingered over those images with my colour pencils, I lived in that reality. I was one of the "little women" with whom I shared my dreams, as years later I would do with the characters of Louise Alcott's novel, certain that I too in time would enjoy such an intense life. I only had to wait and grow up. And yet, I would not ever be able to sit at my mamma's feet and put my face on her lap. I had to settle with conjuring her up at the point of my pencil.

And so indeed I managed to do, when one day I came upon the picture of a woman that troubled me and filled me with inexpressible sweetness. I saw mamma in that face. I continued to stare and lose myself in it until, almost unconsciously, I found myself faithfully tracing it on a piece of paper. As I followed the features with my pencil, I savoured it, I drank it up in me. It turned out a perfect reproduction, like I've never been able to do since, not meant for drawing as I was. That was my little miracle.

All I had to do was to wait and grow up. But for the moment, as from the shade of that long hallway of 1941, another image emerges of three years later, as well dressed in white, but taller, bigger, with her legs covered now by a long skirt, yet with the same lost look of years before. It's the photo of my First Communion. Mamma had the dress made in Chantilly lace by the usual Scappardini in Milano. It had the same name as the sweet cream that mamma used to make, but unlike that, this left a bitter taste in my mouth - mamma was never to see me in that dress, she had died two months before.

That day, I didn't even feel the long anticipated *"joy"* I had been prepared for, when I'd *"meet Jesus,"* in spite of the grownups' assurances. I remember only the fretfulness and trepidation brought on by the many rules, prohibitions, and warnings concerning the First Communion:

> *"Don't chew, don't touch the host with your teeth, don't look at your dress, don't look around, don't talk...."*

Just like the abstract dogmas of Catechism, all these concerns managed to strip away any emotional value from the experience, and any possible comfort for the mind of a child.

Much greater, as I recall, was the anxiety linked to the first Confession, and a negative emotion it was, full of fear. We had to learn which sins to confess, the venial as well as the more serious ones. From the explanations, I understood without any doubt that what that man had shown by suddenly opening his coat, while my cousin and I were walking down the street, was indeed a big sin. I had run away horrified at the sight of that slimy and shapeless thing, amid the giggling of Giuseppina. A really big sin! It dawned on me then, that I would also have to confess having seen my little cousin Enrico peeing. Well, nonna's opinion was that it was only a venial sin, but the priest would decide.

The large Cunardo parish, perched on the hill, at the end of a long flight of steps, was full of children of various ages, due to the delays caused by the war. At seven and a half years, I was a bit old as well for the First Communion. It was beautiful to see that large space filled with girls fluttering like butterflies in their froth of white organza. And how handsome the boys were in their pearl-grey suits, with a tie and a white armband. I watched Carletto, Lucio, Nino Martelli in admiration, they didn't seem themselves.

From that day forth, "taking Communion" became a Sunday ritual. I got used to it, as if meeting a friend. I felt a "presence" within me, with a kind of primitive superstition. To this "presence" I'd confide my fears; I'd ask for favours, I'd beg with cathartic fervour. It was the intermediary between me and mamma who *"lived with Him."* I would cling to it like to an amulet, like something that might materialize my mamma. When something troubled me, I would go to bed holding to my breast the small alabaster and silver crucifix which had been her favourite - she always kept it with her. I had found the courage to claim it for myself when they were about to leave it with her forever. I would squeeze it against my breast like a cilice, till it cut into me with its sharp edges. The torments of the heart thus merged with those of the body, dissolving in it.

That photo of April 1944 was taken in the garden of the villa in Cunardo, in the soft warmth of the first days of spring - a rigid white figure against the dark trunk of the magnolia tree.

The veil forms a skullcap that comes awkwardly down to my ears, and is held in place by a tiny crown, like those of the brides in the 1920's. The headdress is in sharp contrast with the plump cheeks of a child. The pale face has a bewildered and subdued look, as if her questions had died on her lips, knowing already that no answers would be forthcoming.

CHAPTER NINE

A year later, April 25, 1945, Liberation Day went by completely unnoticed by me. I don't know how Cunardo celebrated the event. Only years later, through the movies, I would become acquainted with the by-now familiar scenes of the festive columns of American jeeps passing through cheering crowds. Maybe I hadn't paid attention to it when it happened because I had no reason to run home and make mamma happy with the news. She was gone by then. As for me, I personally did not feel any positive effect. I found myself gradually more alone. At the end of the school year, my friends were beginning to go back to the city. I didn't, because, as nonna explained, our apartment had been taken over by *i senzatetto*, "the homeless" (those who had lost their home in the bombing raids.)

"*My good-hearted Angiola*, nonna would complain, half disapproving half pleased with her daughter, *had opened her home to beggars. She was moved to pity by one and all. Like that good-for-nothing she met on the train, who had persuaded her with the sham of being a poor widow left all alone with a little girl. Ah, I give you 'little girl', the wrong side of thirty! Who, by the way, had been around the corner a few times, let me tell you. But Angiola didn't know how to judge people. She would not have been able to recognize a .... She trusted everyone.*"

And she'd conclude, shaking her head in mock desperation,

"*She gave her the keys to the whole apartment, offering her a room. And that so-and-so carved for herself a little apartment, bathroom and all. And then, wouldn't you know it, that woman let other families move in, certainly not out of mere generosity. They have taken over even the kitchen. Five families in that apartment, and we are stuck here. The children have to go to school, and I can't take them back to Milano. We are stuck here, with the farmers."*

And that's how nonna's umpteenth battle started, the longest and the most difficult: against the Molinari woman, the homeless, and the Housing Commission. The Commission was a war-time institution with the task of requisitioning the few residences left, and to re-distribute them. After the war, we had to appeal to it to reassert our rights over those of the squatters. Getting rid of five families was a daunting task. Just as mamma during the war, now nonna had to travel back and forth to Milano. But unlike mamma, who would always return exhausted, nonna came back elated as if from the battle field, describing clashes, defeats and victories. The story turned into a never-ending saga. Luck would have it – or was it thanks to her unfailing initiative - that she found a champion for our cause: Corradino Oddo, business consultant.

Our namesake Corradino Oddo claimed to be a distant relative. Mamma denied it and, true to the bias in our family, she distrusted him like anyone connected with the business world. She was convinced he was an unscrupulous individual. Later on, we found out that mamma's opinion was well founded. Years later, on a visit to his home, nonna was shocked by what she saw: a display of collector's paintings, furniture, and objects of great value, among which she recognized some pieces she had seen at the Rosenthals' home. I was older now, and able to connect the dots, and understand - the deportation train, the piece of paper I picked up, the contact mamma had made with the Rosenthals, the services offered by Corradino Oddo. The Rosenthals had disappeared to safety somewhere, probably in America. But Corradino Oddo had not acted out of humanitarian spirit, and he certainly did not do so only for the Rosenthals.

In spite of this, nonna had no scruples in seeking his help. *"For two orphans,"* she would justify. The truth is that, to a certain extent, she admired the cunning of that man in facing and outwitting others, without ever giving up. He was her kind of knight, one who enjoyed a challenge as much as she did. In truth, without his dogged help, we would never have managed to reclaim our home in Milano.

Corradino Oddo disappeared eventually from our life, leaving behind a widow with two boys my brother's age, with whom we kept in touch off and on. Throughout the next few years, Giovanni, the youngest, crossed my path occasionally. My adolescent fantasy was bewitched by that foxy face, made even more sharp and cocky by a goatee. I saw in him a reborn Robin Hood, due to the fact that he was an avid and able archer, and that made him even more fascinating in my eyes.

Events far off into the future. My world was for the moment still limited to the streets of Cunardo, always full of restless people those days, noisy, sometimes violent groups, which I couldn't read into at all. As much as during the war, I would hear the anxious voices of adults talk about strange events taking place. Like the incredible arrest of Giacomo Martinotti, nonna's nephew, my cousin Giuseppina's father, famous for being a *"panpist,"* that is a sweet good-natured man, totally harmless. It appeared that he was guilty of having been the town's mayor, or rather *podestà*, as the mayors were then called during Fascism.

"A *Fascist mayor*...." people would say. *"Yes, but he was nominated mayor only because he was a good man!"* Nonna would protest shocked. *"He never hurt anyone. He couldn't hurt a fly."*

Thanks to the many in town who testified in his favour, because everyone in fact knew him as a good and kind man, he was then released from prison.

The end of the war was also the time of the great "returns." There was zio Marco returning to rebuild his family with zia Ida and Pinuccio, though it was anything but an ideal reunion. He appeared restless and dissatisfied, as in fact happened to many young soldiers coming home from the upheaval of the war, unable to adjust to the dull routine of everyday life. Nonna and zia were concerned to see him out of work. He roamed the house like a caged tiger. He quarrelled with zia Ida, accusing her of having failed in bringing up their son. He kept picking on the boy, irritated by everything, imposing on him the strictest discipline, something which really upset me. I tried to justify it, but for the wrong reasons, since my grasp of human psychology was still rudimentary.

I took a long time to free myself of the conditioning of that period, which accepted physical punishment, as well as to understand that certain features of my uncle's character had been magnified by war experiences. A personality that, while still inspiring a certain awe, soon recovered all its easy-going picaresque charm. He was always so imaginative, always able to suggest a game, or come up with a prank. His exuberance was irresistible to me, and apparently to others as well from what I could gather.

Among the various short-term jobs he wangled, was that of ski instructor and most of his pupils seemed to be beautiful wealthy ladies. I myself could attest to the many times zio Marco would be seen in the company of a certain beautiful lady. The familiarity of their behaviour left even me nonplussed. The appearances of the couple along the more out-of-the-way streets in town, which I surmised were supposed to be discreet and which I therefore dismissed, exerted nonetheless an odd interest for me. From all this I derived mixed impressions, something like secret capers that after all could not greatly menace my aunt's life.

Certainly more emotionally intense was the return of my Sicilian cousin Antonino, who had disappeared for years. After his being taken prisoner by the British at El Alamein, we had had no more news from him. My imagination surrounded his figure with a mythical halo. I saw him fallen victim of some spell that kept him prisoner even after almost all other survivors had returned at the end of the war.

In the complex emotional maze of childhood, especially mine with so many voids, cousin Antonino and uncle Marco occupied two completely opposite positions. Zio Marco's image was dwelling into a more concrete dimension, inspiring for me more immediate and paternal feelings. My cousin Antonino, on the other hand, lived in my mind among heroes of tales of adventure, surrounded by a romantic halo, thanks to remarks heard from the adults about the daredevils "Folgore Paratroopers," and the exotic places of battles in which Antonino had taken part - El Alamein, Africa, then the long imprisonment in Egypt, everything so hard for me to visualize.

Perhaps, precisely because I couldn't frame him within concrete points of reference, I often imagined him suddenly appearing from among the flower beds of our garden in Cunardo, waving his paratrooper cap to me as I looked down from the terrace. I would have been happy to be the first to give the good news to mamma, so sad for the fate of her beloved nephew. I could just hear myself shouting, *"Antonino has come back from the prison camp!"* I imagined him appearing without warning, as if Africa were just a skip and a jump from Cunardo... and that's exactly how he showed up, without any warning, standing under the magnolia tree, as if parachuted from a vacuum of time and space. The evil spell had been broken. He had been freed, perhaps thanks to that captivating smile he now turned on me, surely capable of melting the heart of even the ruthless African enchanter.

Mamma, however, was no longer there to rejoice. I lived the experience for her. In fact, my cousin had come for me, for me and Ninetto. He knew we had been left alone, and he wanted to take us under his wing. He became my hero as I listened to his adventures. The absurd long battle of his platoon in the desert, followed by the slow, inexorable, tragic march, withdrawing after the defeat. Dehydrated, exhausted, wounded, but standing up till the last moment of their inevitable surrender. Twelve solid hours of marching in the desert, never falling, flanked and watched by platoons of Australians along the dunes above them, hemming them in, yet not interfering in that last desperate need to save their dignity.

"The Australians were watching us, Antonino would point out, *but they understood and respected this final act of ours. They allowed us to see it through to the end, in recognition of our bravery in combat,"* he would conclude with a bitter sense of pride.

There were also accounts of hunger and humiliations inflicted on them by the British in the prison camps, with no distinction made for officers, or respect of the Geneva Convention. What the Spartan education inflicted on the son by the tyrannical father (the terrible *zio Piddu*) had not been able to achieve, the hardships of the imprisonment certainly did.

The story goes that Antonino had a physiological revulsion for zucchini. He could not eat them without suffering terrible effects. But his father would not relent. Everything served at the table must be eaten. Antonino had to get used to eating zucchini. Unable to rebel against his father, Antonino had resorted to a ploy; he smoothly slid the zucchini on a sheet of newspaper he held on his lap. It's funny to think that, already an adult and a soldier, he continued to use that ploy to avoid his father's anger. However, even he had to laugh recalling the newspaper ruse when he returned from prison camp, where he had known the kind of hunger that forced him to steal cabbage cores and food scraps from the refuse.

Antonino called it *"African fever."* That's how he would conclude all his tales. In spite of all the suffering, my cousin told us that he had really known that peculiar feeling so many talk about, a certain something that stays within you after seeing Africa - a yearning, a deep nostalgia, an almost atavistic, visceral, hard-to-define lure, which never leaves you. Mesmerized by his words, I tried to imagine this strange sensation that would seize his stomach like a sudden nausea, similar to the one caused by zucchini. Only when I grew up and thought back about this concept that had fascinated me as a little girl, by now edified by readings and literary references, did I grasp the sudden yearning that one could feel in recalling dense, wild, primordial jungles, and overpowering fiery sunsets over deserts. Something that seizes us and wrests us from our trite social conventions, and restores us to long lost, dormant passions and ecstasy – a violent wrenching, a fever - *"the African fever."*

The hunger of war times, I certainly remember it as well. For years I did not know what it meant to rise from the table full; and the cream of peas, the rare relief, was our nightmare. It was one of the American products beginning to show up on the black market. Mamma, perhaps already aware that she would not be with us much longer, and fearful for the fate of us children in what appeared to be an endless war, had really stocked up on it. There seemed to be no end to the cans of cream of peas, which day after day were pouring out on our plate their thick yellowish liquid, disgustingly sweet to the point of nausea. Ninetto and I would look at each other sympathizing and pluck up our courage before swallowing that swill. We were never able to forget that taste, and all our life we would remember the torture, turning away with a knowing smile *("Eh, if they only knew!")* any offer of pea soup. Not even nonna managed to win us over with her famous soup of rice and peas.

In the infamous closet of our supplies, (which didn't harbour any more fear of thieves) Nino had managed to discover a rare treasure. It seems that among the incredible number of pea soup cans, there were some of a different colour and content. Quickly identified and "rescued" by my clever scouting brother, they found their way under his bed. I have no idea how many bellyfuls of jam he had all by himself; I only know that every once in a while I would be invited to share in these secret rich banquets. The tin was already open, with a teaspoon in it. These mouthfuls of nectar would go down delightfully, without filling the emptiness of our hunger, but certainly compensating for other wants. I was very grateful to Ninetto for sharing these goodies with me. It never dawned on me that, if nonna had been aware of this, my ration of jam would have been legitimate and perhaps more abundant.

Later on, I began to suspect that nonna was well aware of the situation, but had decided to ignore it. At times I would hear her confide in zia Ida her worries about Ninetto. They would comment on his rather bizarre behaviour since the death of mamma. In fact, he did stay almost always locked in his room. He was no longer an important presence even in my own life, no longer my playmate. Unconsciously, I understood that Ninetto was to be left alone. Perhaps even the presence of that booty under his bed had been viewed as part of his bizarre behaviour, and to be overlooked.

By summer all the families had left. There was no reason to stay in the countryside any longer. The war evacuation was over, and all my friends went away. Only Teresita and I were left. Her family could not go back to her

There's Always the Sea...

city either. Their house was in Trieste, and word was that there the war was not over yet, though I couldn't understand why. I felt sorry for Teresita because I thought she could still lose her house in bombing raids. Maybe this shared fate, which made us feel excluded and different from others, served to draw us closer, to become better "friends." Teresita herself seemed different, less quarrelsome. We spent more time playing on the terrace, also because the adults didn't want us to walk around the town by ourselves, as we had always done before. In fact, it was no longer as pleasant as it had been. The street fights scared us. When we had to pass by the tavern, we'd give it a wide berth. We saw it dark inside, like a cavern from which violent shouts, more akin to beast than man, would reach our ears.

I remember once two huge men came staggering out of it, and almost fell on top of us. Scared stiff, Teresita and I made a run for it. Then we turned around. Two dark giant forms etched against the sky were grotesquely twisted upon themselves, lunging at each other. A raised long arm, a hand grasping a knife. I got home out of breath. The next day, the adults were talking about the fight between two Slavs. One of them had been knifed to death.

Like a slithering snake, this repugnant violence was beginning to creep into my life. My home was no longer spared; there were shouts that made me cringe and I shut myself off from everything! In the courtyard of the house next to ours, the husband would come home drunk every night, his face swollen and twisted. It was a family of refugees from the Veneto region. Word was that he beat his wife, and his continuous, hoarse, choleric barks went on for hours, and seemed it would never stop. It sounded to me like a primeval voice rising from the depths of inaccessible mysterious caverns.

Evil had always been there, just as in the fables I read about witches, dragons, and monsters, but when it suddenly showed itself on the street, bearing the face of Death, it was as if that horrendous black horseman with a skull for a face, its wind-swept mantle blocking out the sun, darkening the earth, ruthlessly mowing down the fields' golden wheat with its long scythe, had materialized out of the pages of the book.

I was on my way to school for my first day in grade four. Unexpectedly, I ran into a restless group of people blocking the way. Someone tried to keep me away, but I was able to see her - her ungainly bulky body lying awkwardly on a stretcher, her face strangely puffy, and the glasses missing on her familiar face. The teacher Casali lay there, dead. In the cold of a still dimly colourless dawn, a Calvary-like scene slowly came into focus, as they pulled me away. They were taking down lifeless bodies from the lampposts and laying them on the ground. Ghostly shadows in the cold foggy morning. I had yet to learn the meaning of "reprisal."

A new bright light came into my world with the pink blond face of Antonietta Mandelli, our new teacher. She was the sister of the fearsome piano teacher Giovanna, yet her complete opposite. She became the first of many persons I adopted as a surrogate mother figure. I became morbidly attached to her, always hanging on to her "apron strings." I can still see the slight embarrassment as she'd gently push me away from her. I adored her. I tried to be the best in the class to gain her attention. Perhaps, I also allowed myself to be enveloped by her soft liveliness in order to erase that other image branded in my mind, of a blonde ashen face that had brought up from the pit of my stomach that familiar sense of nausea.

At first I thought it was a religious procession, with so many people lining the street; but their shrill voices were not intent on reverence, only a few sad faces, a few barely repressed murmurs. Now and then, someone would move away, shaking their head after the cart had passed. Then, I too saw the cart slowly drawing close, flanked by two rows of people. A few excited yelling children pushed me close enough to see. That was not a saint's statue standing straight in the middle of the cart, and those were not flowers being thrown at her. I heard the children yell out:

"*It's Mafalda, the daughter of Mugnin!*"

She was a famous beauty, "*the most beautiful girl in town*," so they said. She was envied by all the girls, admired by all the men for her sensual walk and the jaunty sway of her

There's Always the Sea...

long blonde hair. I stretched my neck, anxiously following the slowly moving oxen. What I saw instead when the cart passed in front of me, was the face of infinite human misery. Beneath the shaven head, two cheeks bled of all colour, two eyes made lifeless by the jeering. Gravely erect, in a final show of will power and dignity, like a Joan of Arc, her hands tied behind her back, the pinched white tunic soiled with the very real and moral filth that human savagery flung at her. The anguishing shock of this other face, immersed in a very concrete realty, became deeply embedded in my childhood conscience. No idealized cinematic interpretation by the intensely luminous beauty of Ingrid Bergman, who would enchant me and make me quiver with emotion at the cruel fate of the Maid of Orleans, was ever able to free me from that traumatic experience.

Soon I would return to Milan to start my fifth grade, already on the threshold of adolescence. Only four years had gone by, but the weight of the events experienced had sufficiently and definitely defined me. Unbearable to me to this day is any scene of violence. I must avoid them, for the images become obsessive in my mind. Perhaps I'm still trying to escape those scenes from my childhood.

Cunardo, however, was not yet coming to an end for me. For another ten years I would return there in summertime with nonna. I would see it and live it, however, with quite a different frame of mind. After all, war-time Cunardo no longer existed. That Cunardo would reach out to me only as isolated movements of shadows and lights, stirring different levels of my conscience. Echoes of a world in which I had babbled a silly childhood jargon - *"Deghedé vogodò pagadà rlagadà rtighidì."* The first syllables of the words would form *"Devo parlarti"* - I must speak to you. The secret code we children used to safeguard our world from the adults, who after all used a language just as incomprehensible to us.

Scenes, voices, noises still reach me like a flash in the dark, like isolated scenes on a stage. On the bright sunny terrace, Teresita pirouettes like the ballerina of a carillon; nonna rips open the mattresses and spreads out its knotted wool to card it, turning it into a soft carpet. A gentler image of her, of would-be maternal feeling, shows her all intent in the delicate work of the *pizzo al tombolo* - the bobbin lace. *Il tombolo* was a kind of hard stuffed cylindrical pillow, covered with pins. Her nimble fingers are knowingly guiding the thread in an elegant dance through the labyrinthine maze of pins. Her profile is etched against the milky white sky framed by the window. In the winter darkness of the house, from a deeper level of my subconscious, a yellow cone of light appears. Standing in it is zia Ida, scantily dressed, as nonna at her feet measures the hem of a skirt. I barely see the scene from the half-closed door of the bedroom, where I'm lying in the dark. Zio Marco passes by, and his hands linger on his wife's uncovered breast. A light slap then follows with a crack. Nonna is shocked, *"Marco! The child could hear."*

I feel a vague sense of uneasiness. I stare at the barely visible fresco on the ceiling. In semidarkness, I trace the well-known figures as I do when I wake each morning. The chubby cherubs blossoming like flowers among the roses, the vine leaves with their slightly faded curls, the crack in the column's capital. I know every single line, every water stain. Soon, reassured by the images of my trusty friends, I fall asleep.

A small ladder at the far end of the terrace takes Teresita and me back up to that attic that used to fascinate and scare us, a place of adventurous explorations and discoveries. Bending low under a ceiling of angled beams, slipping between piles of wood and dusty corners, we used to go hunting treasures in the old chests. Passages illuminated by strips of sunlight would open up like curtains of luminous golden dust, alternating with dark crevices that never did unveil their mystery.

CHAPTER TEN

Just in time for the start of the new school year, our clever Corradino - what a diminutive name for such a large man - had managed to gain entry into our apartment in Milano. He had "liberated" the guest room. The rest was still firmly in the hands of the various families that had "requisitioned" it, according to the bureaucratic jargon of that period. The idea of ending up three in one room, and what's more without the use of a kitchen, was certainly not very appealing. But our champion insisted that we move in. Only by showing our urgent need to be in Milano in order to attend a proper school, and by getting a foot in the door, we would be able to continue the battle with the Housing Commission in an effective and convincing manner.

The famous *camera dei forestieri* ("the room for the outsiders" as the guest room was then called) of my childhood promptly lost for me all the glamour of its mystery as soon as I found myself in a room with a bed short of double meant for nonna and me, and a military cot next to it for my brother. It made me really feel as "an outsider."

We had the luxury of one wardrobe for the three of us, and an electric double hotplate sitting in the recess of the window on top of the wooden crate in which the famous huge crystal chandelier of the salon had been packed. In fact, to avoid the complication involved in moving it with the rest of our furniture as well as for greater safety, that glorious chandelier of times gone by had been hidden in the cellars of the building. But its fate was no better or painless all the same. When we returned from the evacuation and enquired with the concierge, we were told that the precious object had disappeared from the cellar, gone, stolen.

"You know how it is," he had the cheek to explain to nonna, unfazed by her indignation. *"It's been a long time*

since the end of the war, a lot of people have come and gone, a lot of things have been taken away."

Undaunted, however, nonna was not easily taken in. A crate of a ton with crystals jangling inside could not be easily carried on one's shoulders without being seen. It was so difficult to make it vanish that in fact one day, as I climbed the stairs, I noticed objects piled up behind the elevator near a door leading to the cellars. I became suspicious, attracted by a large wooden square box that stirred up long-forgotten memories; I was growing up fast under nonna's tutelage. I ran home and told her. Bursting with pride, I went down with a cheering nonna and Nino to retrieve the stolen goods - in the nick of time it seems, because our treasure was obviously on the way out, and not, as the concierge tried to make us believe, ready to be brought up to our home.

The princely rock-crystal chandelier had to wait a long time before being restored to its former glory. For the time being, like everything and everyone else, it would have to resign itself to the more humble role as a prop for the hotplate, the pots and the pans.

Soon after settling down so precariously, the moment came to go back to school. This time I would be a complete unknown in an important big-city school. I felt at home in familiar surroundings until I got to Piazza Caiazzo. Once there, I can still see myself frightened and alone at the N. 7 tramline stop, on the corner of Via Venini, holding my schoolbag and wearing a black smock under my coat.

Together with the Central Station, Piazza Caiazzo marked the boundaries of the residential area that would be the setting of my existence for the next sixteen years. Characteristic of the neighbourhood were the names of musicians given to all the streets, names that would become very familiar to me: Palestrina, Scarlatti, Benedetto Marcello, and my own street Pergolesi. Via Venini, on the other hand, was a major artery that seemed to go on forever, and I had to take the tramline to reach the other end, where the alien world of my new school was. I had never taken the tram by myself.

It must have been ordained that I should take up the thread of my life in Milano exactly where I had left it off. In fact, behind me, while waiting for the tram, I felt the bulky,

There's Always the Sea...

ominous presence of the portal on Via Venini N.1 - the Sacred Heart Convent where I had attended my first days of school; that first grade interrupted by our evacuation from the city.

Far from being a reassuring presence, I felt no attachment to it at all. That dark heavy doorway didn't bring back even echoes of the unrestrained squeals of the children back then, nor did it appear now to harbour any traces of life within it. Shut away, sealed off forever in its silence. Who knows where my nuns ended up when they escaped the war. Had they even been able to get away? I wonder. I can't remember any of their faces. Perhaps it was for the best that the portal never re-opened, and remained there, impenetrable, to seal away the soul of a vanished era, to protect it from the whirlwind pace at which history was reshaping the face of the outside world. Many years later, that same street corner, that dark doorway, those very same high convent walls would become the backdrop to strolling prostitutes.

What my fifth-grade year in public school at the end of Via Venini meant to me I don't really know. It has faded away into the same haze as that morning, from which no images of places or people emerge. Days of study and human contacts that must have nourished more my intellect than my soul, devoid of joy as well as pain. Strange effect of a selective memory, retaining only my dismay at the initial encounter and my indifference upon leaving. In between, nothing.

Still the school must have had some influence on my intellectual development, since I remember being pressured into taking *l'Esame di Stato* that was not necessary for me since I had been already admitted to Junior High School. They were hoping that by taking the exam I would add prestige to their school. I must have turned out to be one of their best pupils, which might not have meant much anyway. I have no idea whom they wanted to impress. An attitude that still reflected a Fascist frame of mind.

And so I find myself in this final scene in which I feel more than see around me a sense of smugness, while I give the Examining Committee the necessary answer to their enigmatic question: *"How does one form 100 with four 9?"* After quickly answering with a 99, I was honestly a bit stuck, and only after a while I visualized the fraction 9/9. Indeed, I would never excel in math.

It was within the home sphere instead that I lived the most instructive, though not necessarily cheerful experiences of that period of my life. They say that we learn only from our mistakes and painful experiences. Maybe it's one of those bits of wisdom we take for granted and use it to comfort ourselves. Still, I can't understand why no one talks about the great benefits that successes and delightful experiences have on the development of our psyche as well.

Upon our return from the evacuation to the countryside, I was old enough not only to "feel" my apartment as an adult, but also to breathe and engross myself in the life of the building. A microcosm, a small society throbbing with life, where every family and every individual was the protagonist of a more or less colourful story, with dramatic and quaint characters, whom I judged to be fascinating or funny caricatures - all, nonetheless, objects of my insatiable curiosity for people. Those rooms, those walls, those stairways, that courtyard would from then on be inseparably associated with my experiences, giving them a particular substance and personality.

Owing to the presence of so many embittered people holed up in their rooms along the various passageways, scowling as they crossed each other, my apartment had taken on a gloomy and depressing look. From what had been my father's studio, every now and then I would see a stooped, cadaveric figure come out. He would silently cross the reception area, almost on tiptoes as if to avoid being seen, and he would go out, disappearing for long periods of time. He was referred to as *Dott. Lanciano,* a name that fitted his lanky lance-like figure, I thought. Nonna's curiosity for his mysterious activities kept being foiled. On the other hand, his ever longer absences made her hope that perhaps soon he would vacate the room he was using. In fact, he turned out to be the first one to leave on his own accord and, with a sigh of relief, we were able to regain another room, which nonna and I turned into our bedroom.

The salon as well had been taken over by two mysteriously grim and burly men. Even nonna was intimidated by their forbidding presence, only partially mitigated by the rather poor health of the older man, perhaps the father.

The more useful part of the house, *l'area giorno,* "the day area", that included the kitchen, was instead occupied by a whole family with the father, the mother, and two children. Now, aside from Mrs. Molinari *"the shrew,"* with her *"loose"* daughter, as my nonna called them, who, contrary to the dispositions imposed by my mother, had installed themselves in the elegant *ala notte* (night wing), with its spacious bedrooms and on-suite bathroom,

"The horror of it all!" nonna would complain. *"They are fouling it with a cooking plate installed in the entrance hall and with their 'unmentionable activities'."*

Aside from these scandalous beings - as I was saying - what irritated nonna most of all was the Pedrotti family. With impunity they had taken over the kitchen, refusing to share it with anyone and, to add insult to injury, we were forced to share with them, as with everybody else, the only bathroom left, that of the *servitù,* the domestic help.

Still, being my same age, the Pedrottti's daughter became my occasional playmate. Naturally, nonna looked at her askance, while I accepted her with realistic indifference. I remember her clearly crossed eyes, and the odd purplish shiny skin tightly stretched on her face with a large nose. The large entrance hall was our "playground," but we had to be quiet, make as little noise as possible. We would hide ourselves in the dark hollows of the doorways, whose sombre empty spaces we could only populate with our imagination. Our games were of course so quiet that often my worried nonna would come to check on us. It was a refuge from the world of adults, who were always arguing and fighting. The war was over, but every little space had become a battlefield, where people fiercely fought each other trying to survive the worsened conditions.

Once dignified, our apartment building now rang out with sudden outbursts like those I would see in the low housing projects shown in Neorealist films. Exasperated people ready to vent their frustrations and picking quarrels with their neighbours. The excited screams would come in from the window of our room overlooking the large inner courtyard of the building. But the ruckus of those scenes worthy of a marketplace was not coming only from the outside. Our own house was turning into a battleground for what was to become a dramatic and long drawn out conflict between nonna and her openly avowed enemy, the said Mrs. Molinari. Any pretext was good; merely running into each other caused them to show their claws. And invariably these scenes took place in the infamous entrance hall, the unavoidable passage for everyone going out, where nonna would often show up on purpose to confront the enemy with some ready complaint.

I was always waiting in anguish for the inevitable clashes. Though the causes of irritation were valid, these situations seemed to gratify nonna's aggressive temper. I hated those shouts; I shuddered in horror at that domestic violence that affected me so much. Nino was appalled, and at times tried to placate the warring parties, only to end up caught in the middle. Then, in private he would criticise nonna herself, well aware of her capacity to provoke.

The underlying friction between nonna's and my brother's character was manifesting itself more frequently now. Nino was by now a mature young man, with his own ideas and able to form his own judgment, which were naturally destined to differ from those of a much older person. Both had difficult and stubborn characters that exploded at the drop of a hat, if not about the Molinaris, then for matters of finance or decisions about me, or even about playing chess. This level of stress within my own home and, even worse, within my own family, between the two only remaining persons whom I loved so much, greatly dismayed me.

I remember how for years when I came home from school the lump I felt in my throat, standing in front of our door. It would grip me just as I was about to ring the bell, such was the loathing I felt for what awaited me inside; and so I would remain there, hesitating. Then... *"più che il dolor poté il digiuno"* (hunger prevailed on my pain). Which explains why in years to come I would longingly seek "a family" in the homes of my friends, causing nonna to begrudge me due to her obsessive jealousy and her distressing inability to express love.

A long time would pass before the face of our postwar society would change, redeem itself from the destruction and the hatred, and before I would be able to pour into the world of my adolescence my real soul that was hungering for life, for the colour of trees in springtime, the lights of summertime, the good cheer of friends. And yet, that time would indeed come, and they would be for me the fullest and happiest years. Not because they would be rich and fulfilling as they had been for my parents in their best years, but because they would be full of promise, of trust in the future, when for us the young every avenue seemed open and possible. We needed only to choose. That was the positive side of the postwar era, a period of reconstruction that for me coincided with the period in which I had to "construct" my own life... But why then, I would ask myself, so many imposed choices? Social pressures, sense of duty, the odd twist of fate?

Meanwhile, the echoes of the recent horrors were difficult to put to rest. The jarring piercing sound of the factories' whistle at noon, so inconceivably like the air-raid alarms during the war, made me jump and cringe. The sudden bursts of insults on crowded tramline cars, where we were pressed, crushed, and suffocated from a mixture of body odours, where I struggled for every centimetre of space, fought to defend myself from hands trying to squeeze and feel me. I felt as if all the weight of human misery were pressing down on me.

More often than not, the fights were caused by clashes between people from North and South. Refugees were streaming in from the South trying to escape the poverty, and found themselves facing the even more inhuman hostility of those who viewed them as filthy uncivilized beings coming to steal their bread and their jobs.

"*Sodbusters go home!*" was the leitmotiv that I felt like a stab. That word tore into me, I thought of my father, I saw him insulted, offended. I wanted to scream back at them, tell them to stop. It was too much, I couldn't stand it. An outrage against my own roots made by the very city I was born in. I would shut my ears. I didn't want to hear any more, I wanted to run away. At the first stop, I would jump off the tramcar, fleeing those screams, fleeing those hands that sullied me. There I was, tears streaming as I waited for the next tram, or ran alone toward home.

Even children continued to play war games. In our neighbourhood, half a block of the buildings in front of ours had been reduced to rubble, a gap that would eventually be filled in with modern buildings in green granite, and constitute an eyesore in the very heart of a zone distinguished by the gray elegance of its stone. In the meantime, children played in that rubble, in thoughtless imitation of reality. At times, my brother and I would persuade nonna to let us go and play there. There might have been some hazards in that rubble, but it was certainly less dangerous than running in the fields on the city's outskirts, where every day, the papers reported of children having died or being maimed in explosions of abandoned mines.

I remember a distant cousin of mine and how the sight of her legs disfigured by burns had left a deep impression on me. They would often speak at home of the tragedy of beautiful Sonia, and of her *"luck"* in managing to land a husband *"in spite of it,"* an elderly man who *"had taken care of her."*

Whether from school or playing on the street, sooner or later we always had to return to that one room, to those suffocating hours of doing our homework on a wooden board, which replaced the hotplate to make the shaky desk my brother and I shared. We studied surrounded by the smells of what little food nonna managed to put on our plates in those uncertain conditions; smells that lingered unrelentingly in that room, permeating the coverlet of our bed, that heavy silk coverlet with its worn out weave I still feel slipping through my fingers, with its melancholic faded blue that still fills my eyes, and colours that entire dismal experience. Every now and then we managed to escape it, in the always tricky attempt to have a decent meal. That's when we allowed ourselves the luxury of eating at the "Rail Workers Canteen."

How nonna found out about the possibility to get this extraordinary treatment for such little money, I have no idea. She had a booklet of stamps, one stamp per meal, just like the postwar ration books. Who knows, maybe she got that booklet from someone at the railroad in exchange for a stamp for some other necessity. The Rail Workers Canteen was of course only for the employees of the Central Station, which was close to our home. Walking down our Via Pergolesi, we would enter the long Ferrante Aporti Tunnel which passed right under the station and came out in Via Tonale. Much later, after the lean years, Via Tonale was to become for me a gay street where we'd go to the movies; and I would cross that once scary tunnel light-heartedly to go and see my best friend and schoolmate, whose neighbourhood was separated from mine by the very large and long bulk of the Central Station, whose belly we had to cross.

For now, our destination was in the gloomy belly of that "*Geppetto whale*," in its very centre, from where the two exits of the tunnel looked like distant tiny openings, leading us back to safety. From that point, we had to penetrate even deeper in the viscera of the monster. In fact, an internal side gallery led to the underground maze of the station. That was a critical moment for me. Daylight disappeared, and we would move forward between musty porous walls, dimly lit by the rare bulb. I could barely check my fear and disgust, recoiling from the foetor of rats by squeezing myself tightly between nonna and Nino, like a frightened Pinocchio between the two gendarmes.

As a result, I can't remember anything but the three of us sitting around a small table as we decide what to choose from the same fixed menu, day in and day out. Just as repetitive and unchanging was my choice, "*I want the veal medallion.*" It was useless for nonna and Nino to exchange concerned glances and to try to discourage me from having that suspicious looking patty of meat - today we'd call it a hamburger - that to their more experienced eyes must have looked like ground mystery meat. But I couldn't swallow anything else, only that patty dripping with fat that seemed to slide down satisfying my taste buds with a semblance of flavour. Then, I gladly went back to the postwar soups nonna supplied to us together with the nursery rhyme of *Besma Busaruna*, the shrewd cook who knew how to fool hunger with a mere three beans on the bottom of a pot of water. *"Before one got to the beans, the stomach would have been full of water,"* would explain nonna.

As always, however, there were those who fared even worse. The down-and-out homeless, dignified in their poverty, would occasionally knock at our door. Their mortified eyes reflected the void the war had created around them. Seated at the kitchen table, they bent hungrily over the dish of soup nonna had put out for them. Imbued with the classics, in my imagination they appeared like the travelling outlander welcomed by the ancient Greeks as a sacred guest, who often was a god in disguise come to put them to the test. In fact, they reflected much more the parables of the Gospels.

My brother Nino, no longer Ninetto, had taken me once again under his wing, not as a playmate but as his pupil. He was to be my teacher, my mentor from now on. He helped me with my schoolwork, he taught me, and over the years he helped me develop a taste for things of beauty, for art, for music, opening for me doors to worlds of endless fascination through books and reading.

I think his attempts to lighten the hardships of my life had begun already then. I can't imagine how, penniless as we were, he managed to create for me *"la lista delle godurie"* - the list of goodies. He would present it to me every week. It was a list of things from which I could choose at will. It might be liquorice or some other kind of candy; it was hard to choose, but I clearly recall *le treccine* (sweet braids), an early form of brioche which I adored. Much later he added *Topolino* (Mickey Mouse), the popular children magazine that became for many years my inseparable companion. Its appearance coincided with the waning appeal of candy. The list of goodies drew to a natural end, replaced by a subscription to the Walt Disney creations that have brought joy to so many generations.

There's Always the Sea...

Until he was able to, Nino loved to smother me with gifts, which became more and more substantial and fascinating, especially when he began to work and was able to satisfy his adventurous and restless character which led him to frequent travels to foreign countries. Nothing, however, would give me again the pleasure of anticipating with joy those "braids," which sugar-coated the greyness of a life full of hardships. Well, perhaps something did outshine them just when everything was out of reach, beyond our means. It was an unexpected anachronistic experience I have never forgotten, a Frank Capra kind of miracle, - unfortunately, with the same bitter-sweet taste as well.

Within the four walls of that room where we spent our lives in uncertain conditions, the news burst on us like a bomb. It was Nino who dropped it, naturally.

The theatre of "La Scala" in Milano had stood in silence during the long war, and now had finally re-opened in all its glory. The city had been reduced to piles of debris, but its citizens had decided to rebuild first and foremost their beloved theatre. It was of course Toscanini who, in a memorable May evening of 1946, celebrated its moving rebirth with a concert dedicated exclusively to Italian music. As tradition would have it, the opera season instead opened on December 26, with another significant choice, *Nabucco,* directed by Tullio Serafin. And so began the mythical period of the fifties that would bring to the fore names like Carlo Maria Giulini, Maria Callas, Giulietta Simionato, Renata Tebaldi, Giuseppe di Stefano, Mario del Monaco, and many others.

During one of the prolific seasons at "La Scala," *Hansel and Gretel*, the musical fairy tale by Humperdinck, was staged, and one day my brother announced that he was taking me to see it. To say that nonna's reaction was as startling as his announcement would be an understatement. For days afterwards our life was overrun by bursts of lightning and thunders with the same distemper of an angry storm. How could we in fact allow ourselves such foolishness in our current financial conditions? This gave way to one of those long and painful tales of woe nonna regularly cranked out, which oppressed me with a feeling of anguish and rebellion. She would remind us of all the sacrifices she, old as she was, had to make to raise us, of all the physical pain and anguish she endured. Against this, she would of course set the enormity of our ingratitude, especially my brother's, and of his mindless dissipation. Much of this was undoubtedly true, and in fact these were the first signs of Nino's recklessness, totally irresponsibility in matters of money, which would result in painful consequences for him and others, including myself. Of course, at the time I was not able to judge, I only wanted the quarrel to end, even if it meant I would not go to "La Scala." Although I guessed that the truth was more on my nonna's side, I was beginning to develop a sense of rebelliousness against the enormous weight of gratitude and moral uneasiness I felt being placed on my shoulders. After all, I had not asked anything of anyone; it wasn't my fault if we found ourselves in those conditions. In the end, Nino's resolve won him the first of his many victories. More and more his character revealed an authoritarian bent.

Thus, the curtains were raised on a magical moment in my life, and I forgot everything that had brought me to that point. I can't remember who was sitting next to me, whether nonna or Nino, perhaps nonna because my brother knew how to be generous. I could see nothing but darkness suspended in the vast space around me. Below me the tiered slope of the spectators' backs, which I quickly eliminated from my line of vision, aided also by the opera glasses of my mother which I showed off with pride, (Which one was her box where she looked out of, elegantly raising her gloved arm?) absorbed as I was in the magical woods where Hansel and Gretel had taken on a life of their own.

"La Scala" was to become an emblem of my world, as well as "il Duomo," the Cathedral of Milano. Soon I would be proud to be able to say that I had grown up in their shadow, as if they were two guardian angels that gave lustre to my origins. In fact I had been able to enjoy the marvellous secrets of that theatre not only already as a child, but even ten years later as a high school student - a privilege reserved only to the very few.

There's Always the Sea...

I was then at an age when one lives everything and absorbs everything with finely tuned senses and intense emotions. I can still see myself when, for the matinees of the association *Gioventù Musicale*, the entire theatre was placed at the disposal of the youth, and I could enjoy the experience of a concert from *"a box at La Scala,"* symbol of a world of luxury and elegance otherwise preclude to me. And there I would listen to one of the greatest interpreters of Chopin, the already octogenarian and mythical Cortot, who played divinely that music so apt to stir up the adolescent yearnings of my romantic spirit. Later though, in the foyer with friends, we'd put on an innocent show of intellectual snobbism, *"So, how many false notes did you notice?"* And then there was Toscanini, able with his passion to carry me away even in the Teutonic world of Wagner. Finally, the experience that more than any other left heartbreaking impression on me.

There he was, on the front page of the newspaper *Gioventù Musicale,* tall, elegant, his face and arms stretched toward a symphony only *he* could hear. And his picture stayed there on my desk, before my anguished eyes, to renew the painful dismay that repeatedly tore out my heart,

"Guido Cantelli, the promising young orchestra director, pupil of Toscanini and his chosen heir" declared the paper, *"is dead."*

It was we, the young members of *Gioventù Musicale* to be present at his last concert. He had wanted to conduct that last concert exclusively for us, before joining Toscanini in America. He never got there. The airplane fell in the ocean, and with it *"the most exciting promise in the music world,"* and, at that moment, a piece of my heart as well.

That unique magical musical event, that once in a lifetime moment, however, had left in me a lasting mark. The young musician, as if by an unconscious premonition, seemed to have carried the melodies to the outer boundaries of human experience. There was something in that musical crescendo that transcended it, and every one of us felt it. In the atmosphere charged with tension, our young emotions were at unison with the elegantly inspired forceful gestures of the dynamic figure of Guido Cantelli, vibrating beyond human measure. Choked with emotion, I found myself with all the youth filling the theatre jumping to our feet in a continuous thunderous applause.

And one day, a tramline brought me also to the very threshold of that world that existed between the wings of the stage at "La Scala," that world about which books upon books have been written, full of fascinating illustrations of famous singers in theatrical poses, and fanciful choreographed ballets in which the human figures transcend their physical mass to create forms and lines of surrealist beauty - the world of classical dance that fascinated me for so many years and inhabited my youthful dreams. Dance was always a passion of mine, and I had always aspired to become a classical ballerina. Naturally, I could only dream of it.

And yet one day, by a quirk of fate, I found myself in the rear of a city tram between nonna and a tall distinguished lady, her simple attired rendered somewhat austere by the straight silver hair gathered around her face. The two women were chatting, and I was the topic of their conversation. It seems I had stirred the lady's interest. She had started complimenting my thick braids that reached below my waist. Very little encouragement was needed to spark nonna's relish for small talk, and so she did not fend off the probing questions of the lady, who wanted to know everything about me, and seemed to be very moved by my *"poor orphan"* condition.

At a certain point she said her name was Ghiringhelli, the sister of Antonio Ghiringhelli, the newly appointed postwar general manager of "La Scala." I started paying closer attention, and my heart skipped a beat when, with a calm pleasant voice, the lady explained quite naturally that her brother was childless and wanted so badly to adopt a war orphan. She liked me and she was sure that her brother would have been happy.... I have to smile now when I recall how nonna, completely taken aback, immediately wiped out the expression of unsuspecting self-complacency with which she had been chatting. The lady's exposition was cut off by a bristling nonna, who politely pointed out that I still had a family and, in short, I did not need to be rescued from the street. Even so, undaunted, the lady invited us to get in touch with her and meet her brother. Naturally, the idea was not pursued. We all found the thing so out of place that even I, struggling between conflicting feelings, thought it natural in the end to remain in my own home instead of being catapulted among strangers.

Yet, that lost chance, that strange fateful coincidence continued to obsess me with its "ifs" and "buts." I had been so close to entering the very world of my dreams. With the patronage of the manager himself, I could have joined the ballet school at "La Scala," in the world of Carla Fracci, Rudolph Nurejev, Margot Fonteyn. A magic door had been opened for me and I hadn't even been able to look inside. Someone else had taken the most important decision of my life. Done certainly in good faith and out of love, but also guided by a blind conformity and a certain narrow-mindedness, they had excluded me from who knows what life of ease and success. And I would never know. How many more times would I find myself in the back of a tram looking at what I was leaving behind? Places, persons, chances drifting away.

For the time being, the path brought me back full circle to my familiar routine. If not my horizon, my living space at least was gradually increasing, as one by one the "guests" left our apartment. Regaining our own kitchen and reclaiming our furniture was occasion for real celebration. Still, our initial elation was soon followed by the disappointment in noticing all the war damages. Five families living in the apartment, the moving of the furniture, the bombing could not but have left many scars. A cluster bomb fallen on the fifth floor of the building had had effects all the way down to our own first floor. The shock wave broke the glass windows, ripped out the doors, and even moved a dividing wall.

To tell the truth, within myself, I felt sort of proud of having been part of such dramatic events. Of course, those mortifying yellow curtains salvaged by nonna to replace the beautiful frosted glass fallen from the doors in the apartment told a different story; and they remained forever there, sadly wearing out year after year. Not to speak of the horrors we found in those "liberated" rooms, where now we had to deal with much more repulsive dwellers. Thanks to the powerful D.D.T., however, the second "evacuation" was much more easily done than the previous one.

So, finally our furniture had been returned, and... all the mirrors had been stolen. All the bedrooms' wardrobes and dressers, the china cabinets and mantelpieces of the salon and dining room had lost the brightness of the large mirrors and the *charme* of the antique frames. The house appeared wan. Nonna was on the warpath again. She won the battle but lost the war. After many arguments, urging, and an agonizingly long time, the solution of the furniture maker was disastrous. He replaced the stolen or ruined pieces with grotesque copies of what had been majestic lions in bronzed wood and elegant interlace of gilded decorations.

The main thing remained, however, that we finally had once more a home. Everyone had gone... everyone that is except "*le Molinari*," who remained there unmoved and immovable, still filling our lives with zest and colour. To be fair, it should be said that the apartment was really too large for just the three of us, and we could not justify taking it all back.

She, "the Molinari" par excellence, large and conniving, carried her bulk around with the well-fed and satisfied air of a "Madame", and the look of one who seems to know more than she lets on. She was the mother. The other, her appendage, the beautiful Iolanda, a bit long in the tooth, playing up her routine of commonplace seductive affectations, made futile attempts to mask the natural vulgarity of her manners and of her face already worn somewhat. She was the daughter. This odd pair had sunk anachronistic yet deep roots in our home, and had extended poisonous tentacles in our life, especially nonna's. But whether this was disagreeable to her is debatable. In fact, what better relief in her hard and dreary life than something to give zest to her days, feeding her curiosity and the pleasure of exchanging some piquant gossip with the neighbours - especially since the sharp-tongued Mrs. Zaccarìn, a war refugee from Veneto, had come into her life becoming her inseparable friend.

"*Iolanda Molinari hangs out at the 'Green Cat'!*" announced triumphantly one day Mrs. Zaccarin, with the satisfaction of one who saw all her most sordid suspicions about the subject in question confirmed, and had therefore the right to contribute even more. The fact that her informant was her own son who hung out in the same locale was irrelevant - "after all he was a man."

Unable to keep the pleasure all to herself, nonna had immediately passed it on to me. At twelve, I was old enough to understand these facts of life. To tell the truth though, I wasn't quite sure I had understood the meaning of the definition of "green cat"- a wicked place, where one went to dance, and frequented by loose women who were there *"to pick up men."* My imagination went into overdrive, trying to decode this adult language, but it went no further than seeing a group of dark men who'd let themselves at night be taken like a bunch of cherries, and would follow the shapely Iolanda swaying on her high heels. Where she'd take them I had no idea. Nor did it help when one day in the area of the Central Station, I found myself unexpectedly before a neon sign of a scrawny green cat jumping from a wall with fiendish eyes quite similar to those of the Molinari woman. Under the sign, a set of stairs led down to a mysterious passage in the building's basement.

However tentative, these clues were more satisfying for me than the discovery and understanding of the reality, since I found the mystique far more fascinating. People have always been surprised by my lack of "real" curiosity about this type of suggestive allusions. They have never moved me to a morbid desire to know more about them. This explains the state of blissful innocence I lived in for so many years. A strange rarefied condition which I fear I've never been cured of for the rest of my life, even when it no longer had anything to do with my ignorance of the real world. A condition that in fact has often made me feel ill at ease and embarrassed as I discovered the duplicity of the world.

I must confess however that as time went by, the flashy Iolanda with her numerous male conquests piqued my interest more and more, in spite of nonna's severe disapproval of her. My continued state of anachronistic innocence did not prevent me from feeling a distinct attraction for the opposite sex.

Those days I was studying in my room next to the Molinaris' quarters, and I would always hear a pleasant music that seemed to accompany their every activity. Iolanda radiated gaiety and verve, and I felt drawn to the suggestions of the life hidden on the other side of that wall, to which the music seemed to add tones of frivolity and liveliness that were missing in my life. At times, I would interrupt my studies spellbound by those sounds like an Indian cobra. I would even place my ear to the wall and close my eyes so as to lose myself in a different world suggested by those melodies completely new to me. They sounded joyful, sentimental, melancholic. Voices that spoke to me as if in tune with a secret language deep within me, and sometimes they struck me with a blinding revelation - yes indeed, these were the life's promises, what I was searching for, what was waiting for me.

CHAPTER ELEVEN

Like a small, well-disciplined army, with nonna as a leader, and guided by an ingrained sense of decorum, the three of us would regularly undertake the task of maintaining in perfect form all the spacious rooms and reception areas of our anachronistic apartment, or rather of that portion which we found ourselves with, as a precious but cumbersome heredity. It mattered little that those halls performed no longer any function in our daily existence. A staunch and scrupulous defender of the castle, nonna deceived herself into thinking that someday the bright lights of yesteryear would reappear.

And so, this was the scene - like a ruffled bird there is nonna precariously perched atop of a tall wooden ladder, hands filled with rags, cotton wool, and alcohol as she cleans the crystal drops of what for us had become the historic chandelier. In effect, I thought I was right to be proud of it, since it looked to me as a smaller version of the one hanging from the higher spheres of "La Scala." At the lower spheres of our home, however, the chandelier would hang over my brother kneeling on the floor, using all his masculine elbow grease to scrape away with steel wool the stains on the parquet; while, right behind on all fours, I toiled at spreading a thick, smelly yellow wax on the wooden tiles. The task was completed with all three taking turns pushing up and down the huge heavy brush, meaningfully called *la galera* - that is "galley," the slaves' boat – and really feeling condemned to forced labour. I much preferred when, at the end, I had to go sliding with felt runners on my feet like a winged elf on a frozen pond in Disney's "Fantasia." This gave the already shiny parquet floor a final touch.

Once cleaned and shined, the salon would remain closed like an out-of-season theatre. Only rarely do I recall seeing characters appear on the scene, coming from who knows where, and stage-directed by nonna.

The wings show gilded panels, tall mirrors, silken blue draperies, velvet and brocade covered armchairs. In the centre of all this, all the smaller and humble in the vast space, lost and cowed, the Sicilian farmer is standing, rigidly rooted with his heavy boots on the Persian carpet. A coarse canvas bag hangs from his thin wrinkled hand. It holds the lentils he has brought us as a gift. He comes from my father's town, he left his arid fields, and the bandit infested mountains to seek a better life up north. They had told him that in Milano there were relatives of the Oddos who could help him. Choked with embarrassment, I hear nonna, unmoved, explain that we are not in any condition to help him. I see his bewildered, incredulous look. He stretches out his hands to give us the bag of lentils, and then he leaves. I feel sad and helpless. I wonder what I would have done in nonna's place. There, on the kitchen table, the small heap of lentils speaks to us of generosity.

The woman is sitting on the "Empire" settee. Her coarse woollen skirt, too short and tight, barely contains the rather shapely figure, and seems to clash with the damask of the sofa. Her pleasant, gentle, and submissive face does not match the harsh features of her body. The little boy at her side is cute - firm and heavy-set, with a curly set of hair as his mother. He looks to be three years old. I find them when I come home from school. Clearly ill at ease, nonna introduces her to me as *"a friend of zio Marco,"* adding to my surprise and raising more questions than it answers. The woman's presence seems even more out of place and puzzling. Before I am shooed away, I notice nonna's tone of voice: persuasive yet firm, as if refusing something. I am called back when they leave, and I catch something like *"Don't worry, I will tell my son when he returns,"* which leaves me even more confused since I know my uncle is in town. I was never able to ferret out the identity of the woman. It remained one of those "grown-ups' secrets" which I intended to uncover as soon as I reached "the age when I had the right to ask and to know everything," and which I quite forgot then. Who knows, maybe it was what is generally included in the popular saying, "It happens in the best of families."

Ten years would pass before we could see the vast and well-appointed salon used as it was meant to be. Perhaps it was about time with me being at university and wanting to give a party to impress my rich classmates. Nonna immediately agreed to it, perhaps hoping for some "good match" for me. Even if I was not as well off as they were, I too could show off something suitable to their snobbish taste. They would certainly appreciate a ball in my luxurious salon. And that's when nonna was at her best, rolling up her sleeves and getting to work to turn out the most refined delicacies, and bring back to life at least a semblance of past splendours. Tablecloths, services of porcelain, crystals, all the best ... and then in the evening collecting the Limoges dishes left dangerously in every corner of the house, with leftovers of light *vol-au-vent* filled with cream of mushroom and calf's brain. It was the time when hamburgers and hot dogs had already crossed the ocean and were all the rage among the well-heeled youth.

Before retiring for the night, nonna would religiously shut the two wings of the outside armour-plated door of our apartment, the one which showed the Sydol-polished brass plate with name and professional titles of my father. She would sharply bring down the iron bar, like in a medieval castle. With a simple turn of the key, she would then close the shiny interior wooden door. That ritual must have made a lasting impression on my childhood's fantasy. For a long time, the dreads of my life which played out in my dreams took the form of the armour-plated door which I try to close in time against an evil threatening force. Just as I already sense a dark presence, I'm filled with sudden panic that I have forgotten to close the door, and strive desperately to bring down the heavy bar that would ensure my safety. In the real world, however, nothing could check any longer the inexorable decay of the old lifestyle, whose last vestiges those doors were trying to protect in vain.

It was the latest post-war arrivals, the somewhat harsh voices that were bringing us to the present. Like the family living on the second floor above us, who had taken the place of the infamous Livi of the Fascist years, the Quattrinis. They tended to make us aware of their existence over our head to the great annoyance of nonna. Every day, at noon sharp, a series of heavy and insistent whacks like a meat pounder on a cutting board would resound above our kitchen. "*Nouveaux riches!*" Nonna would label them with disdain.

"*Who knows how they made their money during the war!*" she would fume. "*They certainly have an appropriate name.*" (Quattrini meaning "Money") "*They pound on that cutting board to let us know they eat steak every day.*"

What really upset her though was that they had a maid.

"*The world is really upside down,*" she would complain shaking her head.

On the balcony above ours in the inner courtyard, the maid would regularly unroll huge carpets and proceed to beat them.

"*They're making us eat dust so they can show off their precious carpets.*" Nonna would rail furiously.

She found herself torn between flaunting our own "*beautiful Persian carpets,*" and not wanting to be seen beating them like a maid.

To me, on the other hand, the Quattrinis' asset was their handsome son, with those steel gray eyes and the body not unlike the Tarzan of those years, the great swimming champion Weissmueller. It didn't displease me to meet him on the stairs or in the elevator. In time, I think even nonna was entertaining the idea of an "*alliance*"- as she called it - with that family for my benefit. What attracted her was the money, which made Mauro Quattrini the good match she was always looking for. In any event, I didn't manage to grow up fast enough. He was much older, and by the time I reached the proper age, the handsome Mauro had already settled on a splendid blonde.

In spite of all her pride, a strong and lasting alliance grew between the first floor where we lived, which nonna called the main or *"noble"* floor, and the fifth; quite different though from the one she had sought with the Quattrinis.

This was a family from Veneto, one of the many that had poured into Lombardy at the end of the war, fleeing the extreme poverty of their region. They only occupied one of the three apartments on their floor, but in actual fact the entire fifth floor, as well as the whole stairwell on that side of the building were soon associated with the Zaccarin family and their vocal presence. It was my first pleasant taste of the Venetian dialect and its cadence. I was instantly drawn to that sharp-witted, self-deprecating delivery, colourful and rich in flavour, without ever reaching the vulgar level of the *spetascià* Milanese dialect.

The relationship started when I met Edda, the youngest of the family, at school. We were in the same class in grade sixth, *Prima Media*, and when we discovered we lived in the same building, we became of course an inseparable pair in our studies and games, and the best of friends in the process. A natural symbiosis grew between me and the thin, almost scrawny but lively Edda - between her self-confident, clever but trusting attitude and my shy, naïve, but more sensible personality. We made up for each other's shortcomings. The teacher named us the planet and its satellite. And, maybe because Edda was always flitting about like a restless moth around a light, I ended up being the planet.

The odd thing, but perhaps not so odd, was the immediate meeting of minds between nonna and Mrs. Zaccarin, in spite of the difference in age and social origins. A really strange match for nonna this small woman I always found with her when I returned home from school. She was thin, with a "neat and clean" look, her body always bent forward as if ready for the next task, like a busy little mouse, always answering to a query with an *"At your service!"* Inside her house she looked like she was on wheels, going over and over things already sparkling, so clean was everything.

They seemed to have established a symbiotic rapport as well. Mrs. Zaccarin was flattered by nonna's friendship.

She admired her traditional wisdom, the common sense forged from a long life of suffering; she would always turn to her for advice and help, which fed nonna's ego no end. She also loved to listen to her "stories" of long ago, savour a world unknown to her. "Mrs. Zaccarin," as she was always called - her first name never mentioned - for her part, would offer nonna that contagious good cheer, that lightness of being she needed so much. She enlivened her with her manner and her common folk straight talk. She made her laugh with her wit, off-colour words, which gave nonna leave to indulge in some off-colour stories of her own, of which she was fond. As for gossip, nonna and the Zaccarin woman felt free to wallow to their heart's content.

As in every type of marriage, the sharing of life with a certain kind of companion impels us to wear a certain mask rather than another from the vast array of possibilities in our personality. And so, as our living conditions declined, nonna developed certain latent traits of commonness which fell beneath the standards of our family.

There were six members in the Zaccarin family, but it felt like twice that. The oldest son, Sergio, though ordinary in looks like his father, possessed innate manners of naturally captivating gentleness. And the effects were quite evident in the constant to and fro of his girlfriends. As for the second oldest, "Tullio *il bello*," with those velvety seductive eyes that confounded and blandished, every time he showed up, which was quite frequently, he was in the company of a different woman, all of them beautiful and sophisticated, and with one common feature – they all wore a showy hat. That must have been the *sine qua non* to prevail upon the handsome Tullio. I had never heard the name Tullio until I read "The Innocent" by D'Annunzio, which had probably been the source of his name. As a result, when I eventually read the novel, the Tullio of D'Annunzio took on for me the face of Tullio Zaccarin, which after all suited him.

Given the number and the naïve exuberance of this restless family with its various additions, it goes without saying that the traffic in our wing of the building was quite intense and tended to generate complaints from the other more discreet tenants. Gone were the decorum and dignity which

There's Always the Sea...

had once reigned there! *"Where's the elevator!"* was often the desperate appeal of the poor devils waiting in vain on the ground floor, while the elevator was blocked on the fifth floor with its doors open, and shouts came down from above in the unmistakeable Venetian cadence: *"Venimo zo subito, ciò!"* (Coming right down, hold your horses!)

As for the "background noises" in our daily dramas, they were provided by the last male of the family, Mariolino, a fourteen year-old holy terror. No elevator for him, at least for going down. And every day, each of the many times he came down those five flights of stairs, he did it sliding on the edge of the 350 steps, skipping two by two at supersonic speed, obviously with heavy shoes! The effect was that of the arrival of a hurricane, which quickly turned into machine-gun bursts, in a rapid crescendo, and then faded away.

"One of these days he'll break his neck," nonna would exclaim shaking her head.

How far away it seemed now the pre-war world I remembered! The dinners, the receptions, the friends of my father and mother, so few surviving after their death.

"That thick-headed mother of mine!" zia Mariuccia would bemoan. *"She would have done better to entrust you to the Casazza family. You would have had the kind of life Angiola had wanted for you. Wanda Casazza, such a fine woman, your mother's best friend, and with no children of her own. She was so longing to have you. She would have raised you as her own, in the style suited to you."*

That's how I found out much later about these other possibilities available to me, which others promptly dismissed without my having any say. I was perplexed and full of doubts as I considered what different fascinating future I might have had. Yet I also realized I would have been exiled from those walls that enclosed the few memories preserved to create for me a history of love and belonging. I imagined myself walking into the Casazzas' apartment, so gloomy, so empty, so silent, where the sound of children had never been heard, where after school I wouldn't have been able to rush in with Edda Zaccarin into the warmth of a kitchen still echoing the gossip of women, and famished greedily eat up slices of bread slathered with butter and anchovy paste. And I thought to myself, *"A l'é mej ambelessì ch'ambelelà"* - it's better here than there - as nonna would have said.

The Casazzas lived in a twin building cater-corner from ours. One morning I was awaken by the sound of powerful rhythmic blows that shook our walls. I looked out the window and saw in horror they were demolishing that very building. I could see no reason for it. It was like witnessing the destruction of my own building, which for me was a living creature, strong, sound, and beautiful. Swinging from the crane, the huge cement ball relentlessly struck again and again. The ball crashed into the walls, ripping, crushing them, the whole building caving in. I watched appalled. The ball kept striking. I couldn't understand the reason. I was fascinated by that prodigious assault, never before seen or imagined in my life, and whose every blow shocked me for its cruel senselessness. Perhaps the interior of the building had been damaged by the war and was unsafe. As metaphorically for mine, its beautiful and majestic façade had been unable to save its innermost essence from crumbling away. That stony-hearted ball came to represent the visual disintegration of an aspect of my world, of that possible life symbolized by Wanda Casazza and her grand residence - both gone forever from my life.

There were always the Baldonis. That loyal, loving presence watching over us from afar. By common choice, there was no social contact with nonna. Tactful disapproval on the one hand, jealous resentment on the other.

My brother and Mirko had continued to share their life as friends and classmates. Lalla, a few years my senior, was for me like the older sister, who allowed me into her privileged world now and then to tell me about her adventures, travels, parties, and romantic encounters.

Once in a while there would be "dinner at the Baldonis." Vague recollections of my childhood would surface then, as I timidly sat at that glittering dining table, where the maid would display an array of sophisticated pies and delicious desserts. My enjoyment was somewhat muted though by the embarrassment at the elegance and pomp to which I was no longer used, and by the excitement at sitting next to Mirko. He was already a high school student, a self-confident, elegant young man, who managed to stir my adolescent years, and… to take possession of all the *panettone* raisins I had carefully placed in a corner of my plate, planning to enjoy them all at the end. He thought I didn't like them, and I didn't have the courage to speak.

My brother and I would arrive at the main entrance at Via Cimarosa, and as soon as we crossed the threshold, it felt as if all the chaos and ugliness of the world were left behind, while we were enveloped by a shady cool silence, and by the smell of wax and cleanliness. We felt like walking on tiptoes as we passed in front of the concierge's lodge going through the usual ritual. The lanky figure of Ines would materialize in the semi-darkness of the sliding glass-panel, seemingly unchanged over the years, eternal. *"Mrs. Baldoni"* we'd announce, to distinguish her from *"Dr. Baldoni,"* her son Vanni, who lived with his wife in the apartment above, and whom I was quite happy to avoid because, from the years at Loano, I had never overcome the paralyzing shyness I felt in front of him.

As if by magic, the elevator with its shiny brass and the wrought-iron decorations was always waiting on the ground floor, right in the centre of the stairwell. Even if it was a question of merely going to the second floor, we never considered climbing the stairs, almost as if doing so would break an unwritten rule. Although it was essentially quite similar to our building, I felt as if I was in another world. Silence and muffled calm reigned everywhere. I have no idea how the residents were able to efface their presence so completely. A click signalled that the elevator had reached the floor, the doors would open and Lalla was already there to meet us, leaning against the door to her apartment, open just enough to reveal her familiar figure wearing a skirt and a cashmere cardigan, with the unfailing pearl necklace that cast a glow to her perfect smile. She too seemed to remain unaltered by time. Only the hair held back by a ribbon would slowly fade over the years from the bright Titian red to gray, and then to the white of snow. The large portrait in the shadows behind her, depicting an idealized young woman with a book in her tapered fingers, would have underscored the slight changes in her face beneath that freckled ever fresh smile.

It was the five-o'clock tea. There, on her favourite armchair, sat Mrs. Baldoni in the shadowy corner of the salon, with the blinds half closed to keep out the summer heat and the noise of Milano's traffic. In the early years, she had been an energetic presence in our lives, severe judge of our behaviour, displaying her approval or disapproval as Nino and I would give her a report on the events in our life. Then, as the years went by, her tone mellowed. The cross-examination would be always interrupted and rendered more palatable when the tea tray was rolled in, with a wealth of unforgettable things all new to me. First-of-a-kind sweets would appear much before they became accessible to everyone, like kiwis wrapped in chocolate, surrounded by Turkish delight, and my first Coca-Cola, served in a tall fluted crystal glass. *"What is it?"* I asked amused by the fizzle in my nostrils. *"It's a new drink from America,"* Lalla would explain. It would not have ever again that same taste for me; in fact, elsewhere, I never even liked it anymore.

In one of the last images of her I carry with me, I see Mrs. Baldoni seated in that armchair, in the half shadow barely grazed by the flashing light of the television that had been installed in her favourite corner, an anachronistic presence among the gilded Empire-style furniture. A plaid covers her knees. She is watching a concert directed by Zubin Metha. *"She's in love with him,"* comments Lalla with knowing tenderness. Suddenly, I notice with distress that the famous orchestra director has a vague resemblance with Professor Baldoni. An enigmatic smile wafts gently over the aged face of the lady.

When the food shortage of the war and post-war years was finally over - I recall getting up from the table still hungry for years – I did not realize right away that the economic hardships for us were not yet over. I was busy making new experiences and meeting new people at school and in my neighbourhood.

There's Always the Sea...

Life in the neighbourhood was very important then, and it included the parish church and the shops of that area. My horizons were therefore expanding beyond our building to the nearby streets with shopkeepers who knew me and called me by name, and saw me growing up; they would often make comments on my inevitable transformation.

We had to buy fresh bread every day, because there was no way to keep food for long. We felt quite lucky when we were finally able to afford an icebox. Before getting it, we kept the stick of butter fresh by placing it under a constant trickle of water from the faucet. The icebox, however, had to be periodically supplied with huge blocks of ice sold door to door by a man. He carried them wrapped in sheets of burlap, and would break them into big chunks. The iceman, the travelling knife sharpener, the ragman (we sold him our unending supply of rags and old newspapers) were all part of the colourful neighbourhood scene. We could hear them call out from the courtyard below, each with his own distinctive shout promoting his services. There was even the tinker who mended tin pots. But it was the knife sharpener, bent over the great screeching and squeaking wheel that most riveted my attention, and I would proudly return from him with my menacing loot of sharpened knives, scissors, and the *mezzaluna* knife I had been entrusted with.

The shops were in the building next to ours, beyond Via Mauro Macchi, which crossed Via Pergolesi. I had been told that if a block had shops it was not considered *"exclusive,"* because instead of being strictly residential, it allowed trade and commerce. I was happy of course that my block had no such shops. It was however convenient to have all we needed so close. They were all in a row, one after the other down to the end of the street. They went on even around the corner, following the shape of the buildings that curved within themselves to form part of the great circumference of Piazza Caiazzo.

The delicatessen was the first in the row of shops, with its shop-windows dangerously set on either side of the corner, and thus threatened by the constant passing of the trolley line. If the trolley bus driver was not careful as he came down Via Pergolesi and made a turn into Via Mauro Macchi, the long trolley pole would suddenly detach from the overhead wire, and dramatically sweep along the wide curve. The event was quite loud, the more so from my room which looked onto that street. Whenever it happened while I was doing my homework, I went to the window to check on the seriousness of the impact, while the trolley swung wildly to and fro. I loved to watch the frustrated attempts of the desperate trolley bus drivers to manoeuver and reset the trolley pole on the electric line. Often the trolley swung against the wall of the building and ended up against the delicatessen shop window, smashing everything, and making salamis and cheese forms fly out like in a Charlie Chaplin movie.

Every Friday, the prescribed meatless day, the delicatessen would put outside a display barrel of cod, the dried salt-cured cod. Coming home from school, I would be bombarded by its foul smell and would hold my breath, hoping at the same time that nonna had not made it for lunch. Cod and mackerel made in fact frequent appearances in our meagre menu. Every once in a while, maybe the day when nonna cashed her pension as a *"widow of a Great War invalid,"* she allowed us the joy of the *"special treat"* - a small waxed paper cup filled with *Russian salad* – morsels of vegetables and hard-boiled eggs dressed with mayonnaise, all covered with a layer of gelatine. A real delicacy and a novelty for our still inexperienced taste buds.

The delicatessen was next to the haberdasher's, filled with those exquisite fineries I would greatly value in a few years, when I would become a regular customer in need to repair the runs in my silk stockings, joy and bane of my youthful years. Ah, those beautiful silky stockings that flattered the legs but "snagged" onto everything, and there, to my dismay, would be another run that no rubbed soap bar would stop for long. In no time, it would become two, three runs, each costing fifty liras to repair. And then there was the worry of the "seams," having to constantly twist to check if they were straight. *"Are my seams straight?"* close members of the family were constantly asked.

There's Always the Sea...

Then the bakery and pastry shop was a real torture, with its splendid double display windows full of tantalizing treats. Whenever I went in, I would come out with a bagful of the typical Milanese crunchy *"rosette"* buns. Round the other corner of the building, the grocery store and the bar took up a vast area, occupying two separate wings of the same shop. From the two counters, the aromas of espresso coffee, chocolate, and assorted spices blended into a magic inebriating formula.

Finally, right after the butcher - not very patronized by us - came Pino, the greengrocer. Lame and with a club-foot, his grotesque figure broke into my childish fantasy, which struggled to accept as a natural part of human nature a character that seemed to belong more to the horrors of fairy tales. I associated him to the deformed shape of Charles Laughton as the hunchback of Notre Dame. That damp smell of green vegetables, that odour of fruits starting to go bad, those scraps always underfoot on the wet floor, among which his large body moved clumsily, struggling to drag the black bulk of his deformed shoe like a flatiron atop of a high pedestal, would grip every time the pit of my stomach with a vague sense of malaise.

The years passed, and the figures of the greengrocer and his wife (even he had a wife) became familiar and found their proper place in my emotional life, until one day they were gone. They were replaced by a father, mother, and a son my age. I was already around fifteen-sixteen years old. The new arrivals piqued my interest as well, a rather amused one this time, because it seems I had drawn the attention of the greengrocer's son. Nothing strange or bad after all. I didn't mind at all being treated with special consideration. I was flattered and amused. But one day a bomb fell on us. Nonna came home almost bursting with the news swelling up inside her.

"I've been asked for your hand in marriage," she chuckled. *"The greengrocer approached me and practically proposed a match between you and his son!"*

At that instant, I can't recall which was my immediate reaction: laughing or being outraged by such boorishness.

Did he think he could buy me for his son? Did he think he could make a deal between "money and ...coat of arms?!"

"And what did you tell him?" I asked uneasy.

"Well, after the initial shock, I pointed out that you were still young, with many years of school ahead of you, and that any such notion was still very much in the future."

We were later informed that the son was willing to wait. *"Oh, that puts my mind at ease,"* quipped nonna laughing. And from then on, this suitor in waiting became the butt of many jokes.

"So, when are you marrying the greengrocer?", "Consider it carefully, he's full of money!" , *"Have you seen your beau today? Is he still waiting?"*

The irony of it all was that not a word ever passed between me and my "suitor."

Those times, however, were still far off. Now my problems were those of a twelve year old with new classmates and playmates. My interests were limited to the world of the famous, now legendary "Liebig" trade cards. They came with the purchase of beef bouillons. They were the joy of children for well over a century, having first appeared in 1872, and being printed continuously until 1975. They were quite sophisticated.

As I collected those coloured pictures, I began to learn about the world. (Television did not yet exist!). They included many different series, like the fauna, the flora, the ancient knights, the heroes of the Nordic sagas and of oriental legends. Through them I came to know about the peoples of the whole world, seen in their dazzling and exotic traditional costumes: Mongols, Chinese, Turks, Armenians, Persians, Indians, Africans. I was fascinated by the subtitles: "Calmucco", "Ghirghiso", and I would range across the Siberian steppes with my imagination. "Afghan Warrior", "Uzbek Man", "Persian Woman from Iran." Some cards were beautiful enough to seem miniature illustrations of ancient manuscripts, with their gilded arabesque and myriad colours. I would put them in order according to subject in the heavy brown paperboard album, seeking to trade with friends for the cards still missing. *"Do you have the Cruel Saladin?"* I viewed it as a prized treasure.

Later, when my pursuits became less juvenile, the cards were replaced by the more mundane images of Hollywood actors, with their yellow tinged patina, like an old daguerreotype. I had to buy those with my own saving, which was quite an outlay. But the joy of going to the news kiosk and to come back with some new face went beyond the pleasure of collecting. They were the idols I so admired in movies. Stereotypical faces and smiles were for me real characters in a faraway yet real world; a world I would come to know one day, combing my hair like Veronica Lake and having similar adventures; meeting men like Cary Grant or Gregory Peck. After all, wasn't there my cousin Maria Oddo in the flesh, the type of fascinating femme fatale I dreamed of becoming, and who already lived the life I aspired to?

When we least expected her, from Roma she would drop in on us in Milano. She was always in the middle of an important trip or in the wake of a great love. And she would impose herself on our hospitality, with nonna anything but pleased to have to be *"at the beck and call of the great lady,"* as she muttered.

Maria was really quite a character and she soon stirred such excitement in me. A boldly chiselled face, intensely deep, dark eyes, with a touch of burning zeal. A forceful and self-confident stride, slowed at times by a conscious pose of sensuous languor. She moved with the same ease on the tennis court – she was the regional champion – as in the salons, where she stood out for her dark beauty, her intelligence, and her strong brilliant personality. A student of Fermi, she easily engaged men in the field of physics and mathematics. She rivalled with society ladies in the Roman world of artists and intellectuals of Via Margutta. I would look in wonder and admiration at photos of her in the society column, where she had managed to appear, much to our amusement, as "Oddo delle Colonne." A frequent destination of her trips were the United States, where she would go for research as a Fulbright scholar, or for pleasure.

I would look in the mirror to compare myself with her - the abyss was hopeless, and perhaps not just for the age difference. All I could see was a slip of a girl, made even more so by the thick braids that reached my waist, turning me into a sad little orphan Annie, or better yet a *"figlia di Maria,"* (a "daughter of the Madonna," as the typical convent orphan was called in Italy).

As a matter of fact, I actually had my triumphs in the parish church, where I was sought after for my long hair. It was still the Milano of human dimensions, my quiet Milano, almost provincial, that lent its streets to neighbourhood religious processions. In occasion of the parish feast, they always called on me to play the angel. Wearing a white tunic, golden cardboard wings, and my long hair flowing loose, I would cast flower petals on the crowds from atop the float of the Madonna.

When the age of Senior High School came, I was still fascinated by Maria's adventures. One day, during one of her visits, the concierge called me secretly aside, asking me if I knew the name of my cousin's friend, the painter with whom she was about to travel to the United States. I said I didn't, that I knew he was a famous painter but I didn't know him personally. Then, as if he were about to reveal a scandalous State secret, he whispered:

"It's my nephew!"

I would not have been surprised if he had smugly told me of this pseudo relationship between our two families, but instead he was scandalized, and he expected me to be as well.

"But do you understand that it is my nephew? You must tell your cousin!"

I was surprised as well by the news, but I could not react as if it was a case of leprosy. He talked like the butler of "Downton Abbey!"... Upstairs, downstairs....

"Quite a coincidence!" I declared. *"But my cousin's friends are none of my business."*

Naturally, I did not think that being related with a concierge diminished in any way the painter's personal and artistic qualities, though I was certain, as the realistic concierge was, that it would have been quite a shock for my ambitious cousin. I would have loved to have seen her reaction. But I chose not to do anything about it. From then on, however, I saw her in a different light, enjoying the little secret that brought her down a notch.

Smiling, I went back in my mind at the thought of the little girl who, only a few years before, used to cut out from an album for her paper dolls - forerunners of the modern Barbie - a series of dresses modelled on the sophisticated cousin Maria, waiting to be able one day to wear herself that small angora sweater over the polka-dot dress.

CHAPTER TWELVE

"Where do you live?" - *"In the Central Station area,"* I'd answer with a certain smugness.

In those years, the name Stazione Centrale would not have sounded commonplace to any Milanese. The massive imperial style building in the background of the vast piazza rivalled "Il Duomo" in boldness and grandeur. Like Minerva from the forehead of Jupiter, the building had issued from the mind of a mad god, who had conceived it pompous, arrogant, absurd, irrational, thoroughly Fascist. The disapproval and condescending comments of the non-Milanese came more readily than for "Il Duomo." But if you were born in its shadow, if you had passed a lifetime in its company, it was impossible not to love it. It dominated your life, it swallowed you up in its meanders, it pulled you into the whirlpool of its pressing, animated and stimulating crowds.

In that vortex of life, I found it fascinating to pick out one among the numerous railway lines that fanned out towards far off destinations. Cautiously at first, the train slowly wound through the working class suburbs. Shabby sunken lives that distressed me deeply. Then, with a sigh of relief, I felt the train accelerate and take up the race. Whistles, chugs, lights, movement were to become the starting point in my adventures of discovery as a student. I found the *Stazione* faithfully waiting for me at every return home. Getting off trains, taxis, trolleys, it was always there to point the way, to mark my home boundaries.

"Look! A 'fascio'!" – *"And there another one,"* my brother would add.

We raced to see who could spot more of them. And we were scandalized as if by a mark of infamy. But Nino explained that it was not a Fascist invention, it was Etruscan in origin. In ancient Rome, it was the insignia of the magistrates, a symbol of union and strength. I was still too young to fully grasp the whole absurdity of that grandiose flight of steps, like an Aztec pyramid. To climb them was for me the beginning of the adventure. They'd take me up where the trains were ready to depart, like impatient creatures at the ready. I have to admit that it was hard to drag our suitcases, one step after another, and nonna would cuss in Piedmontese. Still, if we had too many, the porter would load them on a big hand-cart and would bring them in the freight elevator up to our platform. But, ever distrustful, nonna would not let her things out of sight, and would follow him with me embarrassed on her heels.

Nevertheless, before being completely won over, when I was all alone, I would approach the monster nervously and fearful. I'd walk warily among the immense pillars, across the dim area of the entrance hall, looking out for unusual shadows along the walls and sculptures, at whose massive glories, degraded by dense layers of grimy dust, I would stare with surprised loathing. I tried to steer clear of the stair cavity leading down to the shady den of the *Albergo Diurno* (daytime showers), every time disconcerted by how anyone could have the nerve to go inside and make use of its facilities.

Beneath that immense portico, the yellow serpent of taxis wound itself. Years after the war they had replaced the old green-black *Aprilias,* a splash of colour in all that dusty grey. The giant's mouth spat them out in the front, and then they could be seen returning from their mission along a wide curve that brought them back to the side entrance.

In a continuous replay, I see a particular taxi enter the curve which signals for me as well the end of the run. The languor of that curve re-emerges, while I feel still pressed by its force into the embrace of a magical encounter. Last desperate moments, a last goodbye kiss before the train separates us once more. A few privileged moments chosen by my memory from the years of my life lost in darkness. An intense flash of life in my soul and in my senses.

Even the piazza had its own eccentric personality. It seemed designed as a track for an electric model train. You crossed it passing precariously from one traffic island to the other over a maze of convoluted streets and rail tracks. You had to constantly look down at the direction of the rail tracks to figure out if that clattering tram heading threateningly towards you would run you over or not. Then suddenly, with an abrupt twist, it would swerve along its own route.

Piazza della Repubblica, back then Piazza Duca d'Aosta. Today the great hotel by that name still rises there, though well past its prime, when it marked an era, now overshadowed by the bulk of the more modern great hotels. I went inside it even before I was born. My mother, in the final month of her pregnancy, had gone there for the wedding of zia Mariuccia. The story in our family was that she had some fun at the poor maître d'hôtel's expense, showing up in all her evident pregnancy and with a distressed look asking for the groom, my future zio Piero. The poor man, fearing some "impediment" to the marriage in the typical melodramatic style of the times, had noticeably paled. And my merciless mother kept him on pins and needles a little longer.

My memories reach down through the depth of time. Images so remote of when even the seasons bathed the city in a different, almost alien colour wash. Laboriously, I work my way through, but at the end of the tunnel the scene is there, muted by the distance, soundless like in a silent film, an unreal black and white frame. This was when heavy snow would fall on Milano, metres of snow blanketing everything, covering shapes, colours, and movements. A white silent city that does not exist anymore. Life would stop; everything would come to a halt. The huge piazza, covered and frozen in white, re-emerges as if from another life. Original as always, eccentric, I can still see Piero Matteotti, Nino's friend, casually moving through the paralyzed city on his cross-country skis.

And then there was the fog, the real Milano fog, that fog which enfolds you, sustains you, fondles you sensuously like the sea. It annuls the solitude of spaces, it fills the emptiness, it wraps you in a warm familiar mantle. It softens whatever it touches, it dampens; the pace of crowds slows down, the muffled clatter of streetcars materializes unexpectedly, a friendly sound, no longer jarring; the shops' lights are a soft yellow, a veiled hint of cosiness, of windows all glittering and mysterious.

Often there were three of us coming back from school, Edda Zaccarin, my friend from the fifth floor, myself, and in the middle Armida Pacinotti, our teacher in *Scuole Medie*. She was strict and commanded the respect of the class with her professorial demeanour and the gaze behind her spectacles. But the moment she stepped away from her desk, her housewife look turned her into a harmless plump auntie, unsteady and insecure, not as much because of her size as for her strong myopia, only just helped by the thick lenses, which made pins out of her eyeballs.

Due to this condition and because we lived in the same area, she often relied on us to escort her home. Edda and I found her then very vulnerable and totally in our hands. This reversal of the traditional roles was rather funny, and it was very difficult not to take a little revenge. The acid test was crossing the famous Piazza della Stazione. Edda and I would grab Armida on either side, firmly under her arms, and we'd make her trot without pity, this way and that way, a bit more than was necessary, in the dusky light of a wintery Milano, with sudden jumps amid the honking of cars and the metallic warnings of tramways, relishing our control over her. That day of thick fog however, our suppressed laughter at her every squeal of dismay gave way to a sense of pity, seeing how thoroughly frightened our hapless Armida was. The fact was that all the extra twists and turns this time were not done out of meanness, but because we were really lost. We could not see farther than our nose and we had completely lost all sense of direction. The sudden appearance of cars and tramways really made us jump, and no labyrinth could have equalled the intensity of that existential anguish gripping us. We felt as if walled inside a void.

"But are we lost?" Armida kept repeating quavering. In part out of pity, in part out of pride, but especially to convince ourselves, we kept denying it. The replaying memory fades out and leaves those three lost souls to find their way.

Edda and I shared the same desk throughout Grade 6. The following year, though, we were separated. The teacher judged the strong bond that we had formed negative for our scholastic performance. She probably felt as well that the unruly spirit of Edda might have a bad influence on me. The quality of our friendship did not change, but new friends as well entered in my sphere of life. I shared my desk now with Clara Lanzara.

What memories do I still have of her? Patches of an unfinished story, "a work in progress" in the novel of my life; yet with her light touch in passing, she left an indelible effect on me. For years she gave me her warmth and friendship, sharing with me thoughts and emotions. Edda was my playmate. Clara was my first bosom friend, a soul mate. Thanks to her I discovered the pleasure of giving and receiving, the comfort of communicating with a kindred spirit, of learning about myself and about life.

Even if her presence has faded out of my life for so long now, her face is not just one of many as I see her bending toward me at our desk grimacing in pain. That face suddenly blanching that filled me with alarm. Clara experienced much pain every month. At times she was forced to stay home from school, or would arrive late. The teacher was aware and excused her. We were at the age of puberty, and the girl who had already experienced the first signs felt grown up and important, and would look down upon the others still young, who *"didn't know."* We were treated with special regard by the teachers, and often we'd take advantage during tests. We had to take care, though, not to fall in the trap of using the excuse twice a month.

Clara was very sensitive and emotional, she lived intensely every emotion. She had the soul of an artist, which she became in fact, and at times she appeared to exist in a world all her own, inaccessible to normal people. One day she came to school very late, bursting in our classroom breezily, right in the middle of a lesson. She didn't appear physically ill. I held my breath wondering what possible justification she might have for such behaviour and afraid of the teacher's outraged reaction. Coolly, as if it were the most reasonable thing in the world, she explained that as she was

There's Always the Sea...

about to leave the house, the radio was transmitting *The Warsaw Concerto,* and naturally she had to stay until the end. I don't remember Mrs. Pacinotti's reaction, but I think she too was somewhat perplexed and deflated.

She was the daughter of two musicians, the father a Neapolitan and the mother a Spaniard. In the home of the Lanzaras, music was the constant background, with only one feature - if you went there in the morning the house resounded at full volume with the Neapolitan songs of Libero Bovio and Roberto Murolo; in the afternoons, on the other hand, the music was always classical. Since then, I have always associated Neapolitan songs with those breezy sunny rooms, in which the matronly figure of Mrs. Lanzara would sweep through singing joyfully, and I would acquire the appreciation for that music.

I recall Clara's sweet face, a bit round, with soft full lips, that I liked even more because it looked like that of Ingrid Bergman, whom I just adored. I gazed with envy and appreciation the already clearly visible curves of her body, moulded by the close-fitting school smock which wrapped around her, closing tightly in the back.

It was a real drama when at the end of *Scuole Medie,* in Grade 8, Clara decided to follow her passion for painting by enrolling in "Brera," the School of Arts. It was our first major separation. In the small album (I still have it) which we passed around collecting the signatures of all our classmates at the end of the school year, her drawing jumps out at you as if she had just done it.

We remained friends for many years and continued seeing each other, but what really creates and maintains a bond are the experiences shared in class during the school years. And so other faces and other relationships overlaid hers. Yet, still all through High School, I continued to go to her home for dance parties, where our friendship became intertwined with the courtship by her brother Davide, known as Dodi. A great big baby, with a nickname that seemed a caricature of my own hated one (on a man, of all things!), the poor devil had no chance at all with me. Sweeter, on the other hand, is the memory of Lamberto, the childhood friend of

Clara, a handsome boy with kind and melancholy eyes, perhaps because a attack of polio had left him lame.

I enjoyed being courted and popular at parties, to put myself to the test and to be reassured. But the pleasure didn't go beyond soothing my vanity. I had no time or space in my life for sentimental ties. That was something important that would come with time and with the right man. Those boys made me smile, they seemed rather immature and unsuitable, my aspirations were quite different!

For the time being, I was satisfied with the moving voice of Frank Sinatra or Nat King Cole. Clara had an intense fascination for Sinatra and a rich collection of his records. A few years later she was in seventh heaven as she told me that she had met a boy from Torino who looked like her beloved singer. It turned into her great love. They married. Clara moved to Torino. Our path diverged from then on, and I didn't see her any more. I learned that soon she gave birth to twins. I was still studying at the university, and I felt a pang.

What did she do with her talent? How thoughtlessly we toss away something as precious as friendship when we are young. How absurd it now seems to have allowed life to distract us, throwing us here and there, without reacting at what we were robbed of, without holding on to that which gave our life substance and meaning. When and how does it happen that another human being passes from being everything to us to being nothing? I stare at the sad lay figure in front of me. One of her first studies done at "Brera" that has followed me all my life around the world. But I've never been able to find Clara again.

During the *Scuole Medie* years, however, great part of my day was still shared with Edda Zaccarin. We went to school and came back together, we shared our afternoon snack and studied together, and then, time permitting, we'd go out to play. In those years, Milano still provided quiet residential streets for neighbourhood children to play in.

I had inherited from my brother an old pair of roller skates, rather rusty, the grandfathers of the modern ones, all metal, four wheels plus the key to tighten them to the size of the shoe. But our races up and down Via Mauro Macchi were exciting in spite of the dangerously precarious balance. We even had our private raceway in the Giardinetti della Stazione. These public gardens were an island of flowerbeds with scattered park benches, flanking the station in the area of our house. You could reach them going down broad sets of stairs, and in the peace and quiet of those days, they were the rendezvous of grandfathers with children, nannies with baby carriages, men taking their dogs for a stroll. Syringes in the grass were then unimaginable scenes of science fiction. We had just come out of the ravages of the war, and we wanted to live. Our area of play was between the two huge fountains of granite tiles towering at each end of the gardens. In those first post-war years they stood empty, their delightful water sprays only a memory. They became for us an absolutely perfect closed circuit, in which to skate round and round the pot-bellied stem with a certain acrobatic skill. How we managed without getting dizzy is one of the mysteries of that age.

But what I still feel in a very real physical sense is the soft warm velum of some summer evenings, when I would go out with nonna to eagerly seize the last minutes of liveliness and human contacts from the day drawing to a close. The day's last exhilaration burst with greater abandon and joy because it was already enveloped in the reassuring stillness of the evening. The blue-rose air swelled in a calm breath.

The concierge was already at the front door of the building, with chairs ready for the other "gossips." And sure enough, there was Mrs. Zaccarin coming out. The trio was complete, as was mine with Edda and Albertina, the daughter of the concierge. A piece of chalk and a pebble, and we'd start jumping like flamingos on one leg on the squares we had drawn on the pavement for the game of *la campana* (hopscotch). Or else, a whole new series of acrobatics could be had simply with a ball and a wall.

I can still hear the swallows in their frenzied screeching in the sky above, echoing our own shrieks below - a rare sound indeed now in our ever more poisoned world.

When we got tired, we'd sit on the curb trying to catch some juicy bit of gossip on the tenants in our building provided in the strictest confidence by the concierge. By pure chance, sometimes the lady gossiped about would just happen to pass by, all decked out for the evening, hissing a disdainful acknowledgment. We, on the other hand, would stare with envy at the older girls who were allowed to go out in the evening. We were particularly curious about Anna Maria Guarneri, the daughter of the orchestra conductor, a new tenant who was a stage actress. We were very proud that she lived in our same building, and we would have loved it if she had acknowledged us at least with a nod. Instead, arrogant, she would pass totally ignoring us, and we got back at her with snide remarks about her bow legs.

Albertina was very unhappy, and we felt sorry for her because her father was an alcoholic. There were horrible scenes when he would come home drunk from the bar and would hit wife and daughter. Tenants had to intervene and call the police at times. In the end, the complaints with the administrator of the building were so many that he was fired and the whole family had to leave. Gradually, the looser tenor which had permeated the building in the post-war period was eliminated, in an effort to bring it back to the propriety it once had. No more children playing and ladies sitting under the porch at the main entrance to have a chat. The mirrors and the brass returned to shine, and a dignified quiet spread amid the marble walls and the hall's carpets. The front entrance, nevertheless, remained open until late at night, as was the custom throughout the city, and life moved in a leisurely ebb and flow between the outside world and the private one. These wide-open great doorways invited the gaze of the passerby on the secret courtyards, where gateways protected unexpected luxuriously green areas. The saying went that *"Milano is the greenest city in Italy, if seen from above."*

Thirty years later, while visiting my city, seeing those heavy majestic entrances always closed, I felt alienated and excluded, as if Milano had closed the doors in my face. Instead it was the silence of fear. Milano had retreated within its fortresses as a medieval town, besieged by violence and criminality. An anonymous, faceless voice answered the ringing of the bell, a small door as in a convent opened with an automatic click. There was no familiar face anymore greeting you behind the glass in the concierge's lodge; the concierge, barricaded as well, appraised you from a narrow opening.

CHAPTER THIRTEEN

Who can remember Milano's Carnival toward the end of the 1940s, still caught in the euphoria of the recent end of the war? The scene is so unreal that I feel as if I have dreamed it. The downtown, closed to traffic, was transformed in a huge salon. Piazza del Duomo, "La Galleria" were all filled with festive people in a masquerade. In "La Galleria" it was difficult to make your way through a carpet of streamers and confetti that came up to your knees. You passed amid jests, witty pleasantries, bows and pranks, while noisemakers blared in your ears and streamers wrapped around you entwining everyone in a lacework of colour, laughter, and joy. The loudspeakers blared out the latest dance rhythms. Edda, Ombretta, and I, dressed up as old-fashion ladies, danced the popular *spirù* right in the middle of "La Galleria."

Ombretta Ludovisi, her face with the features of a bulldog, confirming the stubborn character of the spoiled only child, had forced her company on us much to our annoyance. Snobby daughter of her widowed mother and mama's darling, she was promptly nicknamed *"Ombretta sdegnosa del Mississippì"* (Snobby Ombretta from the Mississippi).

Her mother must have thought that my being an orphan from a respected family made me an adequate and desirable friend for her daughter, and so there was a shower of invitations and demands which I could not refuse. That's how we came to that memorable postwar Carnival. Mrs. Ludovisi decided that she would sew the costumes for me and her daughter. The idea was exciting, but I demanded that Edda be included as well.

When the mother asked if we had at home any pieces of cloth or old dresses, I let it slip out that I had mamma's evening gowns. And so, with some hesitation and reluctance from nonna, the velvets, satins, and laces of the beautiful wardrobe till then religiously stowed away in a special chest,

There's Always the Sea...

ended up in the capable hands of the clever costume designer, who we thought had understood how sacred those things were to us.

At the first fitting, however, we realized horrified that her scissors had carried out a grim operation. The transformation was almost total. Added to the dislike for Ombretta was now our outrage at the shameless flippancy of the mother. Nonna was furious. And yet, we could do nothing about it. I managed to overcome my disappointment more easily when I saw the effect of the final result. I looked pleased as I saw in the mirror an oval face that had acquired some character under the smart feathered little hat; a body wrapped tightly in a long blue velvet dress with even a *tournure* that emphasized my narrow waist; full lips; almond-shaped eyes embellished by mascara; slender hands easing out of lace cuffs. And all of a sudden, with a small parasol in hand, I was part of a Renoir painting. I was beaming to see myself transformed into a woman. How did it happen that I was no longer ugly? Clearly, I was born in the wrong period.

Another figure was approaching from behind. Suddenly, no less than the Infanta of Spain was beside me. A rigid Ombretta had pride of place with the enormous sides of her horizontal dress. It was more than evident that Ombretta's mother had placed no limits in her ambitions for her daughter. On the other hand, poor Edda had been badly treated indeed. Her diminutive figure had not been embellished with imaginative shaping of fabric; for her the improvised designer did not feel it necessary to waste her efforts or creativity. Nevertheless, the day was a triumph for all three of us. We were suddenly cast in a role of beautiful ladies of courting age, free to live it with all the naiveté of our thirteen years of age on that phantasmagorical stage, where every flattery, every gaze, every spiral of stream thrown at us made us feel we were at the centre of the world.

Full of enthusiasm for this unusual experience, on the spur of the moment I decided to include it in the regular rapport I made of my life to Mrs. Baldoni. She reacted with shock and indignation, and a shadow of embarrassment and doubt darkened the joyous moment of that day. Right then and there I did not understand. I was deeply mortified and dejected to see that day so happy for me run down and disapproved of, and to have reconfirmed the ill-concealed censure of Mrs. Baldoni of the way nonna was raising me. As I said, I didn't fully grasp the motives, but in spite of it, I had a vague intuition as I thought of mamma - she would have been of the same opinion, and she would have disapproved of my friends as well. I felt myself in the grip of a painful sense of confusion and pain at the realization that more than one person dear to me was criticizing my beloved nonna.

I have no other recollection of Ombretta, except for the shabby way our friendship ended. This time I was invited to spend a few days with her in their villa in Brianza. I really disliked going far from home, sleeping alone in someone else's house. Even when I went to see zia Mariuccia in Vigevano, I was pervaded by sadness in the evening. In that strange room where I was put to sleep, unfamiliar objects illuminated by the dim light filtering through the shutters would take on an exaggerated physical appearance, and their entire alienating weight would fall on me: the dark colours of the upholstery with stains of humidity, the empty armchairs, the holy pictures on the nightstand. I can still see that silver plate with its carved evening prayers which I would begin to repeat mechanically to keep myself company: "*Jesus, Joseph, Mary, I give you my heart and my soul….*"

To go away from home was like losing evidence of my identity and the safe haven where echoes and memories glossed over the void. They were no longer there, but it was still the home of my parents, and there, I was still someone. Whenever I left it, I was seized by anguish, akin to sea sickness, like on a voyage without any point of reference. Thrown alone in someone else's space, I felt like an orphan once more; I suffered again the sense of being no one's daughter, of belonging to no one.

I don't know how I found myself with Ombretta and her mother in that desolate, isolated villa inside a big park, at the edge of a ravine, with a stream rushing among the rocks, a damp smell of mildew, the walls permeated with cold due to the long winter neglect. The cold begins to go right through my bones, it's a physical cold which soon becomes a chill of the soul. I feel it rising from the pit of my stomach, it has the yellow-green colour of those mouldy walls, it has the smell of those damp draperies. After so many years my well-known nausea clutches me once more. But I cannot cry out "*Mamma, mamma, 'nasua', 'nasua'!*" I am a big girl now and embarrassed. The inevitable drama takes place.

I am taken back home to Milano. Ombretta's invitations stopped coming, and so did my bouts with nausea. But many other times in the course of my life I would feel again that combination of nausea of the surroundings, and melancholy of not belonging.

I don't remember too well the "Scuole Medie Giuseppe Parini" removed perhaps by the fact that "*il Parini*" had always been known for the glorious *Ginnasio-Liceo*, considered the best in Italy at that time. I remember the façade of course, with us going through its humble doorway, as we looked with envy and awe at the "senior" students who instead walked through the impressive front entrance. But the whole area was to become very familiar to me. For eight long years I would walk back and forth along via Solferino, where the *Corriere della Sera* had its head office, the haunt of famous journalists and writers.

On days we had written tests, we'd get off the tramway the stop before, in Piazza San Marco, in order to go in the beautiful red-brick "Basilica of San Marco" to say a prayer. How innocent our faith, thinking we could draw God's attention to a Latin test, in spite of all the unheeded evils in the world.

As I was growing up, increasing the range of my explorations and activities, I acquired more and more familiarity and control of my city. I discovered various aspects of its character, as if it were a living person. Every area, every street, every building took on its own personality by associating them to individuals, historical events, and experiences.

There was the high-class Milano and the low class; the high cultured, sophisticated Milano and the grey and common Milano as well; the romantic one; and it could be snobbish, vulgar, poor, and desperate too. You have to love Milano in order to discover her, and then, in secret corners, you will find her ancient soul, almost discreetly shielded from the hurried look a foreigner might cast. Her art, her history are not displayed as if on a stage like in Rome or Florence. Corrupted by my life in North America, where I was obliged to depend on a car, I recall the happy times when I would cross my city on foot, from one end to the other, stone by stone, with the energy typical of youth. I knew every street, every piazza, every back alley, every palazzo; I lived them, I felt them. Or happily sitting in a tram, time would slow down for me to the pace of its trudging clatter. My eyes could leisurely enjoy the Liberty façade of a building, that curving alley, the piazza with that particular monument, the wisp of a garden, that cluster of trees. I would anticipate the route; I would learn to recognize every corner.

Even among those noble cement structures, spring would suddenly burst out. *"Oh, I see the first buds, spring is almost here,"* I would tell myself.

Every tram number was associated with a particular destination, routes I had done over and over again, each with a different sensation. Number 5 took me to school, with all the anguish of exams; N. 16 took me downtown, with the flashing by of beautiful display windows; N. 33, with its final wide turn, circled the Piazza of the Monumentale Cemetery. It was All Souls' Day and a visit to papa's tomb. A long line of kiosks and stalls overflowing with flowers awaited us at the entrance gate. The sweet smell of chrysanthemum - huge obscene yellow and violet balls - would catch my breath, turning into a dense feeling of melancholy.

From the area of Stazione Centrale, I would drift into the area of Porta Venezia, with its ramparts and gardens full of people out on a Sunday promenade. The odd shape of the Planetarium in Corso Venezia beckoned me, keeping its mysteries of astronomical shows which I dreamed to see in vain. It was also the avenue of the luxurious residential buildings, of the best shops and cinemas, second only to the ones downtown.

It was in one of those cinemas with plush armchairs and red velvet curtains that I saw my very first film, thanks to zia Ida. I was thirteen. Walt Disney's first masterpiece had just come from America, *Bambi*. As I passed under the porticos of Corso Vittorio Emanuele, the huge almond-shaped eyes of the fawn, caught in the precarious balancing of its first steps, were gazing at me in fright. I spent days of anxious, excited anticipation for the weekend when zia would take Pinuccio, Teresita and me to see the film everyone had been talking about, and I could scarcely imagine what I would see.

Finally, sunk deep in a large seat, in the darkened cinema, I found myself immersed in a magic world of images, sounds, colours and emotions. I was immediately caught up in the story and I was pulled along until the final drama of the loss. At that point I recognized myself in the desperate calling out of the fawn for its mother; the wrenching agony chocked me, and I abandoned myself to uncontainable weeping. I think zia Ida never forgave herself for that choice, so poorly suited for me, and she was distressed for a long time. But I was always grateful to her for having given me one of the most memorable experiences of my adolescence.

The cinema remained one of the passions of my life. On Sundays, Nino and I would go through *Il Corriere della Sera* to find in the movie listing some old nuggets being shown even in the farthest corner of our suburbs. Unforgettable experiences in which the gentle face of Ingrid Bergman in *Gas Light* followed an avant-spectacle with a couple of plump soubrettes turning on the local rakes. At times, the sound track of the film happened to be spoiled by the public crunching the apples offered free at the entrance.

On one of our outings, I discovered the *balere* (popular dance halls), the ones made famous by the songs of Jannacci. On a round platform installed in the centre of the piazza, young soldiers clinging to charming girls, and couples of stiff men with full-breasted women in provocative tight pants and body-hugging skirts were whirling to waltzes and sliding into tangos. At the end of their turn, they would be rounded up with a lasso like a herd in the Far West, and forced to leave the stage. To get back on, they had to buy another ticket. Fascinated by this show, I too had to be dragged away by my brother to avoid being late for our own.

Following Corso Venezia, you reached Piazza San Babila, gathering place of sophisticated people, maybe for hearing mass in the basilica where you would find Milano's high society. Their choice was either "San Babila" or "San Carlo" on Corso Vittorio Emanuele. Even more chic was meeting for an aperitif in Via Monte Napoleone, the street which was Milano's drawing room, with its display of expensive boutiques and jewelries not yet behind unfortunate heavy iron grills. These were for me brief and sporadic forays in a forbidden world, before withdrawing once again with a sense of emptiness and unease within my own shell. On our youthful student level, we'd meet instead at the foot of Vittorio Emanuele equestrian statue in Piazza Duomo, or the one of Leonardo da Vinci in Piazza della Scala, alias *on liter in quatter,* as it is playfully called in Milano - a reference to the long-limbed figure of Leonardo symmetrically surrounded by the four shorter statues of his followers. A strange quintet that recreates the shape of the litre carafe used to measure wine in taverns, together with the four quarter litre carafes hanging around it. The shiny "Motta" and "Alemagna" *cafés* and the old "Biffi Scala" with the inebriating fragrances of their pastries would add relish to our student rendez-vous.

The downtown offered the further attraction of the bookshops, with the fascination of the handsome book covers on display, promise of ineffable delights. The whole world of music records would then be added to my passion for books. "Ricordi" and "Messaggerie Musicali" of the '50s released on the market the newest fads from across the ocean: jazz, blues, rock and roll. To invite a boy to listen to the latest by Benny Goodman in the music booth, where you could spend hours without ever buying anything, was the first form of approach permitted to girls.

For me, the romantic Milano was also Parco Sempione, with its paltry tower, which became in my eyes the Tour Eiffel when my junior naval officer taught me from there to recognize the stars. And also the "Castello Sforzesco" with the swallows going wild at sunset. Oh, how I longed to hear that living shrill in the flat silent monotony of Canada!

When years later I returned, the bulk of the castle was waiting for me there at the end of Via Dante (how many times

There's Always the Sea...

had I walked along that avenue!), with its beloved dark shape etched against the cobalt sky. I was just beneath it, and suddenly I was enveloped in the convulsive shrill of swarms of swallows that were stitching the sky with a weave of flight patterns. I had found them again. An experience I thought I had lost forever. With a lump in my throat, I allowed myself to become giddy with their black folly. The last sensations of the day became fused and tempered in the rose-coloured warmth of the evening. That soft golden breath of air - this was also Milano.

That was the time I went to sit on the steps of "Il Duomo" with the nonchalance of a tourist, which I probably was after all. That sense of breaking the rules added to the exhilarating feeling of freedom which I felt being so far away in body and soul from the oppressiveness of my life in Canada. Alone and happy, my sweeping gaze lingered over the cherished and familiar forms. I was breathing through every one of my pores the spirit of that piazza, which was welcoming me to its bosom like a mother. Punctually at dusk, the first neon signs appeared on the opposite side of the piazza. I remembered the first time they had been lit, around the '50s. I think the idea had been to cover up the façade ruined during the war. That cold, mechanical, anachronistic intrusion in the sober warmth of Piazza del Duomo had created a great scandal. It was the future of the modern world advancing and defiling all in its path, until that too would become ancient history. The years would bring even greater havoc. The elegance of the old "Savini" in "La Galleria" would be offended by the presence of a garish America-style fast food eatery in front of it. What a slap in the face to discover in my city the worst of America! At least the *Carabinieri* were always there, strolling in pairs, a fond echo of "Pinocchio," handsome in their parade uniforms; even if they never again would step apart to flank me gallantly while I passed, as they did once when I was young and carefree. Now I was looking at those handsome boys with the eyes of a mother, pleased to look once more on the pleasing features of my people.

They called it *"El gamba de legn"* (Wooden Leg); its cartoon-like snout would suddenly appear under a small arch, popping out from around a curve in out-of-the-way suburban streets. It would trudge along huffing and puffing, pulling its two or three cars on its way to Monza. Those who remember it have known the "real" Milano. We'd poke fun at it singing the Milanese refrain,

"El tranvaìn de Munsa ei disen che posa pian, in ventiquatro ore da Munsa el va a Milan" (They say the Monza train is slow, in 24 hours it goes from Monza to Milan).

Milano could afford these extravagances, like the *naviglio* (canal) Martesana, which I'd cross on the other side of the "Stazione Centrale" before it was forced to conform to modern requirements, and was filled in and changed into an asphalt street. Or the infamous *tombon* in the area of San Marco cathedral. We'd pass in horror on our way to school by its filthy grate meant to filter the flow of the *naviglio*'s waters before it disappeared from sight. It was said that its name (large tomb) was due to all the carcasses of dead animals - and maybe not only animals - which once would pile up against it.

Milano grew with me during my school years, while I discovered its secrets in books of history and literature. In them I followed the adventures of Renzo Tramaglino of Manzoni's "I Promessi Sposi" (The Betrothed), and the feats of the *Risorgimento* period involving Verdi and "La Scala;" and I read with pride the poem *La battaglia di Legnano* by Carducci, the Lombard patriotic song. All at once, I saw my city anew through the words of Manzoni, Verdi, and Carducci. That's how I nourished my youthful hunger for heroism and adventure, with a captivation that few films later on could surpass with their visual version. The literary filter wrapped my real world with awareness, while at the same time the opportunity to physically identify those sites around me gave substance to the imaginative world of literature.

Piazza Cordusio, that rather modern piazza with its unfamiliar name, which I had always vaguely associated with some hypothetical general (may be one of the many failures in our wars), one day revealed unexpectedly to me its absorbing

Lombard history. When Milano became the capital of one of the thirty-six duchies of the Longobard kingdom, the duke established his court in the *Curia Ducis*, that is the Duke's Court; from this the name *Cordusio*. And so the old mystery was solved. In the same way, Porta Romana, Porta Garibaldi, Porta Ticinese, Porta Vittoria were no longer abstract points of exit from the city, but rather milestones of protective walls ringing the city, through which Milano would ride out to meet her role in history.

How many times had I passed by Via Lazzaretto without paying attention? After reading Manzoni, I would then see for the first time that mysterious structure almost covered by greenery; and I would stare at it and imagine fascinated the interior, trying to visualize the ancient horrors inside that hostel for the victims of the plague - there, so close to my home. Renzo's acts of bravado against the Spaniards in the 17th century Milano, narrated by Manzoni in his novel, merged with the deeds of Manzoni's own sons fighting against the Austrians in the *Five Days of Milano* two centuries later. In spite of the efforts of my professor of Italian to create in me an aversion for "I Promessi Sposi" by asking questions like "*the colour of Lucia's stockings,*" I still loved the book.

Milano was all this for me, together with the aroma of roasted chestnuts which accompanied me in the fog.

Little did I know then that only a few hundred meters away from my own home the greatest tragedy of my century had taken place as well. In my times, that event in history, still so recent then, was not yet told in school books.

My familiar, homey "Stazione Centrale," for me a point of departure to exciting adventures, had played quite a different role during the war. It had been not only, as I well knew, a casualty of war as the target of one of the heaviest bombing blitz in Italy, but it had been used to perpetrate the greatest war crime as well. From the deep maze of the station's dark tunnels, truckloads of Jews had been jostled like chattel towards the infamous "*binario 21*" (railroad track) on their way to the extermination camps. Unaware as a child, I had been a marginal witness when they cried out to us from those cattle cars.

CHAPTER FOURTEEN

There was a period when a great part of my life involved trotting along the streets of Milano behind nonna, like an obedient puppy. Before I could consider Milano as my own, before knowing it inside and out and feel completely at ease in it, I had a gradual introduction to it by following her everywhere. In spite of the school, my friends, the constant presence, though on the fringes, of my brother, it was nonna around whom my life revolved for so many years of my life. We lived a life of symbiosis. She imbued my days with her moods, she filled them with her continuous activity – worker and queen bee all in one – whose days were taken up by a series of *"errands", "matters to be settled", "visits to make",* "shopping." Busy and combative as she was, it was a constant thrashing with *"disputes"* and *"bureaucratic procedures"* - a never ending trudging about from banks to city hall and state offices, all part of her struggle for our survival following the war.

Her battlefield covered all of Milano, from downtown to the suburbs. We would literally walk many kilometres, plus endless trips by tramway which we had to take by storm after waiting for it for hours. Whole bunches of us would be hanging outside the door, as we'd slowly try to fight our way through the folding doors snapping shut on hands, legs or arms. And then there were the exhausting lines at the wickets, with me suffocating in the crowd, never seeing the end to those everlasting queues. That's where I learned to fight "for my place in the world." People pressed, pushed, trying to cheat and pass ahead in line. Then nonna would pull out all the stops, and with all her outrage, she would demand with dignity *"the respect due to an elderly lady* "or *"some consideration for an orphan girl,"* which people naturally assumed it had to do with the war and would grant us all *"due consideration."* I don't know whether nonna really intended that, but I felt branded when they all looked at me with pity.

It was a world still embittered by the hardships, the poverty, and the devastation. The war was over, and yet it continued to stretch out its shadow. The shadow of the rubble, brutal gashes in the sun drenched cement, which, like that of our memories, bore continuous witness.

Still unaware of the magnitude of the historical event I had just come through, I would grasp all its horrors in the following years, as the events came up again to my more mature conscience. Just like those long varnished nails torn from the bleeding fingers of a buxom catlike blonde that had jumped out of the front page of *La Domenica del Corriere,* and seized my horror-stricken curiosity. That's how the imagination of Achille Beltrame (or was it Walter Molino?) had dabbled in illustrating with sensational realism the tortures inflicted on spies by the S.S. That body depicted in its recoil of pain like a wounded tiger, that luxuriant blond mane over a distorted face would be for me another one of the revealing images burned in my memory with a mix of disgust and distress. Disgust certainly more naïve than what I feel now in looking back and see, added to the violence of the Nazis, the abuse perpetuated on the woman by the erotic fantasy of men in that intentionally barely covered body. For centuries, from the Christian martyrs depicted in the frescoes of the churches or in the rich residences of prelates to the modern martyrs of the Nazis, pity, like *pietas,* have badly belied what inspiration really moved the hand of the artist.

And so I was back in my city, which I had first known only through the eyes of a child. Away from the rural and provincial peace and quiet of Cunardo, where every spot was familiar and within reach; now I was discovering a futuristic world, multidimensional, a jungle of crowds, offices, streets, a labyrinth of stone and glass. And I was gazing at that new reality trotting beside nonna, and absorbing her secrets of practical wisdom that were to be the key to enable me as well to move deftly through life.

Like an ancient sage, nonna trained me first of all to bide my time with an oriental philosophical patience. And I'm not referring to the unending queues in banks and offices.

There's Always the Sea...

No, I still remember how I had learned to resign myself to interminable marking of time while nonna got caught up in endless chatter at every corner. She inevitably would bump into some friend, and it was imperative to pass in review all the events of the two families, throwing in those of the neighbourhood while they were at it, to conclude with the problems of the world.

She knew everybody, she met everybody, or she went looking for them. Perhaps it was on street corners, or on fruit crates, where I sat more comfortably and resigned, that I developed my bent to meditation, stimulated as it was at such a tender age. I was a lot less philosophical, however, whenever I came home from school to find that lunch was not ready and nonna had disappeared. My brother would inform me that she had gone out to do the shopping some two hours before, and he had not seen her since. Dismayed, frustrated, and famished, I would lean out from the balcony and, sure enough, I would spot her in a heated discussion with Mrs. Zaccarin or some other acquaintance.

Still, my explorations of Milano had their reward. Decades before the modern James Bond-style films, I came to know the fascination of a world that to me seemed larger than life, that seemed built by supermen. I would go down into the heavily protected underground vaults of the banks in downtown Milano. Like a Lilliputian I would face those gigantic revolving doors. It was exciting to figure out exactly when to jump in the speeding vortex of the doors, mindless of the warnings of nonna, fading behind me.

We were then welcomed with disdain by posturing black-suited manikins, to whom nonna with a dignified nonchalance would ask access to her safety deposit boxes, tickled to see them turn suddenly into deferential ushers. Not everyone in fact could gain entry in those undergrounds created solely to guard precious treasures. While our attire did not identify us with the appropriate class, I am more than certain that nonna knew how to assume the appropriate demeanour, leaving no doubt whatsoever as to our rights in the unfortunate employee. After all, aside from the paltry coupons of stocks and Treasury bonds we had to cash, mostly devalued by the war, which were the real object of our mission, our safety deposit box held by full title *"my mother's jewels,"* as nonna would tell me with reverence.

Escorted through elevators, stairs, and claustrophobic corridors, we would finally reach the "sancta sanctorum," the large vault protected by solid bars and the huge round steel door. Every time I stared at its thickness, I could not believe it could be moved. After a protracted ritual of exchanging keys and openings by degrees, our box was extracted from its walled niche, and we were finally left alone in a cubicle with a shiny wooden table and chairs. A long pair of scissors hung from a thin chain attached to the table. Nonna would then take out of the safety box large folded sheets of heavy paper and, just like for the ration books, she proceeded to carefully cut out some coupons. That was the antiquated process for cashing in the bearer-bond coupons in those days.

Once this operation was completed, the best part of the ceremony, meant for my exclusive pleasure, would be solemnly performed by nonna. One by one she would extract from the long strongbox a series of small black or blue velvet boxes; then she would open them with a deferential reverence, displaying to my enraptured eyes the delicate forms of rings and pendants sparkling with diamonds and zephyrs, and she would describe to me the many occasions when mamma had worn them.

Nonna would tell me as well how *"they too had gone through the war."* To save them from potential looting, they had in fact been buried in the garden of the Baldoni's villa on the hills of Maggio, in Valsassina. And that's where they had remained the whole time under a huge tree. The story stirred my imagination. I wondered if they had drawn a map, like for a pirate's treasure, to lead back to them at the end of the war.

So, every once in a while I would share with nonna our moment of glory, grasping with our fantasy or our memory those emblems of a different life, which for a few moments allowed us to escape the hardships of our present one. And there we are once more, the ritual concluded, passing with a degree of smugness by the bank clerks as we head for the exit. Little did they know of the shameful "double life" of those jewels, when nonna would "borrow" a few, taking them to the much more humiliating site of a pawnshop. She resorted to that expedient to supplement the meagre budget in moments of crisis. As soon as she cashed her pension as a *"widow of a Great War invalid,"* as she proudly informed one and all, she would promptly reclaim them before they were sold off. All too soon, however, the to-and-fro would be repeated, and with it the humiliation.

My memory travels back to an adolescence passed through the constant contradictions of abstract venerated ghosts, of forlorn shimmering, which magnified the shadows of an orphaned and wretched present. That's probably the origin of the baggage of insecurity with which I started off in life before I had the possibility of knowing myself. That's why I falsely felt the need of a paternal and protecting shoulder. I discovered too late I had inherited from my father a strong and independent nature in need to be free, which ironically ended up instead serving as a crutch for my presumed protectors.

"Omenoni?", *"Case rotte?"* Which of these fanciful names made us penetrate the labyrinth of narrow streets in the centre of Milano, growing narrower and more shadowy by the minute, until that unmistakable whiff of fried food reached my nostrils?

"Are we stopping at Giuditta's?" I'd then ask nonna, entreating and hopeful.

On such occasions, I didn't care how long nonna would stop to chat. As if issuing from a book of fables, "the *krapfen* den" would appear in front of my eyes in its utter absurdity. No other term could be more appropriate. A cramped pitch-black smoky hovel yawned like a cavern, pouring out its greasy smoke on a filthy back alley.

Once passed through the curtain and gathered the pluck to step inside, I'd find a lean, scruffy woman sitting next to a large pot with the most delicious, inviting and puffy *krapfen* I'd ever seen floating in boiling oil. I had to keep my eyes on those light and crunchy shapes, feeling them already dissolving in my mouth, in order to blot out the dreadfulness of that place and the clear sensation of hearing behind me, where Giuditta was sitting on a rickety chair, the rhyme,

"*Ucci, ucci, sento odor di cristianucci…*" (…I smell Christian blood…).

I can't remember or even imagine what possible connection there was between nonna and that woman, who would not have surprised me if she had pulled from under the counter a tray with the head of Holofernes. And yet I see them hobnobbing in long conversations while I am rewarded at regular intervals with a *krapfen*, in whose fluffy void wrapped by a thin crust I sank my teeth feeling in seventh heaven.

Never again in all my life did I come across such *krapfen*. There is no comparison with those heavy dough balls, those mushy sweet doughnuts that tried to brighten my Canadian existence. Only once, in the most unlikely place, they reappeared for an instant. I was climbing the narrow lanes of Mont Saint Michel, on a trip in France with my husband and my little daughter. Suddenly I caught a Proustian whiff. I took my daughter in hand and headed, filled with anticipation, toward its source. I came back holding the trophy in my hand - only one. I would have eaten dozens just to stuff myself with *krapfen* and memories. I did not dare. I didn't want to show my craving. I would have had to bare myself by describing my childhood experience, and so rendering myself vulnerable. I knew too well the typical distracted and condescending manner my words would have been listened to, thus rendering my story meaningless, and destroying my myth. I walked on with the usual hollowness in my heart. My unfulfilled sweet tooth became a metaphorical echo of that impalpable longing I felt fluttering in my heart along the lonely paths life had set me on.

I remember another scene during that outing to St. Michel. I was leaning against the parapet of the panoramic view at the top of the mount, looking for the sea pulled far away by the low tide and fused with the grey sky. The mount was surrounded by a desert of wet sand. On that open space someone had written in large block capitals, "MAY THE FORCE BE WITH YOU." Smiling, I read that metaphysical message behind which I could see the face of Alec Guinness in his stellar disguise. But I liked that modern way to give a name to the divine, and I took it with me to warm my heart.

If not the *krapfen,* it was *Passerini's* hot chocolate with whipped cream - a rare, very special occasion, though, during my outings with nonna. What could be better on a cold foggy winter day in Milano than to hear nonna say,

"*Shall we stop at Passerini?*"

I don't remember where that famous and luxurious pastry shop was exactly in downtown Milano, famous precisely for its sybaritic hot chocolates served in brimming tall glasses; all I know is that it was always close at hand at the right moment.

To enter from the cold inside the voluptuous aromatic warmth of an Italian pastry café is a unique experience that leaves a mark in one's life, and that perhaps those who have never left Italy cannot fully appreciate. And there I was with a hot cup in my hands, letting the bitter-sweet chocolate seep through the soft white mound of whipped cream, artfully using the teaspoon. This constituted our "*breaking the rules,*" as nonna called it, our small indulgence, which, as usual, she dared only when she had just cashed her pension.

Another "land of plenty" was *Pek,* the old Milanese delicatessen, one of the city's landmarks. But our forays were very disappointing for me. Nonna loved going there to retrace the better days, when she used to go in with poise and self-assurance. She would introduce me in it as in a sacred temple, a privileged place reserved to a world to which we no longer belonged. In fact, it meant leaving much more there than we could afford to take away. I would leave my eyes ogling the many delicacies, the sumptuous richness and variety of the display of coloured dishes, full of mayonnaise and aspics. I would leave my throat choked, and my stomach twisted in spasms. How could a thin 200 grams wedge of the most economical dish ever make up for so much misery?

Certainly not due to indigestion connected to my forays at *Pek* or *Passerini,* but more likely to the last after-effects of the tendency to nausea of my infancy (a case of ketonaemia, according to the experts), there were some dramatic moments during my sorties in town, when I would suddenly be caught by that familiar stomach upset as by a rising tide. Nonna's intervention was rapid and the cure guaranteed, though just as distressing as the nausea - it was *Fernet-Branca* time. I still remember it as a nightmare. With a firm grip I would be dragged to the nearest bar, and with a shaky hand I was forced to down in one gulp a shot of that distilled bitter. If I managed to hold it down, the cure was assured.

"Look, that's Umberto Giordano, who enjoys promenading in the Galleria." Nonna always managed to meet someone famous, of whom she'd tell me stories and anecdotes as if all had been her friends in another life, in a privileged world now gone. If it wasn't Giordano, it was Erminio Macario and Ernesto Calindri, or the incomparable soubrette Milly. And so I began to stare at crowds with a keen curiosity. I peered at passers-by in the hope of discovering a well-known face.

Years later, when nonna was no longer at my side, the best I managed one day, under the porticos of "Il Duomo," was to run across Coccinelle, the famous hermaphrodite, with his blonde seductive good looks. His was the first extraordinary case of sex change to have made the news; he had come to us from the "libertine" France, causing a great deal of uproar.

So much water had passed under the bridges between the times of Milly and that of Coccinelle!

I walked however with nonna for many more years, until I reached an age when a casual encounter, a brief eye contact in a crowd could leave a quite different sign on me. I can still re-live that scene under the rain along the streets of Milano. I, with nonna, he, walking towards us. Our eyes cross, they linger, and sudden, intense my wanting to say:

"Excuse me, nonna, but I must go."

And turning on my heels - the first "high heels" in my life - draw close to him with the greatest ease, ready to follow him to the limit of the Earth.

How much water has passed under the bridges between that me, back then, and the one now?

The tram slowly swept along the wide curve of the great piazza, allowing my mind to pause, to go beyond the

There's Always the Sea...

high walls above which the neo-gothic architecture of the chapels in black and white stripes could be seen. It was "Il Monumentale," whose silent presence dominated a central area of Milano.

Whenever nonna and I took the n. 33 tramway, I caught myself anticipating in a muddle of emotions its clatter as it went along the challenging curve of Piazza del Monumentale, Milano's prestigious cemetery. Its solemn spaces had gathered for more than a century famous personalities, and aristocratic or very wealthy families, until when recently it had closed its gates and had become a national monument. My father lies there.

Influenced by nonna's tales, my melancholy would become confused with an odd sense of pride. Both emotions jumbled up in a heavy sense of anguish, almost a sickness, which again, as so often in my life, I felt at the pit of my stomach; now though, a moral more than physical feeling.

Once a month we would go to the "Cimitero Monumentale" *"to visit papà"* and, without fail, every first of November, the "All-Souls Day." Words whose sound had a vast echo in my heart.

As soon as we took the wide access avenue, lined by a series of dark metal flower kiosks, those abstract words turned into a wave of dense sensuous scent, which surged in me with great force - the smell of chrysanthemum, smell of cemetery, smell of decay for the rest of my life. I recall my dismay when during the years in Canada dinner guests would bring me a bunch of chrysanthemums.

Huge, enormous yellow balls, almost obscene, were the chrysanthemums at the *Monumentale,* larger than any I've ever seen. Maybe they were meant to match the majesty of the place. Luckily, nonna didn't like them, or maybe we could not afford them. She opted instead for a nice bouquet of small motley flowers, tiny roses or carnations or daisies, which I'd put as a dab of brightness in the small vase attached to the marble tombstone next to the photo of my father.

What those "contacts" with my father meant to me I can't say. It all took place in a very abstract grey area. That same image, only more faded, seen in so many other photos, was staring at me with a dignified professorial gaze. It left me with a sense of pride, my father was "somebody," and I unconsciously gained a comforting sense of confidence in my identity. Yet, at the very instant I faced the cold gravestone, those original feelings vanished, and everything was reduced to an empty ritual, frozen in mechanically repeated gestures, which would recall echoes of childhood, similar scenes of "Sunday visits at the cemetery" after Mass, reinforcing the youthful impatient yearning for life.

Victim of secular social conditioning, I was forced to actions imposed on me before I could develop the emotional need for them. A moral blackmail perpetrated by the Church on the basis of its mediating role with God. Much later in life I would learn to *"extinguish with water the flames of hell and set fire to heaven,"* as Jeanne de Lorraine, who already in the XIV century wanted her children to love God for himself.

I was only a girl then, and for me it was like a game when my brother and I would stop to read the rhetorical D'Annunzio-like inscriptions on the gravestones. Some had been personally composed by the august poet. I had fun wandering in that vast, uniform labyrinth of paths, amid marble stones and baroque statuary, where one could get lost quite easily. We competed to see who would first see the point of reference which rose above everything, surging skyward with a pair of wings out of all proportion - it was our "Angel." Whoever saw it first would call out: *"There's the Angel!"* My father's niche was close by.

But my father was not there among all those stones! I would soon dispel from my life forever that obsessive cemetery cult that had accompanied my childhood and adolescence. I carried within me the spirit of those I loved. As for my ashes, they will be scattered in silence over the sea.

At times we would stop to hear Mass in the Chapel, especially if encouraged by the Baldonis when we happened to meet them there. But we did not like it; it was a meeting place for "the élite" and turned into a social gathering.

On Sundays, nonna preferred going to the Chapel of "La Staziome Centrale," close to home. It was a cramped dark cell just beneath the "royal Balcony," famous for the speeches Mussolini had made from there. The attraction was don Miriana, the great Salesian preacher who, from his own small pulpit but with equal passion would launch his anathemas against our society, "*without mincing words,*" as nonna said. I was struck by the unpleasantness of his sweating oily skin and by his bulging neck that protruded naked from the black robe, lacking the freshness of the white clerical collar. Nevertheless, he was exciting, he swept away the audience, he scandalized, he shook our conscience, he mesmerized with his colourful eloquence. The crowds pressed in to listen to him, spilling out on the sidewalk.

"*He really tells it like it is!*" the people would remark with self-righteous approval. I doubt whether it changed anything or anyone for the better, but we would all leave "feeling uplifted."

My days with Nonna included also board games and card games in the evening. As I grew older, I was promoted from the childish game of *Omino Nero* to *Ramino*/Rummy.

I liked the sleepy Sunday afternoons in the chill of winter, when it was pleasant and cosy to while away the time playing endless Monopoly games, gathered around the dining room table under a cone of light. And when my brother and I had to do our assignments, nonna would play solitaire. She played with passion and doggedness because she had always the same goal. If she could "finish" the solitaire, it meant that something she really wanted would come true, otherwise… But then she could not allow herself to fail. Looking up from our books, we would see her do the forbidden move, cheating in order to reach the desired conclusion. If we caught her red-handed, she defended herself like a child by lying. Those were nonna's small white lies, deceiving and deluding only herself, a child-like way to conceal her own vulnerability. After lunch she'd fall asleep on her chair and start snoring. If we urged her to go and lie down, she'd defend herself offended,

"*I was not sleeping. I don't need to go to bed. I heard everything you said.*"

She loved bananas, which for us then was a rare treat. When we'd tease her for her gluttony, feeling guilty, she'd justify herself saying,

"I don't like them; I eat them because I hear they are good for you."

But if she pulled her little shams to avoid defeat while playing with us, serious quarrels would break out with Nino. The bickering occurred mainly during their intense chess games, or when all three tested our mettle with the "Shanghai" pick-up sticks. In his youthful intolerance for any form of injustice, Ninetto was merciless, insisting that a stick had moved, while nonna kept denying.

We also spent many evenings listening to the radio, the main form of entertainment then. A booming voice would announce the famous debates *Led by Carlo Arturo Jemolo,* on the *Terzo Programma.* Fortunately, both nonna and Nino were very keen of this programme and they shared the same reaction to the socio-political issues debated.

Then there were the plays, my favourite. I had by then reached the perfect age and romantic stage to be moved by the melodramatic decadent plays of Sem Benelli, like *La cena delle beffe,* later on enjoyed once more in the film version with the popular actor Amedeo Nazzari, who was to go down in history for the famous melodramatic phrase spoken in a deep, roaring voice, *"E chi non beve con me, peste lo colga!"* (And may those who won't drink with me catch the plague!)

It will be under my brother's guidance that, during my last years of High School, I would share with him and nonna some of the most sophisticated experiences. I recall as if in a dream the evening when the three of us, deep in the large leather armchairs, in the dim light of the living room, listened in silence to the saga of "Peer Gynt." Lulled by the mesmerizing voice of the narrator Arnoldo Foa, by the musical suasions of Grieg, and by the refrain of the singers, my imagination meandered for hours in the impenetrable mysteries of the Nordic forests, stirred by Solvey's sweet lament. Late that night, the three of us found it difficult to emerge from that draining rapture.

That large leather armchair continued to be my favourite whenever my mind meandered. I had the most exhilarating encounters with literary masterpieces in its comfortable arms. I remember the epic marathon when my brother handed me "War and Peace." A beautiful edition in four small red leather-bound volumes, taken from my father's huge library. The text became even more precious when I opened it and saw his name written in black ink with a firm hand. I picked it up in awe, thinking that he too had held it in his hands, losing himself in that story.

The title page read, *La Guerra e la Pace, Romanzo storico del Conte Leone Tolstoj, Milano, Fratelli Treves Editori. Nono migliaio. 1909.* It was part of the *Biblioteca Amena* that included Dickens, Balzac, Maupassant, etc., each volume costing one *Lira*! It was a Saturday. I spent the entire weekend reading it. As my brother had warned me, once I got over the first pages, in which the reader is introduced to a long confusing list of high-sounding names, I was not able to put it down until the end.

I used then to go back to it once in a while, as if wanting to stay in touch with old friends - Pietro, Natalia or Prince Andrea, with whom I identified,

"He was not able to control himself, and he wept tears of tenderness and pity for humanity, and for himself...."

It was the first of a long series of readings, memorable especially for the freshness and the enthusiasm that are reserved for all first encounters: the Ibsen of "Hedda Gabler" and "Doll House", the "Winter Tales" of Ann Blixen, down to the very first bewildering science fiction explorations with Asimov.

It was the start of a lifelong comforting friendship with books, thanks to my brother, my mentor.

CHAPTER FIFTEEN

"*Nonna, how does the story of Ciciu Berliciu go?*" Patiently nonna would start the nursery rhyme, and I had her repeat it until I knew it by heart too:

Ciciu Berlìciu a l'avìa 'na fia
Tòni Balùni a la vulìa
Ciciu Berlìciu a vulìa nen dèjla
Tòni Balùni a vulìa piejla
Ciciu Berlìciu a l'ha daje n' sgiaflùn
Tòni Balùni a l'ha mandalu an përsùn.

I had fun challenging myself with the Piedmontese dialect which I had never learned. Although nonna was proud of her Piedmontese, in our own upbringing dialects had always been associated with a lack of education. But she'd claim that "*even the King spoke it!*" Nevertheless, my brother and I thought of it as a funny trait of nonna, a prerogative all her own that did not concern us, which was, if anything, beyond our ability

The fact is that nonna was right to be proud of her language, because as I later learned, it was anything but a dialect. For over a thousand years it had been the literary language of culture of the Kingdom of Savoy, the famous *lengua sabàuda* Vittorio Emanuele II used in his address to the first Italian Parliament in 1861, at Palazzo Carignano in Torino. What an auspicious beginning for a nation just unified having a king who didn't like to speak Italian, and who preferred even French to the language of his own nation!

Nonna was a bottomless source of anecdotes, nursery rhymes and amusing recollections with which to constantly feed my childhood fantasy. *Berlìciu* must have been related to *Pepina*, who "*a l'andava an campagna con la scua e la cavagna,*" and who "*fasiva 'l cafè con la cicolata përchè a l'era mesa mata."* Her stories came up in the oddest moments, stirred by hidden promptings of her fancy. To this she'd often sprinkle quotes from lyric operas she loved, and a vast repertoire of old proverbs that she would bring out at the appropriate moment. An entire cultural heritage which coloured all my life and now my memories.

"*Tanto va la gatta al lardo che ci lascia lo zampino!*" The image of that cut off and discarded cat's paw was enough to graphically discourage me from wanting to do something wrong or forbidden. Nor could I afford to persist in wanting something because, of course, "*L'erba 'voglio' non cresce neppure nel giardino del re.*" ("The grass "*I want*" doesn't grow even in the king's garden.") Occasionally though, she tried in vain to slow down my youthful exuberance with the questionable wisdom of "*Chi va piano, va sano e va lontano.*" ("He who goes slowly, goes safe and sound and goes far.") Which I would interrupt with: "*...and never gets there.*" The years, whether for better or worse, would prove me right, thus challenging this old way of thinking, which taught us that we could go "*far*" only by going carefully, discreetly and prudently. What an abyss between that and today's world where one goes ahead driven by wanting, demanding, daring, in search of an instant gratification.

This steady trickle of warnings would come from our elders to shape our thought and behaviour, influencing us and reining us in. In addition, for us girls there was another continual reminder,

"*Good girls don't behave like that... It's not nice for a girl... If you want to become a good little housewife.... You look like a tomboy... Sit properly, close your legs! One can see all the way to Paris!*" Etc. etc.

But how could I not laugh when, seeing me sad for some reason or other, nonna would come near me and whisper "*Pissi, pissi bao, bao, are we blue my cavalier!?*" Someone should make a serious study of the origins of these "cultural" pearls.

Nonna loved lyric opera. She knew them all, and had seen all of them. She talked about them comparing various performances, referring to this or that famous tenor. She needed only two notes to tell the voice of Tito Schipa or Enrico Caruso. She loved them and she'd lose herself in them, especially because they had marked the most dazzling years of her life: first, when as a girl she accompanied her father who, as a Member of Parliament, travelled frequently throughout Italy and France and attended the various Opera theatres; and later as a young bride before the Great War. After the war, everything changed, and though she lived in Milano, "La Scala" became a dream, the music only a memory relived through the illusion offered by the radio.

She knew by heart all the libretti. Of course she did not sing arias, it would not have been dignified, but she could quote and strike up phrases and the first lines of famous arias. They would come out as a more or less appropriate comment on the situation at that moment.

One of her favourite operas was *L'Andrea Chénier*, whose composer, Giordano, was the very one we had run into in "La Galleria" of Milano during his last months of life. The continuous references to the despairs and loves of *Madama Butterfly*, the *Lady of the Camelias* or of *Santuzza* roused my imagination. I was fascinated by *La Fanciulla del West*, by the thrilling intrigues of *Rigoletto,* of *La Forza del destino,* of *La sonnambula*. I would visualize the dramatic fate of *Aida* being buried alive, of *Tosca* throwing herself from the battlements. So, as nonna told me these mesmerizing stories, my world became filled with their characters. When I was old enough to warrant her trust, she allowed me to look at her precious collection of libretti, an account of rare and prestigious performances, often enhanced by a dedication. She kept them lovingly collected in her house in Cunardo, inside the *tabouret*, the black piano bench whose lid would open to keep all the libretti with the vocal scores. These were my very first "romantic novels."

Then, there was the circle of her real friends, strange individuals met during her eventful life, in so many different milieus, each with a bizarre life story which nonna would freely dispense, and which hovered in a confused dimension somewhere between the real and the imagined. She must have had three lives in order to have known all those people!

She assured me that she had two very best friends, *signora* Stringa (shoe lace) and *signora* Scarpa (shoe). Both of them had ended up in an Italian colony in Africa, and she would chuckle at the idea that once there, they might have become friends and had naturally decided to "*join forces.*" Then, there was *signora* Bevilacqua (drink water) who had married *signor* Pisciavino *(*piss wine), and *signorina* Vacca (cow) whose parents had baptized her as *Bianca* (white).

Once, on a train she had met a woman who full of self-importance had introduced herself "*I am Signora Trabattoni di Seregno,*" with the same tone of voice and expecting the same reaction as if she had claimed to be a reigning princess. Nevertheless, her reputation was assured in our family because from then on every time we would refer to someone who affected importance, we would say, "*Sono la* S*ignora Trabattoni di Seregno!*"

If I happened to start speaking and leave the sentence in mid-air, the inevitable comment at home would be "*Che bel prato...*" *(*What a beautiful grass field...). It seems that in another encounter on the train, an absorbed and meditative man, who was looking at the green valleys out the window, suddenly had exclaimed "*Che bel prato...*" adding, some ten minutes later, "*così veeerde!*" *(*so greeen!), when everyone had already forgotten what he was talking about.

Whenever nonna wanted to say that someone was a bit strange, she would bring out the story of another of her acquaintances who during an unusually long winter would go for his constitutional dressed for spring, donning his new Florentine straw hat and his elegant Marquis cane, mindless of bad weather. If anyone pointed out this to him, he replied that if the weather was crazy, he saw no reason why he should be!

From her childhood memories, some unusual characters of farmers on great-grandfather's estate in Piedmont would emerge, like the respectful estate manager Aristide who, while the owners were travelling abroad, had felt the need to send them a telegram to inform them of *"the tragic death of the white sandpiper."* The poor thing had been attacked and devoured by a fox and - as the distraught man dramatically concluded in his message - of the sandpiper only *"head, tail and little more"* was left. Or the ninety-year old Artemisia, who seeing how every day nonna's little brother, the last of ten siblings, was given a bath, would exclaim scandalized,

"Col fiolin tùt ij di ant l'ava! Pòvra masnà! Mi, a novant'ane ch'i son ant ës mond i l'hai mai avù dë feme 'n bagn!" (That poor little thing every day soaked in water! In the ninety years I've been around, I've never had to take a bath!)

Then there was that hapless woman who sent her son to study for the priesthood to use up all the buttons she had. *"Is that a jest or folly?"* I would say echoing one of her favourite lines from *Un ballo in Maschera*. Yet there were also some sad stories, of real poverty.

"The farmers were so poor," nonna would tell us, *"that quite often there was only a dried salted codfish hanging from a string over their table, and all around the children would rub on it their ratio of polenta to flavour it."*

"A l'era Bruneri o Canella?" the phrase had become symbolic of the eternally unresolved doubt. This was a real story of deceptions and mistaken identities that shocked and divided the entire country during the '20s. Hoping to somehow untangle the mystery, I never tired of hearing nonna who had lived through it, tell it again and again. It dealt with a wife and her husband missing in action during the war, who finally reappears affected by amnesia to the point of raising doubts about his identity: "Was he Bruneri or Canella?"

They called him *"lo smemorato di Collegno"* ("the forgetful" - the lost-one - from Collegno) because he had been released from that town's Mental Illness Institute. But thanks to the publication of his photo in the column *"Has Anyone Seen Him?"* of *La Domenica del Corriere*, he was recognized as Professor Giulio Canella of Verona, missing in action. He was therefore happily reunited with his loving wife. Time goes by, then... a dramatic turn of events! A police report identifies him as Mario Bruneri from Torino, with a criminal record.

A real thriller begins, with romantic twists and turns, because it seems that in spite of the fact that the stranger had been identified as Bruneri by "his own" wife, by his brother and even through his fingerprints, Mrs. Canella became an accomplice of the impostor, with whom in the meantime she'd had three children. Attracted perhaps by the more inspired and daring personality of the mystery man, she was unwavering in declaring him her own true husband. The threat of a scandal went then up in smoke by the timely flight of the entire family to Brazil, where *"lo smemorato"* lived happily for the rest of his life as Giulio Canella. *"But was he Bruneri or Canella?"* remained the question. Yet the bigger mystery remained Mrs. Canella herself.

In spite of being a strict disciplinarian (how many denials, how many things forbidden in my adolescence!), nonna never forced us to eat something we did not like. Perhaps she recalled the nightmare of her own childhood. Whenever she refused to eat her cabbage soup which she could not stand, the same soup would be put in front of her for eight straight days, until through hunger, nausea and tears, she swallowed it. This in spite of being in a well-to-do family. This iron discipline had tempered my ancestors from the Alps down to Sicily. The character of the recalcitrant Sicilian cousin was forged with zucchini, while cabbage was used for the wilful Piedmontese nonna. I almost ended up having a "Nonna *rampante*" like Calvino's famous "*barone*" who, to avoid eating snails, climbed the trees and never came down again!

My brother and I, however, did not run the risk of being served something revolting, because nonna was not only an excellent cook, but she prided herself in making for us all those delicacies she knew we loved. She reserved her greatest achievements for the Christmas holidays. That was her forte, for which the whole kitchen was turned into a serious workshop. Christmas dinner was an operation which required three full consecutive days and one night. Yes indeed, a night was required to make her famous aspic. Traditionally, "the capon in aspic" followed the first course of home-made ravioli filled with meat specifically roasted for them, and spinach.

The lean post-war years were a thing of the past. We were not any better off economically, but at least things were now available, and with zio Marco's contribution, who would then join us for dinner, we could splurge a bit.

The excellence of the aspic depended not just on the intense flavour of the sherry-based consommé, but particularly on its clarity. To obtain it, the capon broth had to be strained through a napkin of nothing but the finest Flanders linen. The process took a whole night. Nonna would set up the apparatus on the kitchen table - a chair was laid on its side with the napkin tied by its four corners to two of the legs. The broth poured in this trough slowly dripped through the cloth into a bowl sitting below. This birthing labour was watched over religiously until we all retired to bed. Fearing the severe judgement of her son Marco, her equal in gastronomic sophistication and, as a typical man, demanding and very critical, it was understandable that achieving perfectly transparent aspic became a point of honour for nonna.

On Christmas morning, if the aspic had been a success, nonna was very happy and pleased with herself. But to achieve this stage it had to pass through a series of tests to determine the right amount of sherry, and my brother and I happily took on the role of tasters with all the necessary gravitas. Once this phase was complete, nonna would proceed with the final part of the dinner, and the house would be perfused with the appetizing smell of the *fritto misto*, the Piedmontese specialty.

On a large oval porcelain platter, she would put a display of breaded and fried baby artichokes, cauliflowers and veal brains. On another platter she laid her pièce de résistance - the *bas-de-soie,* boiled pig's feet, painstakingly de-boned (dozens of tiny microscopic bones), ennobled as well by pan-frying them breaded till they were golden brown. The *fritto misto* was not complete without the "sweet fritters"- sweet, gelatin-like soft yellow dough, artistically cut into small rhomboids and then fried to a perfect crispy golden crust. Finally, the dessert: with pride of place on a stem serving dish: the "two-colour mould," the result of a careful overlay of *pannacotta* and chocolate cream.

Christmas in those days glowed with the chestnut-brown hue diffused by the red fringes of the wrought-iron chandelier in the dining room. A soft light that warmed the reddish purple of the silk wallpaper and brought out its golden threads. The dark bulks of the heavy credenzas seemed to grow in the penumbra. A *Presepe* filled the large space between the two levels of the buffet, separated by the two regal lions that held up the upper level.

The closed shutters and the tall full drapes isolated us from the wintry grey of the streets below. All around us the aroma of the consommé simmering in the kitchen. Those were the nights filled with anticipation, the nights before Christmas Eve, when we'd finally prepare the gifts.

The gifts were placed on the large table in the centre of the dining room. The surface was divided in three parts: one for nonna, one for my brother and one for me between the other two. The ritual began with nonna and I placing the gifts for Nino, then he and nonna laid out my gifts, and finally Nino and I would plot how to arrange things for nonna. The gifts, which in those days were not wrapped in paper, were simply then covered along the way with a heavy tablecloth to hide them from indiscreet eyes.

It was not difficult to please nonna, because her great passion was Salvator Gotta, who as a prolific writer would supply us with an endless choice of novels Christmas after Christmas.

"*What are we getting nonna this year?*" we'd query each other with a knowing smile.

"*Salvator Gotta, of course!*"

To me Salvator Gotta remained just a name, or the hint of a title, "E le stelle stanno a guardare…" (And the stars are looking…) - the name of an era, of nonna's days. I never read him, scorning him with a youthful intellectual ostentation, undoubtedly influenced by my brother, "*Mawkish, sentimental mush.*" And yet I too would go through my own phase of "romances," the last of which was, with me already a mature woman in Canada, being caught up in *Days of Our Lives,* one of the popular American soap operas.

It happened while I was taken by a period of intense academic work. I was writing my first book of literary criticism. The soap opera acted as a sort of brain wash, the only way to take a complete break from the intense research and writing. When the book was already published, I was still hooked on the melodramas of women possessed, rising from the ashes, buried alive.... A kind of Carolina Invernizio, compared to whom Salvator Gotta was something quite serious. But back then I was too young to pass judgement on books, as it turned out the one time I dared to buy one on my own.

It was during a summer in Cunardo. While walking along the streets of the town, I was drawn by a book with the haunting title "The Voice in the Desert" in the display window of a stationary bookshop. I thought it was just the sort of adventure book that Nino liked. It sounded like the Jack London novels he read, books like "The Call of the Wild."

"That's just the right Christmas gift for my brother," I thought.

No sooner said than done. All excited, I walked into the bookshop and bought it. I felt so proud to have made such a brilliant "adult" decision! For the next six months I couldn't stop touching it and caressing it anticipating Nino's surprise at Christmas. The problem was that the voice in the desert was that of St. John the Baptist! In any event, it was the good intention that mattered. Afterward, Nino gently suggested Woodhouse, a prolific writer as well, who would solve the question of his gifts for many years to come. I think Nino ended up reading all his works and I with him. Woodhouse marked an era of our life as well.

To the books for nonna, we were sometimes able to add with our meagre savings a shawl or a pair of gloves, and we were then all happy. The gloves had to be wool of course, because leather gloves were beyond our pocketbook. Actually, all three of us almost always received something to wear, in other words *"something useful."* For Nino it might be a sweater or a scarf. For me a pair of gloves or a beret

Nonna had knitted. And I was happy to show them off at Christmas mass, always in the hope of meeting Mauro Quattrini, that handsome boy living above us, but unfortunately so much older than I.

I too had by then been bitten by the passion for books. Under my brother's guidance, my library started expanding with the dearest friends of my life, those that would mark moments of unforgettable joy, those that have generated a rich legacy of memories forever mine. The mere thinking of them makes me relive their fascination, when I explored fantastic, exotic, mysterious worlds.

I can still feel in my hands the collection *Libri della Scala*, with the coloured illustrations of "The Baron of Münchhausen", "Till Eulenspiegel", "Little Lord Fauntleroy" on their rigid covers trimmed in grey. Which was the first to enter my life? Difficult to say: De Amicis, Salgari, Dumas, Dickens? When did the ineffable encounter with "Sans famille" take place, in which I lost myself in a flood of tears? I loved them, savoured and collected them all. Each new series represented a more mature phase, each one identified by the colour of the covers: green for the *Medusa* Mondadori collection, with Daphne du Maurier; grey for the small paper back collection *la B.U.R* with Oscar Wilde.

I remember one of the most beautiful Christmases ever when, like an unveiling, we pulled the tablecloth off the gifts on the table and I saw the most beautiful book I had ever desired. I had thought I would only be able to dream of it when I first saw it, elegant and lavish in the window of "Paravia," the luxurious downtown bookstore. I had stopped in front of the window with Nino, enraptured by a bound book with the gilded spine, its colourful cover filled with damsels and knights in oriental dress, surrounded by exotic animals in flowered gardens. A unicorn peered from a bush. "Persian Tales" read the title in illuminated letters. And now it was there, on my table, one of my very own gifts.

Not always, however, did our wishes come true. Often our economic straits forced us to make sacrifices. Once, I suffered what to me then seemed the greatest injustice in my life.

For years I had dreamed of having a pair of ice skates, and one year, before Christmas, my cousin Antonino had come up to Milano from Sicily. When he asked me what I wanted for Christmas, I could not resist. Nonna was to buy them for me. But Christmas came and went with no ice skates in sight. The twenty thousand *Lire* my cousin had generously left, an enormous amount of money in those days, well beyond the cost of the skates, had been used for other more pressing needs.

I was assured that the purchase had been only deferred. But months and years passed, and with them my desire for those skates as well, not the burning sense, however, of the injustice suffered. The beautiful novel "The Silver Skates," which I read, lost in the magic of a Nordic fairy-tale and its limpid and enchanted landscape, reflected all my adolescent despair for many reasons. Since then, it has remained for me a metaphor for all that life denied me.

Christmas morning mass at the San Camillo De Lellis Shrine had become a tradition. A long walk in the crisp Christmas atmosphere. The preciosity of the name kept the promise of originality. We loved that tiny castle with its whimsical intrigue of pinnacles, resting in an exquisite niche, with high Rococo lattices isolating it from the modern reality surrounding it. A small inviting capriccio, a sanctuary quite different from the usual solemn places of worship.

We went there to see the *Presepe Mobile,* the mobile crèche set up there each year. Man-size statues revolved along the underground walls inside the small shrine, passing through valleys and mountains, vanishing and re-emerging among rocks and caves. I was enthralled watching shepherds and sheep, all moving toward the large grotto where baby Jesus lay.

Our own *Presepe* was also nice. The pleasure of erecting each year that large detailed landscape would never be equalled by the Christmas tree that a consumer society would impose on us in the years to come, together with the crass Santa Claus, more suitable to the American society than to the ancient patina of our homes and cities. When we were children it was baby Jesus who brought us gifts - the act of love of a poor child like ourselves.

As early as summer, during my vacation in the countryside of Cunardo with nonna, it was my responsibility to go into the woods to gather whatever might be useful for our *Presepe*. I would return to Milano with a stockpile of pieces of bark, leaves and dry twigs, pebbles and soft moss which at Christmas would take the form of huts, tiny bridges, woods and bushes surrounding silvery lakes made with tin foil. Villages plotted the roads winding along the length of the large buffet, all converging on the large thatch-roof hut, Nino's architectural masterpiece. Joseph and the Madonna, the ox and the donkey would breathe over the empty manger until Christmas at midnight, when I was granted the privilege of laying the Baby in it. The three Wise Men would have to wait until the day of the Epiphany, just to put in a brief appearance before everything would be taken down. A real shame to my way of thinking - they were so richly dressed and handsome.

I would have liked to hold those moments suspended in the domestic warmth and enriched by a vague festive spirit. It seemed that everyone felt fulfilled and well-disposed toward each other, and the table games were played in peace and harmony, as if we all would want to enjoy that sense of "goodness" in the air, or in our soul, fearful of spoiling it.

Mercante in fiera (Merchant at the Fair) and *Tombola* were played using Christmas chocolate coins wrapped in gold foil under the circle of the reddish light on the table cleared of all gifts and dinner. Tired, we'd then end up sitting in the armchairs listening and laughing as Nino read aloud Jerome K. Jerome's "Three Men in a Boat," or the feats of the scoundrel Gian Burrasca, "Viva la pappa col pomodoro!" (Long Live Tomato Soup!)

In the street below the sound of the last *cornamuse*.

CHAPTER SIXTEEN

The curtain opens on another scene - nonna is riding a mule bareback through the mountain trails of Sicily.

1948: for the first time we crossed the whole length of Italy to *"go and see the land of papà."* I was eleven when I made this big first voyage of discovery of the world.

Travel by train in those post-war days was certainly not a pleasant prospect, what with the taking by storm of the few cars available then by the many desperate people, with the many interruptions along the rail lines, and the fallen or precarious bridges. But the idea of getting to Sicily from Milano was close to pure folly. Nonna, however, had a lot of nerve, and for me it was all one big adventure. Glued to her side, I had already faced trips in cattle cars, sitting on suitcases, or standing pressed by a horde of soldiers: the groping hands…the overpowering acrid stenches.

The trip to Sicily involved a twenty-four hour train ride. Second class was all we could afford. Coal-burning trains with the nightmare of the tunnels. From Rome down it felt like a never-ending tunnel. And this in the sweltering heat of July.

Every other minute the shout *"Tunnel! Close the windows or we'll die of carbon monoxide!"* We'd close the windows, and we suffocated in the heat. *"Open the windows, we're suffocating!"* We'd open the windows and a coal-black gust would invade the compartment. Coughing and chocking, we'd close them, and the agony would start all over again.

Finally, we would arrive at the Strait of Messina, and amid shaking and rattling the train moved onto the ferryboat. At that point, we would all rush into the open air, cheering and breathing in a lungful of fresh sea air, in the bright sun and a blue sky.

But we could not believe our eyes as we stared at our faces! We looked at each other, seeing ourselves reflected.

There's Always the Sea...

We did not know whether to laugh or cry. Nino was black and dirty like a chimney sweep, with great big eyes staring out of his coal mask. Too bad that American tourist in Rome who had asked nonna if he was an *"Indian prince"* couldn't see him now! Even our smoked *nonnina* was something to be seen.

After having crossed the Strait, we'd start again going into tunnel after tunnel until we reached Termini Imerese, where we got off, filthy, hot and totally wrecked.

The following two summers, we allowed ourselves to do the trip in stages, stopping off in Rome and Naples as guests of our Sicilian cousins.

The trip became for me an unforgettable gradual discovery of the marvels of Rome, Tivoli, Naples, Pompeii, Capri, Ischia. I found myself wandering spellbound amid the splendours of the Vatican, the churches, the museums, the piazze of Rome. Led by my brother, I learned to love the art, to be fascinated by the *Mosè* and the *Pietà* of Michelangelo. When years later I studied art history, I was thrilled to discover in books that which I had already seen with my very own eyes.

Our *pensione* opened into the splendid Piazza Santa Maria Maggiore, where in the early morning sun we would sit at a *Caffè* and start our day with the fragrance of a *cappuccino* and some *"maritozzi,"* for lack of the *"mogliozze,"* as Nino would quip. On one side of the piazza we would notice every morning a number of men hard at work with picks around a hole. When we enquired, they said they were digging for the new subway! We never found out if, typical Romans, they had been pulling our leg.

Our cousin Maria, who lived in Rome and worked at the prestigious C.N.R. *(Consiglio Nazionale delle Ricerche)*, would join us on weekends. I was happy to trot alongside her. After the death of my mother, I instinctively clung to any young woman, whose presence would bring a sense of glow in my life. And glowing indeed I recall my excursion with her to Villa Tivoli. I can still see her with her youthful smile and her typical decisive and spirited stride, framed for a picture against the cascading triumph of water of those famous fountains.

My roaming through Rome was not always carefree. One summer I was forced to avoid the sun, which I adored, in my walks around the city. I had to slink along the shadow of the walls like a mouse, all because of a recurring nose bleed. I had almost died from one the previous winter, or at least so I thought; so much that, in my role of moribund, I thought it best *"to ask for a priest,"* as was the custom in similar circumstances. I can still see two large blue eyes looking at me up close, not those of the priest, but of Doctor Cazzaniga, who *"saved me"* by tamponing my nose, as the grownup later informed me. *"As deep as two lakes,"* I kept saying to myself fascinated, and I felt I was drowning in them.

In Naples, our other cousin Anna, Maria's sister, would welcome us. Her husband was a biologist working in the famous *Stazione Zoologica,* and the director of the adjoining Aquarium, which I remember visiting as his special guest, entering spellbound like Alice in Wonderland in a surreal watery world.

The Zoological Centre had been founded almost a century before by the German Anton Dohrn, to be followed by its twin centre, the Marine Biological Laboratory of Woods Hole at Cape Cod in the United States.

Anna had also a summer home in Ischia, where we would stay for a few days. The eldest sister, Giusi, used to vacation with her. Anna and Giusi would always be waiting for us, there on the dock, all in white, one blond, the other brunette. Anna with her sweet face, her blue dreamy eyes, and a natural noble demeanour, which suited the young bride of a prince. She had in fact married Prince Alberto Monroy, who belonged to an ancient Spanish lineage that went back to Hernan Cortés. (What a delight for my childish imagination! I was bursting with pride.) Theirs, however, had been a simple, almost furtive, wartime wedding among the ruins of a devastated Palermo. Both their families had just lost their home and were all dispersed.

I remember Giusi standing beside Anna, taller, severe, her beautiful graceful body moulded by her linen chemise, her classical face like that of a Greek statue. Giusi, Anna and

There's Always the Sea…

Maria, the three striking Sicilian sisters, *"Le belle sorelle Oddo"* as they were called, were the ideals of feminine beauty to which I most aspired.

We would take strolls all over Ischia and Capri, excursions in a buggy up the hairpin turns amid bursts of oleanders, or on a boat to the Grotta Azzurra. The mystery of those grottoes, and their water diffused with a light of an unreal, almost glazed blue like in a painting will remain for me as a background for the classical myths I would later study in school.

We went to Pompeii, which I still see beneath a dramatic sunset, with its dim colours scattered in huge brush strokes of red and black clouds in a boundless low-hanging sky; sombre as the mortification I suffered that day. All alone, I was contemplating it from the small square with the Faun, being the only one to be excluded from a visit to a certain "house." No one had wanted to give me a reason. They had only made me feel very "little" with their barely hidden smirks. I was particularly furious with the guide, who had excluded only me, but took in Maria and even Ninetto, who after all with his 18 years of age was still a teenager. For many years I didn't know what they had gone to see.

Our trip would then resume towards our final destination: Caltavuturo, in the Madonie Mountains, my father's birthplace. As in Quasimodo's poem *Vento a Tindari,* the wind in Sicily would suddenly take me, sweeping away that damp fog-like sense I had been carrying with me since we had left the North, ever more distant and alien to me. Suddenly, I felt wrapped by the warm mantle of the sirocco, by the clear skies, by the emanations of that rich and fertile soil, intoxicated by the intense perfume of the flowers, and of the rosemary and boxwood hedges; enfolded in the warmth of a maternal bosom, feeling a deep sense of belonging. *"Il mal di Sicilia"* had taken hold of me, never to leave me again. It was impossible not to forget Milano; to live in Sicily meant identifying completely with that land, it meant an immersion in the chasm of time itself.

We were living in my ancestors' house, the very same where my father was born. In the morning I was awaken by the sound of the hoofs of mules slipping on the cobblestones, down along the town's steep lanes: toc, toc, toc, truum… toc, toc, toc, truum. At the first light of dawn the farmers were off to work their fields in the distant horizon. I would see them return in the evening, their backs bent over the mules, the dark profile of a slow caravan etched against the blood-red sky.

Each morning a flock of goats would crowd our doorway, and I was offered foamy milk, with a bewildering salty tang, still warm, drawn as I looked on. I was even happier when the farmer showed up with small barrels of salted anchovies. I could not believe such abundance, I loved them and I would wolf them down by the handful, no longer restricted by the small and costly tins in Milano.

The interaction with the street occurred in both directions, taking on forms which revealed a rather unexpected pragmatism. In the evening, all the vegetable scraps were tossed out the window, and were invariably cleaned up by the pigs set loose in the streets at dawn.

This prompted the most riotous act of vandalism thought of by my brother. Our wise Piedmontese nonna was convinced that the Sicilian diet provided by Caltavuturo was not the most wholesome for us young ones, especially because of the lack of beef. In those days, all that was available was a nauseating roast of mutton, which we snubbed. As a result, she would force us to suck every day a revolting "*ovetto fresco*" (a fresh egg, raw!). A pin hole was made at each end, and with a few practiced pulls the egg was sucked clean. Of course, I could not manage it in one go, so that disgusting glutinous liquid would linger in my mouth all the more. The distress was compensated by collecting many empty whole eggshells, so lovely that neither Ninetto nor I wanted to throw them away, sure that sooner or later they would come in handy for some game. So we collected day after day, hiding them in the drawer of an old abandoned bureau.

Summer came to an end, and we remembered our secret hidden treasure. Somewhat anxious, and in a quandary as to what to do with it, we found ourselves in front of a mountain of eggshells.

"*How are we going to get rid of them?*" ... "*The pigs!*"

We crept out of bed that night, and from a window - the farthest from nonna's bedroom - we enjoyed the best and the longest shooting gallery imaginable. When we had exhausted our artillery, we went to bed, trusting in the proficiency of the pigs. The story does have an ending. When we returned to Milano, I developed a nice case of jaundice, either as punishment by the gods of ecology or as a result of the rather unguarded measures taken by nonna, however well meaning.

In a carousel of temptations and repulsions, of attractions and contradictions, I was experiencing the pageant of a primordial world, with its myriad of inebriating perfumes ... a thousand nauseating tastes, which would put my yet unformed taste buds to a cruel test. The nightmare of zia Cornelia's dinners! Tears would choke me as I faced the umpteenth dish drowned in black squid's ink, or the sugary taste that the tomato sauce would give to pasta, meat, or fish. Everything seemed cooked in sugar. Everything ripened by the Sicilian sun was infused with a flavour of molasses. The same scorching sun that made *uva passa* ripen on the vine itself. We would pick in delight those shrivelled golden raisins, bursting with a dense muscatel flavour.

And the confectionary was something else: the multi-coloured display of fruits sculpted in almond paste, the pyramids of *pignolata* dripping with honey, the *cuccidrato* - that mouth-watering pastry roll filled with figs - the *cassata* coated in the green mantle of marzipan, the *brioches parfait,* the colourful nougats bought in country fairs. It was the legacy of a hedonistic Arabian lavishness. All these wonders were made for us children by the nuns at the convent, where my father's sister, zia Vincenzina, was the Abbess.

The little sisters would swoop and flutter around us children like swallows during those few days permitted to them. For them it was a welcome departure from their monotonous days. Destined most of them by poverty to that semi-cloistered life, young and old they were all happily chirping away. But they didn't seem to begrudge it, as they formed a blissful community with their unendingly adolescent innocence. There they were, all sitting around a bare room, busy embroidering, or up on the sunny terrace running and playing with the hoop like little girls. The fresh simpleness of someone who had never known anything else - their gowns as breezy as their soul.

We'd leave loaded with sweets and peacefulness; and when the convent closed its doors during their retreat period, the gate-keeper nun had instructions to slip the package through *la ruota* - the foundling wheel - a tenuous point of contact between the turmoil of the outside world and the mysteries of a peace protected by the high walls of the convent. As in a magic ritual, I hesitated while reaching out to turn the ancient wooden shelf along those same tracks that spoke centuries of stories of forbidden passions, of abandoned infants, of perilous secrets.

Caltavuturo – "the Castle of the Vulture," with its beaked *Rocca* looming over the downward sweep of roof tiles, an imposing presence even from the terrace of our home. The ancestral home, later divided between the last two heirs: papà and zio Giuseppe, commonly known as zio Piddu.

The house bordered the town's main square, together with the *Chiesa Madre* and the staircase leading up to the piazza. There was, however, a small drawback, living as we did in the shadow of the bell tower: its clock, that is the bells, rang out every hour and every quarter hour, repeating each time the entire hour itself. It seemed they had just finished, when they would start all over again. At noon then, there was a festive wild outburst of bells to announce the break for lunch to the farmers labouring in the distant fields. At midnight, unable to distinguish the twelve daytime hours from the nighttime ones, the concert would explode once more, making us jump in our sleep. Naturally, at dawn we were awaken by the calling to mass, which on feast days would be repeated until sunset. Perhaps, this was also a reason for zio Piddu's anticlericalism and his futile struggle against… the intrusions of the Church.

Beyond the bell tower was the green scrub of *Terra Vecchia*, the plain which, like an appendix to *la Rocca*, flows gently from its flank, hiding the ruins of the ancient Norman settlement with its pines. My ancestors had settled there in remote times, protected by the cliffs, until in the 1500s, the settlers had moved down and spread out over the slopes that now enfold the houses of modern Caltavuturo.

After the heat of the day, our panoramic terrace welcomed us in the unruffled quiet of the evening. During the two months of our stay, the terrace was transformed in a drawing room in which almost the entire town would come to *"pay their respects,"* much to the satisfaction of nonna and the frustration of Ninetto and me. We were the summer attraction, *"the foreigners."* Everyone knew us or wanted to meet us. Everyone desperately tried to prove they were related, however distantly, to "*the children of Bernardo*": *"...because your grandmother, Giuseppina Comella, of blessed memory, was the cousin thrice removed of Concettina who was the daughter of the brother of our grandfather Beppino, who had married Rosina, the aunt of the sister of...."* And every new encounter gave birth to a whole new genealogical marathon. We were even stopped on the street: *"...but you are the children of Bernardo, God rest his soul. I remember him, I knew him well when I was little, because my cousin Vincenzino...."*

With all the men at work in the fields, or emigrated or dead, the town seemed inhabited only by women. For "decency" sake, they always went around in groups of three and were all dressed in black, either because they were old or because forced by their widowhood to lifelong mourning. Wrapped in large shawls and long skirts, strolling three by three, they transformed the town in a nest of crows or black vultures, as if they had swooped down from *la Rocca*.

The traffic in the terrace increased during the town's various religious feasts, when the parish priest managed to keep all the faithful constantly engaged, so that they had no choice but to remain "faithful." Every couple of weeks there was a new saint or Madonna to celebrate: processions, municipal band, midnight fireworks on *la Rocca*. Our terrace offered "orchestra seats" and the local gossips came like bees to honey. Fortunately, the social code made us only object of homage, and we were not obliged to return the visits, except for…the dead. In case of a death, whoever the departed soul was, even a stranger, (but who could be considered a stranger? We were all related, weren't we!) condolences had to be offered in person.

We had become quite adept at the ritual, which didn't mean that my brother and I were able to keep a straight face during the ordeal. The ceremony was as follows: my nonna, Nino and I would arrive at the home of the bereavement and knock on the door. A person unknown to us would come to open and, for a few seconds standing on the doorway, nonna and she would engage in a silent dialogue carried out with the facial mimicry suitable to the occasion. In fact, it was categorically forbidden to make any sound or to utter any word at all. Absolute silence during the entire visit. The silent exchange of a frown and a twist of the lips or a gesture were sufficient to express something like *"The poor man…"* … *"What a tragedy!"*…. *"We share in your grief"* … *"Thank you"* … *"Have a seat, please."*

The scene we faced and in which we had a part to play was a large room with chairs lining the walls, and where all other furniture had been removed - an obvious echo of Arabian customs. Visitors filed in and took a seat in silence, their face a mask of compunction, hands folded, their neck twisted for the occasion. We took our place, stiff and poised, without uttering a word, waiting for the expected ten minutes to pass. Every once in a while, someone would get up and gravely walk out. My brother and I didn't know where to look to stop from laughing, how to avoid looking at that array of silent faces painted with mournfulness, how to suppress the itch of the giggles that provoked us without mercy. Then, finally freedom: someone would knock at the door and, our time being up, we took the opportunity to make our escape.

But those times were modern by comparison with the stories we heard from zia Cornelia, zio Giuseppe's wife. When she was young, funerals were more like Greek tragedies. In fact, they hired *le prefiche* (mourners) women who for money would "weep." They'd follow the funeral procession, howling and wailing, tearing out their hair, throwing themselves on the ground, with fake thrashing of pain. They even carried phials in which to collect their tears; the more the tears the more the money they would be paid.

Zia Cornelia remembered that when women remained widows, even if young, not only they had to dress in mourning the rest of their life, but they could no longer participate in any feast, not even a religious one. When processions would go by, you could see these cloistered wretches discreetly spying from barely opened shutters. Pale, tragic resonance of Arabian harems, as the use of words like *persiane* and *saracinesche* (shutters) would confirm.

The strictness of the tradition could have cruel implications. A woman's beauty was like a death sentence because, out of envy or jealousy, it easily became synonymous of loose morals. And a woman considered "easy" was finished.

Zia told us the story of one lovely girl of her days, the daughter of a Postal official, the beautiful Sara. All the men desired her, all courted her, and the resulting stigma discouraged anyone from marrying her. But someone from a nearby town dared, and the vengeance of the town befell on him: along the entire route of the wedding procession, the couple was forced to pass between huge portrayals of horned bill goats - the symbol for a cuckold.

In this backward and bigoted society, my family must have been viewed with alarm and horror for its open anti-conformism. And its "anti-clerical lair" rose, of all things, directly in front of the parish. "Alas!" the priest must have bemoaned the fact that the family was too influential to be undermined and lose the respect of the people. And so, high on the terrace, the irascible and commanding figure of zio Piddu continued to thunder with his anathemas, competing with the sound of the church bells, whenever the commotion in the piazza caused by the religious feasts disturbed him in his studies.

Too recent were the memories of the war time and the German occupation, when Giuseppe Oddo had been the town hero, so much so that by popular acclamation, after the war, he had been elected mayor of Caltavuturo. Unfortunately, his first official act had been the removal of the crucifix from public schools, implementing to the letter the separation of Church and State proclaimed by the new Italian Republic. And so, by popular outcry as well, he was promptly dethroned. The town school, however, still carries his name.

The poking fun at the bigotry of the world continued anyway unabated in this family of men of science through the generations. And there was Alberto, Anna's husband, "the mad scientist," as they called him, with his contagious laughter and the looks of Groucho Marx. And on top of that, he was a communist, whose code word was: "Death to Fascism, to the Church obscurantism, to the war," which had robbed his generation of its youth.

He would include even us kids in the hilarious open-minded words and actions with which he enjoyed shocking the moral majority. *"Let's do a bivouac!"* he would suddenly propose to us when tired of waiting for his wife, who had been "kidnapped" by the town gossips; and flashing a sardonic grin between his teeth and his walrus moustache, he'd grab us by the hand and have us all sit on the sidewalk, legs crossed like Indians, while he entertained us with his hilarious stories. And if the ladies dared to look at us, scandalized by a behaviour unbefitting the Prince Monroy of Pandolfina, (blissfully ignorant of the fact that he was called as well "comrade Alberto Monroy") unmoved, he would simply stick out his tongue like Einstein. The horrified gossips couldn't believe their eyes, and would leave indignant, followed by the guffaws of Ninetto and me, incredulous and fascinated by our crazy cousin.

Forty years later, in that very same church square, in those same narrow streets, now sadly paved and congested with cars, I saw once more the statue of the saint carried by raw muscle power, along the ancient tradition. Following them, however, were lively girls in mini-skirts, blowing trumpets in the municipal band to which they belonged. Modern times had arrived at last.

CHAPTER SEVENTEEN

In Sicily I had my brother all to myself for a whole two months. We passed the days playing games or hiking. We'd climb all the rocky crags in the area. We had even conquered *la Rocca*. On the day of an excursion, we would set off early at dawn in order to avoid the worst heat of the day, but even so we'd reach our destination under the dog days' sun. The landscape was sun scorched, harsh and rocky like the Far West of the American movies, ideal for our battles as Indians with bows and arrows. The huge dark *carrubi* were our oasis in the desert. Alone, in their majestic solitude, they offered a wide blanket of shade in which we'd take refuge, climbing on the lowest branches to have our lunch - zia Niccolina's famous salty fritters! We'd find them ready made in the morning, lined up on the table to drip off the hot oil that filled the kitchen with its aroma. From the drawer we'd take out a large loaf of rustic bread wrapped in a piece of cloth. From the cupboard came the cheese: *caciotta, primo sale, pecorino* with its familiar whiff. All this would be eaten with thick slices of bread. Later, on the *carrubi*, all this would be shared with the ants!

Zia Niccolina was the first of ten children and, with zia Vincenzina the nun, and zio Piddu, were the only three who had survived. Having been left a widow without children, papà gave her the use of our house. And so, during the summer months, there was an inevitable stressful confrontation between her and nonna, contending the running of the house and the love for us children. The fate of the other aunts and their progeny was a mystery. All that was known to me was a cousin Peppino we had once met in Rome, but that soon after had disappeared with a hint of scandal, a subject avoided at home. It seems he had run off to South America with a married woman, who had abandoned children and husband for him. The last news from him was a postcard from Genova, before boarding the ship, and then he had vanished. All enquiries came to naught.

On the other hand, when grown up, I heard talk of zia Rosina, the most beautiful, the great socialite, and the one who had managed the best marriage. We'd be shown her genteel palace on the *corso,* the main street of the town, with its row of balconies onto which opened beautiful salons dedicated to grand balls and parties. Offering as they did the best view on the *corso,* those balconies were sought after and would host the town's most prominent families whenever there was a parade or a procession. I tried to imagine the rustle of crinoline gowns, the gaiety of the waltzes... behind those windows now closed on a world of silence. Zia Rosina had not had any children, and when I reached the right age, my cousin Giusi finally shared with me the most piquant family gossip. It seems that one day zia Rosina went to the doctor with her husband, who was anxious about the lack of heirs. Pressed by the doctor about her intimate rapports with her husband, indignant she had finally burst out:

"*Gesummaria*! *What are you saying, Doctor! When my husband comes close to me, I start screaming. Never! Never!*" And so this all-purpose Sicilian *"Gesummaria"* would echo from the wife of the *Gattopardo,* the prince of Salina, to zia Rosina - same cry...with different results.

What I remember of our house in Caltavuturo was its vertical layout: all small rooms on different floors, connected by long narrow stairs all the way up to the terrace. Small drawing rooms in purplish red brocade, in the shadow of drawn shutters; gilded frames and mirrors, the sparkle of antique porcelains in the tall china cabinets. The mysterious captivation of the distant landscapes lacquer painted on the black head and footboards of the beds. In the large kitchen, the commanding iron stove set between blue majolica that covered the surrounding working areas. In the shadowy corners of the terrace, the *giare* to keep cool the rain water collected in the reservoir on the roof. And then, spreads of *fichidindia (*prickly pears*)* brought by the farmers.

The layout of the house allowed Ninetto and me to give free rein to our imagination, running up and down; and at every landing along the stairs an ambush, an Indian arrow whistling by, a shout from our despairing nonna. When the heat of the day waned, we'd go down to the torrent, in its wide dried up bed, strewn with rocks on which to jump like goats. The bed's bottom was of marvellous clay, which we'd gather and, following my brother's instructions, we'd mould into ships and tanks, soon after destroyed in mock battles.

Clever as he was, Ninetto had no trouble making up new games and plots: a few bamboo canes for bows and arrows, a jutting rock, and we were in the Far West; a bit of clay for tanks and battleships, and we were in the middle of World War II. Perhaps it was the lack of ready-made toys that stimulated his imagination. When a child is surrounded by a profusion of toys, his mind becomes lethargic and surrenders to the object. Closed in our modern materialism, we seem to have forgotten that the greatest pleasure lies in utilizing our own internal resources. A child needs so little to be happy, and yet we deny it, smothering his imagination with a multitude of objects and readymade video games, which stimulate only violence.

Occasionally, a big thunderstorm would suddenly turn the dry bed into a rushing torrent, flooding the streets as well, forcing us to run home. But the most exciting and adventuresome excursions were those to our "properties" with the exotic names of *Sciara, Cerasa,* and *Giambretti*.

We had to set out at five in the morning, escorted by the farmers already waiting at our door with the mules. That's right; we were facing a four or five-hour mule ride! I always wondered how my classy nonna was never dismayed. Instead, I remember her dignified and dauntless, caracoling without a complaint in the middle of that odd-looking caravan, passing single file up along impracticable tracks.

Terror stricken, I'd peer down the crag on my right, along whose edge my mule stubbornly insisted on going, even though every few steps one of his hoofs would slide. To no avail the farmer riding with me on the same mule tried to reassure me. On the contrary, his wry smile under his mustache persuaded me that it was he who led the mule so close to the edge just to scare me. After a while though, I got used to it and began to enjoy it. I also noticed that the less fear I showed, the less the mule and its owner tested me.

I was barely twelve when I had the first - and perhaps the last - feeling of authority in my life. My age allowed me to enjoy this sensation innocently, though not totally free of a sense of unease.

For those farmers I was *"la padroncina,"* (the young landowner) and I was treated as such. Sharecroppers and tenant farmers would place themselves at our service. And when I was gallantly helped down from the mule by my young escort, I'd revel in it, completely oblivious to my age and the obstinate animal. Fairy tales and romance turned me into a damsel who was trying with the utmost elegance to dismount her horse with the help of her knight. What did not fit the fairy tales was the scene that followed, when an old farmer, who seemed carved from an olive tree, greeted me on the doorway of his home bending down in front of me and murmuring,

"Bacio 'e mani a Vussìa!" (I kiss your hands!)

At first my heart skipped a beat for the emotion, but then my northern democratic spirit had the better of me, and I blushed for the embarrassment and outrage, grasping all the incongruity of that scene if seen from without: an old man humbling himself in front of a two-bit girl simply because I was "the daughter of the *padrone*". Still, it was so nice to eat the *fichidindia* the old farmer handed to me, after taking off their thorns with a few practiced flicks of his knife.

Wheat fields, olive, orange, mandarin, and lemon trees were for us city kids an enchanted garden never seen before. With an almost incredulous pride we felt it ours, the heredity of our father, which came to fill the void left by him with a feeling of roots, of belonging, of continuity. Little did we understand how all that was losing its value. The neglected land was gradually becoming barren. It was in fact absurd that it should belong to someone who was not able to work it, and in the course of a few years, we had to get rid of it for little or nothing, and everything vanished into thin air. We had just the time to savour the dream, to live the adventure, even to have the thrill of bandits.

That day we had gotten up even earlier than usual, so we could reach the most distant property, *Giambretti*. It was the largest: wheat fields, olive groves, orchards, and a small stone hut used by the farmers to shelter from the heat. It was reached following trails between rocky gullies.

In the early morning silence, as we were rushing to get ready, we heard a great commotion in front of the house and then the imperious voice of zio Piddu booming more than usual. We came down with our hearts pounding and found the farmers nervously confabulating, and zio Piddu enraged, his grey eyes flashing. Finally we understood that the excursion might have to be cancelled. Rumour had it that the bandit Giuliano, constantly on the run from the *Carabinieri,* had hidden in our property. I was bursting with excitement and pride. The legendary hero who was fighting against injustice, that hare no one could catch among the mountain crags, pursued even by English journalists in love with him, had chosen my property as a hideout! Zio Piddu was angrily trying to make the farmers talk, but they naturally were bound by the unwritten law of *omertà* and, as well perhaps, by complicity with the bandits. I hoped in vain for an exciting encounter, but as usual the dull good sense of the grown-ups prevailed. I had at least the satisfaction of leaving my classmates in Milano filled with envy.

And so for three years we enjoyed the idea of being "landowners." We'd come back home with the fruits of our land, with the rents of the *mezzadri* (sharecroppers*)* and above all with what was even more precious in those times: olive oil, green and mellow like the olives themselves.

We carried as much as we could manage. We had to conceal it, however, as if it were *"stolen goods"* as nonna cursed, because the customs duty was still in effect. Our baggage was checked as we came off the ferry in Naples.

Ever since we had "grown wealthy," thanks to the rents of the tenant farmers and the revenues from the farm products, we had allowed ourselves the luxury of the Naples-Palermo ferry, to avoid…a few tunnels. Our return then was a complete pantomime put on by nonna with her two "little orphans" for the benefit of the indulgent Custom officers, while our suitcases were bursting with tin cans of oil hidden under dirty linens to discourage any search. And in the anxious rush to close the suitcase before getting off, my brother would find himself holding an extra pair of socks.

Was *"l'Ingegnere di Termini Imerese"* my first crush? Probably. I was only thirteen. He called me *"treccine"* for my braids, and he had taught me to swim with the *cucuzze,* dried out gourds he tied around my waist. How could I not love him? He had taken a liking to me. During strolls with my family, he would play and banter with me, while I trotted next to him like a faithful puppy. Actually, I had already given him all my heart. It didn't matter that he had a fiancée - an annoying but trivial presence - I "loved" him and felt him "mine" by right.

He had invited us to his seaside villa and would have wanted me to stay on longer than the others, but nonna explained to me that it wasn't possible because I was *"at the age of development,"* and I could expect the first embarrassing incident at any moment, which would require her assistance. For the first time I felt a victim of life's injustice towards women.

In fact, it was that very summer that my famous "development" occurred, and from then on life, it seemed, led me along different paths, drifting away from "that" Sicily.

The summers in Caltavuturo were over, as were the trips to Sicily with nonna, who started going to her hideaway in Cunardo. I did go back for a few summers in the Fifties with Nino, but only for brief periods. I was in *Seconda Ginnasio* (Grade 10) by then, and he was already in University, so naturally he preferred the social life of Mondello, the beaches of Palermo, the girls, the sea. I had lost my playing mate.

It was with my brother as a guide, however, that in the following years I was introduced to another facet of Sicily, that of her art, her architecture, and her century-old history. Unrolling before my unspoiled fifteen year-old eyes, was the millenary history revealed by Phoenician walls emerging from

There's Always the Sea...

the basements of palazzi, by Greek temples, by Roman theatres, Arab cupolas, Byzantine mosaics, Swabian and Norman towers, by the Angevin castles, the Spanish baroque of churches and mansions, and the eighteenth-century villas.

A well-known story in many other parts of Italy, of course, perhaps even embellished with greater splendours. And yet, in this small triangle of the world, where so many civilizations had carved the passage of time, one lives an exceptional sensation: the magic of timelessness. Due precisely to its insularity and to its remote barren lands, ignored by the developments of modern civilization, the voice of the ancients reaches us in uncontaminated spaces. This is the miracle of Selinunte, of Segesta. This was the miracle for me at least, in the Fifties.

It was sunset when I climbed the hill of Segesta. Suddenly, the temple emerged magically at mid climb. Not a soul around, not a house in sight. Green fields rolling far off in horizons of hills and clouds. A mirage for us alone - sitting on the grass, at the foot of the enormous columns, immersed in a millenary silence broken only by the chirp of swallows whirring around the capitals. No one will be able to enjoy it like that ever again.

Near Selinunte, at the caves of Cusa, where the tuff stone for the temples was extracted, there still lives the instant of the dramatic and sudden flight. Enormous stone wheels of columns are lying along the paths, as if ready to roll in the incredible march that would have brought them to the distant Selinunte. Other wheels half buried, not yet freed by the chisel, reminders of Michelangelo's *I prigioni* (prisoners*)*. In the spell of the silence, one can almost hear the distant echo of the clash of arms, as the Carthaginians take Selinunte by surprise, putting it to sword and fire; and sense the terror and the flight of the labourers called back by the screams.

In Agrigento's Valley of the Temples, a valley of almond groves in bloom already at the first warm breezes of February, the sleep of the *telamuni,* the stone giants, lies among huge fragments of columns. Powerful witnesses to broken glories. On top of isolated hills emerging from the valley in bloom, the temples are etched against the blue sky.

The medieval peak of Erice materializes enshrouded in fog. We have to wait until her beauty sheds her veil before we can appreciate her mysteries. And I saw Cefalù, a crèche lying at the foot of its architectonic *Rocca*. Above the town's rolling roofs, rises the immense cathedral built as a defensive fortress against surprise attacks by Saracen pirates. Its apse serves as a jewel box for the majestic Pantocrator Christ, with whom Monreale will want to vie, building its own jewel: the Cathedral completely lined with its golden mosaics all ablaze.

I left Sicily, which remained there in its vulnerable beauty, in its century-old solitude, retreating more and more from me in a mythic dimension.

Images remained fixed in my heart. The blue bus honking insistently at every hairpin turn as it toiled ever higher, bringing us to the last stretch of the trip, to Caltavuturo, to "*Palliduzza te truovo,*" the inevitable welcome of zia Niccolina who always found me too pale. The statuesque image of zia Cornelia, zio Giuseppe's young bride from Como - who had then identified herself so completely with this land - all dressed in black as she slowly spreads on wooden boards the red tomato paste to dry in the sun. The white panama of zio *Piddu* dressed in white under the parasol on the sun-bleached terrace. The somber farmer closed in his diffident silence: "*Cà, 'nu saccio!*" (I don't know anything). Scared of the *Mafia,* scared of anyone, he wouldn't help a stranger find his way. The storytellers on the street corners of Palermo, who recited the colourful deed of paladins and the madness of Orlando at Roncesvalles. The sirocco that blew infernal breaths and made us gasp for three days. The luxuriant cascades of bougainvillea which intoxicate you with their colours and perfume. The entire family for the evening stroll along the county road: zio Piddu's figure now curved over his cane, leading us to see the sunset over the Madonie.

To the myth seemed to belong my own paternal grandparents, whom I never knew, and whose unimaginable Germanic physiognomy I had never seen even in reproductions. Only two dates: 1836 and 1838, their birth, on a tombstone in Caltavuturo. Exactly one century separated me from them.

"*l'Albino*" was the nickname given in town to the father of my father - my cousins told me - because of his extremely pale blond hair. My grandmother's hair was tawny, of which my father, to his great pleasure, found traces in my own black hair. These grandparents seemed to be more part of a distant Nordic saga than of my Sicilian reality.

Where then did my dark colours and Mediterranean features come from? Most certainly, the result of the eventful history of Sicily. I gave free rein to my imagination: Arabs' invasions, rape of ancestors, or thwarted multiracial unions followed by romantic escapes?

All this then vanished, swallowed by forty years of living in which I lost myself along the roads of the world. I thought I had forgotten it. But the day came when I was free of the mistakes of my life, free of the Canadian bonds, and I hungered to rediscover myself, the one I had been forced to deny. I was standing still and alone on the edge of the valley, facing the mythic cliffs, a silent sunset, and I was breathing the air of my fathers. I could hear the distant echo of a saga started in the warring of Arabs and Normans.

With the cemetery at my back - a soil nourished by their bones - I felt like the Indians venerating the sacred grounds of their forefathers. In the distance, the sheep looked like daubs of flowers dotting the green meadows. Suddenly, a quiver ran through that white mantle like the wind in a sea of grassland, and like a wave the mantle began to roll till it touched another knoll. As in a movie, I saw myself with my red car, futuristic metal sliver fallen from space in a land standing still for centuries - a strident note in an ancient harmonious symphony, which I was echoing from the other shore of a millennium.

For an instant, I felt the very soul of that land sweep me away with the call of distant voices.

CHAPTER EIGHTEEN

Sicily remained a sunny interlude; it was Cunardo that saw me grow and mature. Though nonna lived with us in Milano, this was the place where she kept her nest in which to defend her memories. And even after we returned from Sicily, it was to Cunardo that we went in September to see the autumn colours, until in the end it became the regular summer residence for nonna and me, while Nino, already a young man, went on his journeys abroad.

It had been there, in the microcosm of Cunardo, ensconced in valleys and mountains where, having reached the age of reason, I had opened my eyes to the realities of life, which till then had simply washed over me. Cunardo had already offered me a preview of the vast gamma of human drama: war, illness, death. It was my first world, that of my childhood, but already fraught with all the lights and shadows shed by human experience: the despair for a loss, the melancholy, the loneliness, the joys of friendship, the jealousies, the disappointments, which would then be rendered even more complex by the adolescent stirrings that would lead to maturity. After that, as Pavese says, there is nothing left to discover, there are no new horizons to explore; we merely repeat the same experiences in more meaningful depths, reconfirming the same truths.

Cunardo had very quickly taken hold of my heart and sunk its roots in it. It was there that nature first came alive for me, turning into an enchanted realm to discover. Roads and trails reached out from the epicentre of Cunardo towards the various wonders of the surrounding woodlands.

I remember that ravine overlaid with blackberry bushes; the patches of raspberry bushes all around the *Rungia*, the irrigation ditch; and that hill with a rise called *Schienafredda* (Cold Back) because it never saw the sun, where we'd go looking for mushrooms in the musky moss;

and I remember the grove going down the *Bulgheroni* slope, a fragrance rush of cyclamen. We'd pick them with their roots for nonna to plant them in pots on the window ledge. The grove of chestnut trees was my favourite, with filtered sunrays gilding the paths of yellow leaves, through which we'd rustle our boots searching for the large shining chestnuts bursting out of their green husks. I was fascinated by everything, I had everything to discover. I explored and learned with Ninetto as my guide. A real symbiosis, a physical connection developed between myself and nature. As in the early morning hours, when the fresh air you breathe becomes the fresh breath of your soul. Something hovering, pulsing in the air echoes the beat of your heart.

Places, countries and cities have always affected me almost physically, transmuting almost into a taste, a languor that I feel in the pit of my stomach. Taking on their own definite character, they either vibrate as one with mine or they repel me. Whenever I recall them or see them again, either a feeling of heaviness comes over me, almost revulsion, or a sweet yearning. The flavour of Cunardo was that of the mist that wrapped me in its soft cool mantle. It was an earthy essence, a grotto-like dampness found in the mushroom-scented woodlands of fairy tales. Its densely earthy spoors, as primal as a womb. Everything was damp and fertile because water oozed even from the moss-grown stones.

Leaving the city of Varese behind us, as soon as the bus reached the threshold of the valley of Valganna, we found ourselves in a gorge hemmed in by cliffs, where the water ran in small streams and waterfalls that had hollowed out grottos, and carved eerie caverns.

The colours of the day, the changes in the weather, the awareness of nature, everything which in Milano went by unnoticed in its pale-grey flow of time, here in Cunardo became a vibrant experience which excited all my senses.

In the morning, snuggled in the warmth of my bed, I'd listen to the sound of the rain on roof tiles, and its patter slipped into the hollows of my torpor, plunging me into an even deeper slumber than sleep itself. When I then opened the window, I breathed in deeply the scent of air and damp earth which filled me with the stirring of all things. My eyes coursed down over the town's last houses as they gently descended into the valley below, at the foot of the surrounding hills. I kept my spellbound gaze on the far-off valley of Valcuvia, on those last emerald-green meadows, which in the vivid unspoiled distance exuded a mystical sense of peace: *"How green was my valley!"*

That window looked out as well on the autumn show, when the hilltops turned colour. It was as if in those first years of our return to Cunardo after the war, I was seeing all my days filtered through that autumn light, that warm golden glow that lights up the early morning dew. Autumn meant for me the last chance to lazy about before going back to school. The white fluffy clouds chasing in the terse blue sky above the hills filled my mind for endless moments, and caressed it like the verses of Baudelaire: *"J'aime les nuages, les merveilleuses nuages, les nuages qui passent là-bas."* The thunderstorms were heralded by skies shot with thick threatening black and purple curtains of clouds, like in the paintings by Vlamink, and they thrilled me. From that window, I could plunge into the very heart of thunders and lightning, in the dramatic spectacle of thunderbolts ripping the entire breath of the sky. And after the thunderstorm, a fresh caressing breeze would stir in me unknown yearnings. Maybe the same that years later would come to life in a curly-haired boy, who spent hours repairing his scooter in the courtyard below my window, and whose eyes met mine.

The idyll became real during evenings of playing *scopone* around the table with nonna and *Tota* Olimpia! Until one day, returning to Milan, I received a phone call from a certain *"Italia."* That's how the girl's voice identified herself, as she pounced on me, accusing me of threatening her happiness for a whim. What use could I possibly have of a young factory worker, while for her Franco, her fiancé, was her whole life! As Teresa in the nursery rhyme, who had caught the poor butterfly: *"Confused and contrite I blushed, pried open my fingers, and away he rushed."* Though not as easily as that. For the moment, anyway, my gaze from the window rested only on the depths of the forest, where perhaps... a prince would pass in search of Sleeping Beauty.

The perfumes of Cunardo were also those of our garden, in whose centre a majestic old magnolia tree held court, surrounded by bushes of blue hydrangeas, like a queen and her handmaids. The scents of camellias and mimosas created a splash of colour against the green ivy cascading from the high enclosure wall. In one corner of the flowerbed, against the house, a bush of long stems ended in corollas of pink flowers. I would try to pluck those buds without being seen. I'd put them between my lips and suck their pale dewy colour and nectar, the taste of summer.

And then there were the sounds of Cunardo: the sound of church bells at dusk, reaching out over the valley till it filled the whole countryside. Sound and space would merge and swell until they faded into infinity. I felt then a tug at my heart. As darkness fell, the barking dogs would echo from one farmhouse to another. Yelps far down in the valley. They seemed in tune with the mystery of secret lives hidden behind the windows that lit up at night - a warm welcome to the evening hearth. They suggested intimacy, the glow of family life. Houses which I imagined more filled with people and love than mine was. Voices from the valley, like a melody issuing from a far off piano that seems more evocative than if coming from one's own home. I'd gaze out of my window... In the end, I had to tear myself away and go back to the nervousness of nonna, the bored unease of my brother, who eventually left, to find his own way in life.

I loved Cunardo from my first waking moment in the morning. I'd open my eyes within the cracked walls of that old villa, and the arabesque frescoes on the ceiling gave me a familiar greeting. They were always there, the same *putti* and flowers spying me, as the first light filtered through the shutters. I never tired of tracing with heavy eyes the crisscrossing of lines, of settling my astonished gaze on the very cracks which glossed it with melancholy.

At times a shadow would take shape in the darkness next to my bed. It was nonna. She'd bring me the *panna,* just skimmed off the pan of milk she had filled the night before. The milk was not homogenized and we'd go and buy it at the dairy. With metal beakers of a quarter or a half-litre, it would be measured still lukewarm straight from large milk cans just arrived from the stable. We had to boil it, of course. Then nonna made the *panna* by letting the milk stand all night in a large flat container. In the morning, we'd find it covered with a thick tasty layer of cream. Nonna would then skim off the cream and bring me a large spoonful of that sweet buttery *panna,* which sensuously filled my mouth. Ah, to wake in the morning to that taste!

I knew every corner of Cunardo. I'd slip through the houses up and down the narrow lanes, feeling safe and protected. It was like moving in a closed environment, an extension of my home. I knew everyone and everyone knew me. I liked doing the shopping in the morning. The shops ran along the main street which, snaking through town would widen here and there or open onto a piazza. The main street even passed along one side of the enclosure wall of our villa. In the mornings, streets and shops became a crowded stage which, as I grew older, I valued even more, seeing it as a theatre of characters worthy of the *commedia dell'arte.*

For bread, we could choose to go to the piazzetta, where there was the old baker's oven since before the war. Like a jack-in-the-box, with his floppy cap all dusted in flour, from behind the counter would pop up the spry baker, next to his imposing looking wife, equally floured. Always ready to spar with each other, they offered constant entertainment, with him trying to stem the aggressiveness of his wife with his biting wit.

After the war, though, a "new bakery" that made *le trecce,* twisted oil bread, had opened up. For me it was an irresistible temptation, to which nonna gave in only now and then, because it cost too much. It never reached home "untouched". I'd nibble on it still warm, along the street. The perfume of bread fresh out of the oven would mingle with the stimulating scent of spices and coffee from the nearby grocery. This one as well threatened now by the competition of the rival store, opened by Oliva at the other end of the town. Many had grown rich with the war and the town was expanding, bringing in modern times.

"I wonder how Oliva made all that money! After all, she was only a washerwoman," the town would gossip. *"Maybe it's thanks to those eyes that fit her name!"*

But I liked Oliva, young and cheerful she always welcomed me with a smile. I liked her shop as well, with those mounds of wrapped fruit drops of different colour inside glass bowls, where every once in a while she'd let me slip my hand. Behind the counter there were wood boxes all lined up, with sugar, flour, rice and legumes in bulk. The long-handled dipper she used to measure out quantities reminded me of the "grocery shop" I used to play with when I was little. But I didn't have the large measuring scale nor that nice azure paper - *carta da zucchero,* as it was in fact called - with which she shaped the holding cornets.

"La Bonora," the fruit vendor, was always standing still like a caryatid by the open door of her shop. Every morning she served the women doing their shopping. She was ready not only with all the freshly-picked vegetables but with the latest gossip in town. If I went with nonna, it was sure to be the longest stop of all, and I'd sit on a crate of fruit and used the time to ruminate.

The pharmacy was in one of the most respectable buildings in the centre of town, sitting on a spot slightly above street level, reached by two lateral flights of steps. It was a characteristic landmark, with a large poplar tree on one side. Its door was always closed, and when pushed open, a small bell jingled our presence. It was a very familiar sound to me, and even the pharmacy itself was like home, with its unmistakeable odour of medicines, its walls lined with dark wooden cabinets with glass doors, and at the very top large ceramic jars painted with blue flowers, containing herbs with exotic names and assured magic powers.

As a child, during the war, I used to go to see nonno, and, fascinated, I would spell out those names: cassius, tamarind, gentian extract, populeo ointment, basil ointment. Mrs. Nella, the owner of the pharmacy, for whom nonno had worked, was still there. Always there, behind the counter, with her white lab coat, deafer by the day, with her blond hair fading into white. Her husband, tall and thin, would loll around her now and then, but in town he was known as the "prince consort" because he did, in fact, nothing at all.

The butcher was at the opposite end of town from *Olivas's* grocery. Instead of a door, it had a strand curtain to let in the air but keep out the flies. I hated going there and being surrounded by all those butchered sides of beef. I didn't even like the butcher, sanguine like the meat he sold wrapped in thick yellow paper, with his bristly red hair and his hands always bloodied. Luckily, nonna almost never asked me to go there. In fact she didn't mind going there herself, because Cecco the butcher had a hidden quality: he loved opera. That blood-spattered man hid a sensitive soul.

And one summer, the season's great event threw the whole town into turmoil: the parish theatre was going to put on nothing less than the opera *Rigoletto.* And who was going to play Rigoletto? No less than Cecco the butcher... *"le roi s'amuse"...* and nonna and I even more so.

An unforgettable experience, and for me certainly a damaging first encounter with lyric opera. I was horrified by that appalling melodrama in which Verdi's opera had been drowned, and at the same time, I was fascinated by the fact that this grotesque mise-en-scene had nonetheless something of the sublime. I can still see a bright whirl of bizarre gaudy costumes, the perfect counterpart to the screeching voices; and the hectic movement of the characters between the scenes, none more so than the butcher who, looking more like the grim hunchback of Notre Dame than the pathetic Rigoletto, was dragging bodies into a bag. That's how my fantasies about the opera were brutally dashed, and from then on I found it difficult to take the melodrama seriously, though still appreciating its music.

In the midst of so much confusion, stood out as incongruous the beauty of Gilda, played by a real "Gilda", the beautiful daughter of *Barba* (Beard*)*, the rag dealer who, gossip had it, by dint of selling rags had become the richest man in town. Gilda had a twin sister, and they were both the talk of the town. I remember them together in another parish play: two curvy supple figures, draped in green chiffon costumes, which set off their long blond hair. It was a wonder how those two parents had been able to give birth to such a miracle. The mother was a drab dumpy housewife; the father was a kind of overbearing Bluebeard, who went around town with a shabby musketeer's hat, a shotgun slung over his shoulder, the cartridge belt flopping over his belly. Word had it that wild game was not the only thing he went hunting for. He was a well-known womanizer. Maybe those splendid daughters were due thanks to him; women considered him fascinating, no less than did his own wife. She was proud of her handsome man and did nothing to hide it. She found him so handsome that she considered his flings as expected and readily excused him. As she saw it, it would not have been fair to keep him all to herself, other women should have a chance to enjoy him as well, because *"l'era 'nsci bel!"(*He was so handsome*!)*

On Sundays, we'd wake to the bells of the *chiesetta*, the little church near the cemetery. From the moment they started to peal, we had three quarters of an hour to get out of bed and get ready. But sometimes our sluggishness made everything more difficult; and despite the urgings of the ringing every quarter hour, we were unable to make it.

There goes another ringing, *"Hurry or we'll miss mass!"* nonna would spur me, because she didn't want to have to make it up by going to "high mass" up in the parish church. That was the solemn mass at noon, which seemed endless. We'd reach the *"Ite, missa est"* with a big sigh and a grumbling stomach. It wasn't easy having to fast until one o'clock just to take Communion. When we couldn't have it because we had had breakfast, I tried to convince nonna to slip away before the long ceremony, in which the whole congregation filed up. We ended up sneaking our way out through the crowd, like thieves, embarrassed, with our heads hung low as we crossed ourselves. It was of course not polite to leave without waiting for the priest's blessing, which was in a sense an acknowledgment of our having done our duty, and in fact gave us a sense of well-being. We'd leave the church "cleansed" to face the day serenely. Waiting for us was the *risotto* with *ossobuchi*, our traditional Sunday lunch.

It was really exhausting going up to the Mother-Church, the parish, especially for nonna, all the way to the top of the hill at the end of town. We'd climb the uphill streets that gave onto a final wide and endless stairway. Late as always, footslogging along, we'd arrive there out of breath. In spite of it all, I preferred it. It was a loud and festive pealing of bells which beckoned us up there; it offered the friendliness of a Sunday feast and the brilliance of the midday sun. That stairway brought us to a wide open and breezy space, a large church full of elegant Sunday goers, vacationers from Milano.

By contrast, the *chiesetta* was a melancholic place, where the smell of incense so early in the morning always gave me nausea. It was the mass for the town's old peasant women, all in black, who muttered their prayers in a dog Latin; it was the church for visiting the dead in the adjoining cemetery. I'd wake to a morning of gloom at the faint sound of those bells.

In that small countryside cemetery, two granite headstones leaning back to back (there hadn't been room enough to place them side by side) marked the graves of mamma and nonno. Every Sunday after mass, we had to stop *"for a visit."* I can still see myself in that awkward and absurd ritual, forced to pass from one tomb to the other, unable to include them both in a single embrace of my gaze and of my heart.

How many minutes for each? What thoughts? How should my feelings change in passing from mamma to nonno? And what was I supposed to feel? Something different from the anguishing void I already felt all the time for my mamma that was no longer? Why? Was she in fact there, perhaps?

A confused discomfort and a sense of malaise, that's what I felt, because despite all my efforts to put on the pious and contrite demeanour of the "little orphan," which I felt was required of me, an unclear sense of rebellion was already coiling inside of me. I didn't understand what it all meant, but I was sure of one thing, that mamma and nonno were not "those things", they were not there. And I only wanted to run away.

CHAPTER NINETEEN

The time had finally come when I was no longer just the little girl who had lost her mother, and Cunardo was no longer what it had been during the war. It now meant summer vacations, excursions, games, and evenings of card games, of which nonna and I were avid players.

For the foursome of the *scopone* we'd recruit *Tota Olimpia* and *Tota Anna*, the only trouble being that one liked to go to bed at sunset, and the other was always involved in the parish activities. The scandalmongers in town claimed she was in love with the parish priest.

One summer, quite unexpectedly, a vacationing Milanese couple rented a small apartment on our same floor, on the opposite side of the terrace: *i Signori Rossi* or to be more precise *i Sciuri Rossi,* with the funny typical Lombard accent, and a totally Milanese mind-set. A couple worthy of a sociological study. He went always around in his undershirt, with the look of a typical Milanese boor, loudly rebuking his wife. She was large and heavy, humble and submissive, always trudging along behind him with a slight limp, leaning on a cane. An unlikely duo to strike a friendship with nonna, but the unpredictable old lady always managed to surprise me. There she was, happily bonding with S*ciuri* Rossi as if she had known them for a lifetime. Anything was better than loneliness. In fact, they turned out to be a pleasant company and two good partners for our evenings of *scopa.*

Sciura Maria was as good as gold, and he was a simple soul underneath that rough exterior. One night I heard him throw open the window on a starry sky and give out with his loud voice in the most emphatic Milanese: "*Ma che bèla stelàaada!"* (What a beautiful *staaarry* sky!) A phrase which promptly became part of our family lexicon.

Soon after, things began to stir up even more with the sudden arrival of *Sciura Adalgisa*, Maria's sister. I have no idea what quirk of nature had made those two women sisters. Adalgisa was the complete opposite of Maria: tall, alluring, squeezed in loud tiger-stripe materials; she'd toss her platinum blonde mane with brazen sassiness, in short she was titillating. Next to her was her man, *Sciur Brioschi*, lean and well-groomed, the typical Milanese businessman, all efficiency and affluence, with a ready rejoinder and a rich repertoire of jokes. In their tow the son, Carletto, a boy somewhat ungainly and awkward, a couple of years my senior. The town's gossips were on full alert in front of such a scandalous presence.

"*There's never been anything like this!*", "*But how can she possibly be the sister of that saintly Sciura Maria?*", "*That's a fallen woman!*"

Poor Annetta crossed herself every time she saw her: I wonder whether anyone has ever considered how easy it is to be "saintly" when you are as homely as *Sciura Maria.*

That trio, however, brought gaiety into our lives, turning *Casa Rossi* into a gambling hall, without the risk of perdition, and our evenings were full of carefree laughter. They were all card enthusiasts. They taught us a whole series of new games: *Dubito, Famiglia*, games of deceit and cunning that made me ecstatic whenever I managed to trick one of the grownups. In the breaks between games, *Sciur Brioschi* would entertain us with hilarious stories.

I have another memory of the summer. One evening, while we were playing at the Rossis, I had to dash home to get something for nonna. Since I had to cross the terrace in semi-darkness, Carletto offered gallantly to escort me. As soon as we got in the house, Carletto grabbed me and planted a kiss on my cheek. I was shocked and speechless. When we got back among the others, I think I was still as red as a lobster. I told nonna everything, fully indignant: "*How did he dare?*" But nonna didn't seem to take his affront very seriously. It was my first "affront" at the hands of a man. I was fourteen years old and very far from imagining of what else a man was capable.

There's Always the Sea...

The following summer brought among us another surprising presence: Dottor Carmelo Lo Riggio, the new Cunardo City Councilman. It was the great event of the season. Short, plump, with a jovial smile stamped always on his ruddy face that matched the wily spark of his lively eyes. In spite of the joviality and his limited height, he gained our respect with his dignified demeanour and impeccable attire. A particularly heavy Southern accent completed his portrait. The warmth he aroused was immediate and everyone fell in love with him, the young, the old, and even the children. And he was single. A rare palpitation snaked through the scores of the town's "eligible young ladies." As soon as he arrived from the South, he rented a room from *Signorin*a *Olimpia*, on the ground floor of our villa, and we were swept away by a thrilling gust of novelty.

The nightly gathering moved to *Tota Olympia's* home and the group swelled. A large table, a circulating deck of cards, and in addition the exciting grand finale, the novelty introduced by the new guest: the penance. Whoever lost the game had to suffer a punishment, determined of course by the lively imagination of Dott. Lo Riggio. One had to go around the garden with a mattress on his head. Another had to chase and catch in the dark a squawking chicken, running amok in the garden. His imagination knew no bounds, and neither did our hilarity.

I remember one night when Ninetto was there as well, and he was forced to dress as a girl and recite *La Vispa Teresa* in front of all of us, to the discredit of his nineteen years of age. The top was when someone had to go to the pharmacy and invite poor Savina, *Signora Nella*'s maid, who was convinced she was a great opera singer, and as soon as she could, she'd launch into piercing highs worthy of a throttled soprano, and pathetic scales. So that evening, she was invited as the guest of honour to entertain the gathering. The naïve Savina, flattered and unsuspecting, arrived with proud bearing and gave way to the performance. At a certain point, Ninetto got up bent over and rushed into the nearby kitchen, unable to stop from laughing. From the kitchen we heard dramatic choking fits. It seemed rather excessive, and nonna, quite embarrassed, sent me to tell my brother to calm down. But in the kitchen I found instead the cat that was vomiting. Was that due to Savina as well? I had to stifle my laughter as well at that point.

Those summers are some of the best memories I have of nonna. She was always cheerful. In Cunardo her character softened. She seemed to be able to cast off something that prevented her from being herself. For sure she was not the nonna always dressed in black, when for the many years of mourning she had had all of mamma's clothes dyed, including "the red jacket," the one in which I had seen mamma so radiant. Then, splashes of black had seeped in to extinguish even the colours of my memories.

Perhaps it was Milano that hardened nonna, perhaps the passing of time. In fact, all three of us were changing; she was getting older, we were growing and no longer children. Nino, more of a man with every passing day, needed to be more independent, tired of the rules and of nonna's way of life. The strain at home was constant, the arguments more frequent. The two of them were poles apart. The reckless and ambitious exuberance of youth against the prudence and frugality of old age. Nino wanted to live, to dare, to enjoy, and nonna reined him in. I was in the middle, torn between the two. I felt sorry for nonna, and felt I should listen to her; but Nino was fighting for me as well, for me to have what he felt was just, but which perhaps we could not afford. I wasn't able to judge. Back from school, standing by the front door, I'd long stare that anachronistic brass plate: Prof. Bernardo Oddo. I got a lump in my throat just thinking of crossing that threshold and finding myself once more surrounded by unkind words or the heavy silence of resentment. I could not find the strength to raise my hand and ring the doorbell.

I would see nonna's other face, that of the recriminations, of the endless complaints for the sacrifices she had endured for us, for the suffering she still now tolerated. I can still see those poor hands, deformed by arthritis, doing the housework and tiredly washing the bed sheets in the bathtub. I'd then help her to wring them out. But where was my brother? She'd ask me to thread the needle, but she'd continued sewing in spite of her painfully contorted right thumb. And she'd take quinine. All this was ruefully held against us.

I saw my brother transformed into a monster of ungratefulness, and I felt crushed by a sense of guilt. Something inside me screamed out that we had not asked for all this, that it wasn't our fault. Why - I kept asking myself - had nonna taken on the responsibility for raising us, against everyone's opinion? Out of a sense of family, a sense of duty or a bent for sacrifice? Was she moved by fear of loneliness or more simply by love? But it wasn't love that she showed me - I told myself - by tormenting me with her jealousy, with her rancour that gave me a sense of guilt whenever I went out with my friends.

That jealousy which had already afflicted her married life was tormenting her more and more. I had to grow up a lot to start to understand the depth of the tragedy of her life, how it could have hardened the best of characters; the pain when she must have understood that she was losing us, that her task was over, that we did not need her any more. With the insensitivity and the self-absorption typical of youth, we were slowly turning our backs to her, drawing away toward new emotional needs, toward our friends. She was seeing the end of our "friendship," that had seen us travel hand in hand down so many roads. All she faced now was loneliness and vulnerability.

Life demands that we move on from one role to the next, that we change, and if we refuse to, we may lose it all.

Just the same, many more years would still pass between Cunardo and Milano, between the various "faces" of nonna. Then one day, she picked up and left, just like a slighted wife who "goes back to her mother." She gathered her things and left. She went to live with her son. The saddest thing was that I reacted with a sigh of relief. And yet, I ended up with the responsibility of the entire household, plus a demanding brother to care for, while I attended university.

Time, however, would eventually give back to my memory the image of the pugnacious nonna that had accompanied and guided me during an important part of my life, continuing to be its emblem, just as she was the emblem of an historical period which was coming to an end. Obstinately monarchical all her life, clinging to her past, she continued to live in the cult of the Savoia, the royal family, faithful to the historic *Partito Liberale* of her father, standing firm against all of Nino's social democratic attempts to persuade her. On the day of the 1946 Referendum which changed Italy into a Republic, she proudly hung from the balcony the flag with the royal coat of arms, heedless of the risks she'd run in that turbulent period. After all, she had survived the greatest family tragedies and two world wars.

December 6, 1956: Nino calls me to the dining room where in grief he is listening to the radio. The voice of Indro Montanelli from Budapest, above the rumble of the Russian tanks, is describing their relentless advance. I stand there listening, transfixed. Tears well up in my eyes. It was my twentieth birthday. Nonna had left us just a few days before.

A new period of my life was starting. But I never lost my ties to the past. I spent summers abroad, I took long trips, but in the end the road always brought me back to the familiar outline of the hills of Cunardo. It was my autumn pilgrimage to nonna before resuming the school year in Milano.

Year after year, everything looked a little older, smelled a bit more musty, and I would gaze at the immutable symbols that halted the rush of time. Ever so slowly I'd push the heavy green lacquered door that gave onto nonni's bedroom, where I slept on nonno's bed next to nonna. The first thing that struck me was that hook, that enormous ridiculous hook that jutted out at right angle next to her dressing table. On that hook nonna used to hang old hydro bills. I'd see them there, hanging in their dusty fate, in all their incongruity. She used to hang on it her everyday purse as well. I'd see it every time with a sense of melancholic understanding, that greyish parallelepiped, pressed against the wall, greyer and more wrinkled by the day. Those things were my nonna, they were her face, and they were her very soul. That purse always remained there, absurd and anachronistic, even when nonna no longer used it. The yellowed hydro bills kept peeking out behind it.

There's Always the Sea...

It was at that point that I was finally able to give her the love and tenderness which she so craved, condemned as she was to alienate the very people that could have loved her. I repaid her for the love which, though unable to express it, she had given me. I was now the stronger and more self-assured of the two, while she was slowly reduced to the more child-like and vulnerable essence, to the slightness of a body ever more fragile, like a sparrow losing its feathers. It was I now who cooked her favourite dishes, and naturally at night there was the ritual of the camomile tea with a peel of lemon.

We still went to pick cyclamens. Before going back to Milano, I'd make sure her windowsills were filled with flower pots. We'd go looking for mushrooms and chestnuts as well. But her favourite afternoons were spent at the *Caffè,* watching black and white television, which had just reached Italy. Not everyone could afford it, and so we'd go to the *Caffè* for the shows. Even Cunardo's most elegant *Caffè* had set up the "TV lounge." The five o'clock appointment was with *Perry Mason.* We'd sit at our favourite table with palpable anticipation, and we'd order a *Chinotto. Perry Mason* would long remain a fixture even in my future life in Canada, but it would never again have the flavour of those first encounters, together with nonna in that corner of the *Caffè.*

When visiting with nonna, I also had to think about my university exams due in October, and I liked to go looking for the perfect secluded spot where I could study. It was a chance to re-discover Cunardo on my own. I'd pack up my books, retraced the streets I had once known, and I'd go deep in the woods all by myself. There I felt my spirit breathe, free to be myself, to feel, to think, in perfect harmony with my surroundings. I had rediscovered the mulberry grove where, as a little girl, I had gone to pick leaves for the silk worms. A brook thread through the rocks and its gurgle underscored the surrounding silence. Sitting on those rocks I would immerse myself in the poetry of Shelley, Keats or Wordsworth.

Then one day, as I crossed a hedge of hazel bushes, I passed from the shadows of the wooded area to a small sun-drenched clearing, a patch of sunlight perfectly surrounded and protected by the hazelnut bushes. It became my second retreat. Stretched out on the soft carpet of grass, the sun enfolded me in a deep sense of well-being, and the blue sky drank in all of me. With my spirit and my senses so intensely alive, I felt as if suspended, as if detached from the world, in a space and time folded onto themselves. That's how death should come to us, I thought, while the source of life is shining bright upon us, so the transition would not be frightening. To die in the sun, losing oneself in the light.

Only Canada was able to tear me away from Cunardo, as it did from everything else, against my will. There must have been a day in which I said goodbye, but I erased it from my memory. Yet I know quite well what that tear must have been. How was I able to shield myself from the pain nonna felt when she saw me leaving? Now my own lacerations are superimposed on hers. Now I know.

I never saw nonna again. She closed her eyes at the hospital, under an oxygen tent. That image, which I never saw, has obsessed me. How long did she wait for a final goodbye from me? Why didn't I reach out to her? My husband didn't make it easy for me. For three days, when I opened my eyes in the early morning shadows of my Canadian room, I sensed her presence, I saw her, I felt her, a shadow at the foot of my bed.

That day, I was leaving Cunardo with my loneliness. I saw an old woman struggling up a road out of the woods. The apron over her long black skirt, the grey hair slipping out of the kerchief tied at the back of her head, a long rake in her hands resting on her stomach, her back bent under a long basket full of wood. It's one of the distant faces of Cunardo that I carry with me.

CHAPTER TWENTY

That first morning, I crossed the imposing entrance hall full of trepidation. The day had finally arrived when I could cross the threshold of the "Liceo Ginnasio Giuseppe Parini" in my own right. For three years we girls of *Scuole Medie*, relegated on the far side, much smaller and humble, of the majestic building of Via Goito, had watched with envious awe the coming and goings of swarms of *liceali* through the doors of their sacred temple. Boys and girls would cluster along the stairway at the end of classes, to banter and flirt free and easy.

Now I was in *IV Ginnasio* (grade 9*)*. I had good reason to feel intimidated and shy, and not only because of the well-known strictness of that *Liceo*. It had a glorious history - as my brother informed me - it had been the first public High School in Milano, dating back to the period of the Austrian domination. It was in fact Maria Teresa of Austria who had founded it in 1774, as a "Regio Ginnasio" *(*Royal High School*)*. Its origins however were even more ancient. It had been erected over the famous "Scuole Palatine" during the period of the Roman Emperor Augustus. Then, under Napoleon, it became the democratic *"Liceo di Porta Nuova."* After his fall, it was renamed *"*Liceo-Ginnasio Giuseppe Parini,"* because in the '700s it was that poet who had made the inaugural speech and who later taught courses in oratory.

Among its alumni, were the greatest protagonists of the history of Milano, such as Alessandro Manzoni, Tommaso Grossi, Carlo Cattaneo, Luciano Manara, till the more recent ones like Clemente Rebora, Carlo Emilio Gadda, Dino Buzzati, and Giorgio Strehler. There were famous names also among its professors, as the Latinist Luigi Castiglioni, the political scientist Ferruccio Parri, the writer Guido Piovene.

La Zanzara (the Mosquito), our own student newspaper, was the first of its kind in Italy. The title derived from the satirical and biting tone of its articles. It had even been sued. Among its copy editors, there had been Vittorio Zucconi, who later became a very well-known journalist.

Only three of us went there from the *Medie:* Vanna Austoni, Maria Grazia Mazzoli and I. Our other classmates had taken different paths, *"easier,"* as we three declared patronizingly: *Liceo Scientifico* or *Artistico* or *Linguistico*, or the even more humble *Magistrali* (Teachers College) as chosen by Edda Zaccarin. And even those who had chosen *Liceo Classico*, they had avoided "Il Parini," which at that time, was considered *"the toughest one in whole of Italy."*

If truth be told, I hadn't chosen it either. Nino had chosen it for me. It was inevitable: it had been mamma's *Liceo* in the years of the prestigious Latinist Castiglione, who had been her professor, and whom I managed to meet thirty years later, although briefly, as Chair at the "Università Bocconi," where I registered just before he passed away. For that short while, I felt with pride that frail bond that tied me to my mother, almost as if I had been unexpectedly brushed by her diaphanous presence. There was a photo of the *III Ginnasio* class published in a newspaper of 1922, in which mamma appears next to one of her classmates, Edda Mussolini, the dictator's daughter. A tradition of almost historic roots in which also my brother had been a part, leaving a series of successes in his wake that now I was supposed to retrace! There was no escape. I had to follow in those footsteps.

Clara Lanzara, with whom I shared desk in the *Medie,* had enrolled at "Brera School," following her artistic talent. With Austoni and Mazzoli I had never really been friend, but suddenly feeling like fish out of water, alone and intimidated in that unfamiliar environment, we developed a close and spontaneous bond of familiarity among that throng of new faces.

It was the first day of school and we were all congregated in the school atrium. My gaze followed the beautiful marble floor that broadened at the foot of a wide double staircase leading to the mysteries of the upper floors,

There's Always the Sea...

where my new life as a Liceo student would start. For five years I would go up those stairs, in a walk more familiar with every passing day. Under my feet I stared fascinated at the spiral impression of a seashell fossil which spoke of a million-year old history, when that shell had been under the sea, as Ms. Cavallini, the new science professor, would eventually explain.

Every once in a while a professor would arrive with a list of the students in his/her section, and would call them to form the class. Section A was exclusively boys, and they had the best professors: Cantele, Vicinelli, Binni, renowned names in classical and modern literature. They had been my brother's professors. Then came Section B, the mixed one, said to be the one with lowest quality, as if whoever chose that section did not have serious intentions, but merely sought the chance to be together with the opposite sex. Finally, Section C for girls only, to which I and my two friends had been assigned.

While anxiously waiting, we caught here and there rumours about this or that professor. They spoke with terror especially of professor Carbone.

"Let's hope we don't have Carbone, they say she is a holy terror."

Our turn finally comes, and Austoni's name is called out. This is it. The voice comes from the top of the staircase, where we see a woman with a firm tone, not too tall but dynamic on her lean muscular legs. Even her face had decisive features that with their lively expression revealed a beauty just recently faded. Her no longer glossy blond hair was gathered in a coil in the back of her head, except for some rebellious locks slipping out here and there. The easy and energetic look was borne out by a simple attire of skirt and blouse, and the practical laced ankle-boots. The green-blue eyes suggested an unusual personality. That was professor Carbone. She would be our professor of Italian.

There were no half measures with her - either you loved her or you hated her. I loved her. To be liked by her, it was not necessary to share her tastes and her ideas; it was enough to be direct and sincere, assured and coherent with yourself. She was the best teacher I've ever had. It was she who taught me to have the courage to be myself. She was stern, demanding but fair. I'll never forget the two years she gave to me.

The 1950-51 academic year - the textbooks and the programmes were just beginning to shed the rubbish of Fascist rhetoric. The programme of Italian literature ended with the dignified Carducci and the querulous Pascoli. Then one day, professor Carbone took the chalk and wrote on the blackboard:

M'illumino d'immenso
(I grow radiant/ in the immensity of it all)

And that's how it started. It was the beginning of my passionate discovery of poetry, "real" poetry. At fifteen, I was thunderstruck by Giuseppe Ungaretti, and by a passion for life. He was not part of the programme, he did not appear in the textbooks, but our professor had us taste it like nectar by writing his verses on the blackboard. After the rhetorical rhapsodies of Carducci, Ungaretti surged clear and intense into our very soul. I faithfully copied his verses in neat handwriting in a small checkered notebook, which I still have next to the rich Mondadori editions I bought many years later.

Professor Carbone told us how she had spent the period of the war in Africa. She had gone among our suffering and confused soldiers, and brought them comfort by reading Ungaretti, the poet who had argued the anti-heroism of war, and had sung the desperate clinging to life in the midst of the atrocities of trench warfare.

Who could have imagined that some twenty years later I myself would mesmerize my Canadian students with Ungaretti?

I recall another event connected with professor Carbone, which has helped me ever since to lift my self-esteem in moments of need. It was during the period of the "Trieste Question," whose territory had been constituted as a "Free State," with the city and the port administered by the Allies, pending an accord with Yugoslavia. Rallies had been organized in Milano to demand the return of the city to Italy. I decided to join the march in favour of Trieste. Not an easy decision, because it meant skipping school without permission from the Principal. We were still living in a post-war period when tempers ran high and there was strong political bad blood. Even the slightest incident could spark a street clash.

I think this was the reason why professor Carbone, however bold and militant, had tried to discourage us from taking part in it, when she had first told us that a rally was in the offing.

"I inform you that you are free to choose, but if you miss class, you will be reprimanded. These are the guidelines I have received from the Principal."

Passionate about the Trieste cause, I took part in the march, but with far less trepidation than when I faced professor Carbone the day after. As soon as I sat down, she calmly did the roll call, and then with a fierce look she asked me to stand and to explain my absence the day before.

"I went to march for Trieste" was my wretched reply, trying then to overcome my nervousness in order to mention the reasons why I felt it was the right thing to do. She motioned me to sit, and then called on another girl who had been absent for the same reason. In a faltering voice, the poor thing began to explain that she hadn't really meant to, that she felt it was important not to miss class, but that she had been swept along by her other classmates, etc., etc. At that point professor Carbone exploded out in a loud voice,

"Oddo, explain to your friend what it means to have an opinion! She doesn't seem to have understood that the question is not whether it's more important Trieste or the school, but rather to be able to maintain the respect and coherence of one's own ideas. When one has chosen to act in accordance with one's beliefs, one must have the courage to defend them all the way, to defend one's own convictions, cost what may. This means acting morally. This is the choice, not whether to skip school or not, not whether to obey or not obey."

A particularly significant lesson in the aftermath of Nazism. I felt bad for my classmate, but inside I was bursting with pride for the show of esteem I had received from my beloved professor. I would never forget her words, nor would I ever forget professor Carbone, "the holy terror."

"Vite! Vite! Vite!" We had to get back in the classroom after the break, to start the French lesson. The sharp and tetchy voice of Madame Roland was trying in vain to call to order the girls scattered along the hallways, more concerned with exchanging the latest gossip than to follow the agitated bulk of the French professor. Her hour was in any event nothing more than a extension of the break.

Though speaking in French, which in the end achieved the aim of making us learn the language, her lessons dealt mostly with her personal flings with a series of husbands. We called her "the black widow," or "the praying mantis," because she seemed to have buried so many, and she dressed always in black. Her powerful bulk wandered around the classroom, fluttering the folds of the wide black cloaks that opened with a generous décolleté on her heaving bosom, together with the black feathers of her showy wide-brim hats.

Disorder and confusion were for Madame Roland an hilarious condition that kept her constantly fluttering about, and made her easy prey to our manipulations. Though she surrounded herself with hundreds of small notes, she would misplace everything and could remember nothing at all. It was such a child's game to distract her from pre-set written or oral tests, assignments to hand in,

" *Mais non, Madame Roland, vous vous trompez bien sûr. Vous aviez dit différemment l'autre jour....*"

In the end, however, the gods had their vengeance. For the final exam, which was in reality an internal exam to decide whether a student would be promoted from the *Ginnasio* to the *Liceo,* Madame Roland, out of the goodness of her heart, had decided that each of us would prepare just one topic, handing in an essay on it. Unfortunately, on the day of the exam, we found ourselves facing not only Madame Roland, but the terrible Marchesi as well, our future professor of Math at the *Liceo,* who, maybe to show off her ability in French, didn't just attend and observe the exam as she was supposed to, but began to ask questions. Seeing my dismay, Madame Roland anxiously began to go through her pile of papers, trying to find my essay and the presumed topic of the oral exam. Naturally, it was all in vain, as equally useless were all my attempts to give her a clue and bring the discussion to a comparison between Racine and Corneille. All the while professor Marchesi continued to talk heatedly about Baudelaire, and to wallow among the "*fleurs du mal,"* pleased with herself like a convent school girl, with a flash of prissy malice in her owlish eyes.

Within the "Parini" institute there were two other "institutions" or "national shrines," as good old Guareschi would say: the janitor Mancuso and the Principal Garavoglia. Omnipotent, omnipresent, all-able men and for all seasons. One presided with enviable efficiency and infallibility to all technical, mechanical and bureaucratic problems. The other, with his superhuman powers, presided over our intellectual and moral needs. An unusual twinning of two elderly venerable figures. Only in cases of extreme need did one dare disturb them in their sacred temples.

Such did in fact appear the janitor's lodge, beyond whose glass door one could see a small altar, always lit by a flickering glow. It was for Mancuso's son, gold medal, fallen in World War II, a few months before the Liberation. The *fasci littori,* which had been placed on either side of the *Liceo*'s entrance with the usual fascist bombast, after the war were replaced with a laurel crown in his name. An aura of pride surrounded the figure of the father, rendered even more tall and lean by his dignified bearing of sorrow.

The figure of *"il Signor Preside"* was the personification of the "*Parini"* itself: discreet, aristocratic, always dressed in grey, with glasses in a light metal frame, he looked like Malenkov. An old-school gentleman, whose cultivated speech had an elegant, smug Tuscan lilt, the *Duecento* poets became *"I Dugentisti."* For us Professor Garavoglia was *"il Signor Dugento."* We were intimidated by his voice, but we loved it when it would materialize as if by magic in the classroom through the loudspeaker, placed on the wall over the head of the professor teaching at the moment.

In the middle of a lesson, the loudspeaker would begin to sputter and crackle. It was the first sign, which our own light coughs would echo in an attempt to cover up our satisfied gabble. At that point everything had to stop, though some time would still pass between the first and the second crackling. Then, finally there was Garavoglia clearing his throat, the prelude to one of his long and cherished speeches. The teachers' eyes would grow dark as they tried to hide their disappointment. With his *"important communications,"* our dear Garavoglia would conveniently shorten our lesson, and so also the homework that would have been assigned, or better yet, it would interrupt an oral examination.

Garavoglia had a particular significance in my academic life. At the end of the first trimester, he would show up in class to wish us a happy Christmas and to comment on our achievements during the first part of the year. Each of us would be called by name, and while standing, would in essence suffer a public trial, anything from a dressing down to praises and an assortment of advice. I looked forward to these solemn events with ambiguous self-satisfaction, mixed with fear and embarrassment. Finally, there was my name emphatically announced: *"Oddo!"* I'd get up, my heart beating, my legs shaking, though I should have been used to it.

"Honourably, Oddo, honourably!" This by then traditional refrain had become part of the ribbing phrases of my classmates, and gave way to the usual praise which made me out to be one of the characters in a tale by De Amicis: a poor little orphan, who despite life's misfortunes, achieved honour in her studies, keeping high the name she bore, and following the example of the brother who had preceded her, and winning year after year the bursary for orphan children of university professors. A real tearjerker, which despite incredible efforts, made me shed hot tears of self-pity. And so I'd sit down amid flatteries and shame.

At year's end instead, the tough verdict appeared on the notice boards hung on the corridor's wall. We had to elbow our way through the scrum of classmates, necks stretched out and faces tensely deciphering those tiny numbers that signaled our fate: "Passed, Re-sit the exam, or Failed?" But even from afar the "insufficient" mark for subjects you'd have to be re-examined in at the end of

There's Always the Sea...

summer would cruelly stand out in red. And if the "insufficient" subjects were many, it meant repeating the entire school year. I was able to achieve every year the dream of every student: having my summers free.

The years of *Ginnasio-Liceo*, however, were not free of struggles and mortifications. The label of "Sans famille" that had been pinned on me still oppressed me, and I had to deal with the typical adolescent existential crisis when life on the outside does not match the life within you, and your spirit suffers without being able to define the pain.

I recall a recurring dream during that fifteenth year: in the shadows of a forest at the end of some solitary path, the image of my mother would appear from behind the trees. I would call her, look for her, follow her until I would wake with a start, while still calling out her name in my sobs.

Maybe it was that black school smock, threadbare and dull, which fell on me like a sack, while, much to my envious admiration, many of my classmates wore it tightly wrapped around their already feminine figures. Maybe it was that everlasting Scottish skirt with a no longer white blouse, which I had to wear day after day, and which according to nonna, no one would see under the smock. Maybe it was those braids which fell heavy on my still flat chest and made me hunch my shoulders. For sure it was the holes in my knee socks which peeked outside my shoes, a real nightmare during oral exams, when I had to stand on the platform by the professor's desk, and I felt everyone's eyes were looking at my heels. Perhaps it was the constant comparison with Vanna Austoni who, I don't know why, had wanted me as her desk mate, rather than her great friend, Maria Grazia Mazzoli. Tall, blond, refined, daughter of one of Milano's most famous surgeons, Vanna represented everything which to me meant beauty, class and wealth.

From the very beginning, a lavish box of colour pencils by the prestigious Swiss brand *Caran D'Ache* was what symbolized her in my mind. Still now, whenever I think about Austoni, I immediately see that large metal box open on her desk during Art class at *Scuole Medie*: a rainbow of colours, passing from one to the other in a thousand hues; a display of thirty well sharpened long tapered pencils, of the most incredibly delicate tints that took away your breath. I stared at them, rather than looking at my nine or ten stubs held in a simple wooden box.

And then it happened! Vanna invited me and Mazzoli to her home, and on the soft carpet in her room she insisted I take off my shoes, as they had done! With a distressing lump in my throat, I tried in vain to avoid the shame of my well-known socks.

Vanna Austoni did not complete the *Liceo*; she was sent to a college in Switzerland. As for Maria Grazia Mazzoli, with her dark womanly beauty, rumour had it that she had become the mistress of a rich elderly man. These things affected me in a confused way back then, and I could not imagine their significance. But I did imagine that something rather mysterious took place in that gloomy apartment, where Maria Grazia lived alone with her ambitious widowed mother.

As for me, in *V Ginnasio,* two more modest events sent my life in another direction. The unforgettable day I had gone to see zia Mariuccia in Vigevano, and the two of us decided to rebel against the absolute vetoes of nonna. Zia took me to the hairdresser to have my braids cut off. Two firm and fateful snips took half a kilo off my shoulders. The two stumps were in fact placed on a scale and weighed to everyone's amazement. This marked the end of the ugly duckling.

The second event was the arrival of Antonia Romagnoli in my class. I can still see her sitting down there, in the last row of seats, the first day of school. She was assigned to the last row because she was taller and more mature than the rest of us. She was joining my section to repeat the *V Ginnasio.* She was sitting there alone and a stranger to all. During the break I joined her, I sat with her and we talked. We had an immediate liking for each other, which turned into a lifelong friendship. The thing that immediately bound us was discovering that she spent her vacations in Ganna, only five kilometres from Cunardo. She had a large ancient villa, which would open every summer for her big family of four children, her parents, nonno, aunts, uncles, cousins, and for her friends.

At the end of the academic year, I was invited to join her there. I see myself getting off the bus, dressed in my best, a white and green checkered *tailleur* that Lalla Baldoni had given me. I was now old enough to wear the beautiful things she wanted to discard. From then on, I would have a nice wardrobe provided this way by her. But that pimple, which had appeared on my chin at such a bad moment, was agonizing me. I can still feel the emotion as I climb along that street Antonia said it was jokingly called "*Sali e Tabacchi,*" curving between villas and gardens, as I followed the instructions she had given me to reach her house:

"Sali, *Sali, Sali,*" in fact all I did was climb, climb, climb, "*until the last curve which ends in front of the gate of a villa with a plate bearing the name 'Tabacchi'.*" That's why the epithet of that street, *"Sali e Tabacchi,"* as the sign of the shop selling salts and tobaccos.

Shortly after, I found myself in front of an enormous solid front gate with wrought iron knockers. It was clearly something medieval. Its dark archway in fact, meant for coaches, allowed passage through the solid wall of a Spanish-style villa on which the date of 1406 was carved. Everything was sombre and imposing, different from what I had expected.

I knocked with some uneasiness. A small door was opened within the huge portal, and I went through. A burst of light hit me, and I found myself among flowers, plants surrounding the confusion and gaiety of young people laughing and joking, as they followed a game of ping pong on the table that took up most of the portico at the entrance. I was introduced to everyone, hugged by the solid matronly figure of the mother, who would become for me "*Mamma Carlotta.*" In an instant, I had become part of all that.

Little by little I soaked in the environment which surrounded me, and in which I could already breathe vitality, an intensity of lively human beings so unusual for me.

A garden opened in front of the portico; a large table was already laid out under a pergola of grape vines on the right, and bounded on the left by large terracotta amphorae and flowerbeds. From the railing of the balcony that overlooked the portico, running along the entire length of the house, there was a cascade of wisterias. On the right wall of the portico, a baroque frame in wrought iron closed the opening of a mysterious well of unplumbed depths. Who knows what secrets were hid in its abyss. Right next to it the guest quarters…a perfect location for the requirements of a mansion built in those "Borgia times!" On the left side of the portico there was the door to the kitchen, and then you'd come to the dining room and finally to the large living room with tall stained glass windows. One entire wall in the kitchen was taken up by a huge ancient fireplace, flanked by tall, dark wooden settees, where we'd encamp in the damp autumn days, enveloped by the steam of the polenta or the fragrance of roasted chestnuts. Around the large table in the middle of the kitchen, the mother-mistress of the house kept busy for hours to turn out fresh *tagliatelle*, *agnolotti*, breads, cakes, and various other delicacies to feed family and friends. Beyond the perimeter walls of the garden, a slope led to an orchard and to the space laid out with stone tables and benches surrounding the brick oven, where on warm summer evenings the pizzas would be turned out.

Antonia was solid like her mother, physically and morally, statuesque, buxom and athletic at the same time. She was a firm presence in my life. She encouraged my self-confidence. With great patience she taught me to swim, helping me overcome the fear implanted in me by the rash exploit of my fascist zio.

A limpid still surface, spread with the green reflection of weeping willows and silver birches, was our cherished *Lago di Ghirla,* which reflected the peacefulness of the Valganna woodlands. All for us, before the tourist developments would later ruin it. We enjoyed it in the best years. The twin-hulled rowboat would glide, steadily propelled by Mamma Carlotta, while Antonia and I would swim in its wake across the lake.

That's how the series of summers during the L*iceo* started, my life being driven with the confident force of my sixteen years. Day after day the youthful enthusiasm of a group of friends on the threshold of adulthood, to whom everything seemed possible, would pour out in a cascade of emotions in that villa in Ganna. On rainy days we'd bicycle, riding along paths in the woods, then warming up by the fireplace, while telling stories or strumming on a guitar. We launched ourselves into everything and everywhere, with constantly renewed energy and curiosity: swimming, running, climbing, exploring, singing, dancing, play acting.

Those wonderful days on the shores of the lake flowed as gently as the leaves of the weeping willows on its surface.

CHAPTER TWENTY-ONE

Was I ever aware that those were my happy years? Having overcome the childhood traumas and the adolescent melancholies, I was now open to all the stimuli life had to offer me, enjoying the delight of a group of young people who lived convinced they held the future in their hands. We worked and we studied hard, of course, but we were also sure we'd get our fair rewards, knowing we were following a path of our own making; a path freely chosen, without the problems and uncertainties of today's youth. As a result, we could indulge untroubled in fun and games. Our secret lay in knowing how to have fun, enjoying simple things in a playful and carefree camaraderie. I had all the ingredients for the magic formula: youth, freedom and health. Was I ever aware of it then? The irony of letting the best years of our life slip unaware through our fingers! Still, a trace of it did remain in my soul, a balm to ease the years to come.

I would experience other moments of happiness in my life; instants perhaps, intense like the passion with which I've always lived life. Every moment, however, had its bitter side, because years and experiences had scarred my soul and dampened the ephemeral sense of joy. I ended up blurring *"pleasure and pain in that total absence of discernment, which is the only condition in which a person dares to say: I feel happy!"* as Brancati observes in "Il bell'Antonio." Never again could happiness be as uninhibited, as pure as it was then. Sooner or later there would be a price to pay. It would have shown up together with, or overlapped by, the dark aspect of life, until it became, as Leopardi observed, *"the mere absence of pain."* The moment comes when one must assume the responsibility for one's own life, even without having complete control over it, and live it in a dubious freedom full of consequences. Back then, I was still favoured by a life of free-flowing actions, devoid of any negative consequences for me or anyone else. I lived happily because I was making the most of my emotional, physical and mental capacities.

At school, Antonia and I formed an immediate alliance, even though for that year I had to stay next to the Austoni girl. After that, the two of us became "desk partners" for the rest of the *Liceo* years.

We were in the third row centre. In front of us were two names that belonged to the élite of Milano: Enrica Melzi d'Eril and Simona Massa Saluzzo. When we approached them, they didn't act haughty in the least. Fascinated by Enrica's flair and Simona's spirit of adventure, we forged an inseparable foursome. We'd share a cigarette in the washroom; we'd gossip in the hallways; we'd clap eyes on the *"Liceo boys;"* we'd play mock naval battles during the dullest moments of our classes. We were thick as thieves and called ourselves *"Il Ganglio del Gran Simpatico,"* to show off our recently acquired scientific notions about the glands system.

Simona was the first to go her own way after *Liceo*. She had a special beauty, a full head of tawny hair, porcelain-like skin, blue eyes shadowed with green. She never forgave us for thinking she used eye shadow; hers were natural tints. She did not continue her studies. Soon after she got engaged and married. When Antonia subtly probed her about married life, Simona, disappointing her expectations, echoed a famous phrase: *"Frankly, my dear, sex is highly overrated!"*

His vast torso rising over the desk, professor Canesi called out our names in a booming voice in the Latin and Greek class, as he handed back our tests, piled neatly in front of him in the order of descending marks. The nervousness of waiting to hear one's name grew with the anguishing drop of the marks toward failures. The "6" were done, even the "5"; finally my name echoed in the silence of the class, and my heart was as tiny as a pea.

"Oddo! Four minus! Team work! And we know for whose benefit..."

Then came the "4" of "*your friend Romagnoli*". Little did it help the professor's attempts to separate us. Even putting Antonia at the rear of the class, we still had a perfect system of wireless communication. The agreement was that I would help her in Greek and Latin, and she'd help me in Mathematics. With Antonia in the last seat of my row, the message reached her through our classmates: imperceptibly my hand stretched and tapped the knee of the girl behind, and so on, until the message reached its destination. We didn't lose heart even when we were in different rows. While the professor was immersed in his reading, the message flew across the classroom in a conveniently rolled up little ball. Everything ran smoothly, except when I'd make a blunder in the translations from Greek, and the glaring error would stand out equally in both our works. In any event, I continued being professor Canesi's favourite, and Antonia the "favourite little donkey" of the hated Math professor, the thin and beaky Marchesi.

School represented our first trial with reality. It was like a microcosm in which to expand our emotional world in dramas, comedies and farces; experiencing friendships, loves, joys and sorrows, achievements and failures; creating the most intense emotional relationships with professors and classmates, who became an extended or, at least for me, an ersatz family.

The figure of professor Canesi was that of a giant, both physically and intellectually. But, like the Colossus of Rhodes, it rested on feet of clay. The powerful torso rested in fact on two pathetic legs paralyzed by polio. He'd walk into class dragging them with crutches clasped under his wide shoulders. But his wretchedness was forgotten as soon as it disappeared behind the desk, and the upper part of the body towered above it together with his mind, which swept us like an exciting wave into the world of Classical culture.

His voice thundered, plunging in the tormented maelstroms of the tragic characters of Aeschylus, Sophocles and Euripides; and it softened in the rich tenderness of Greek lyric poets. When, on the other hand, he entertained us with Aristophanes, his clear articulation would suddenly drop into embarrassed slurred sputtering, and he coughed trying to save the innocent ears of young girls from the vulgar jokes and the many obscenities, amid our stifled laughter. We forgave him also the hundreds of verses from "the Iliad" and "the Odyssey" that we had to memorize on a regular basis. To cheer us up, he'd tell us that someday, somewhere in the wide world, we would conquer the heart of a rich Texan reciting the verses of Homer, Alcaeus and Sappho.

I remember his smile of delight as I rattled off Greek etymologies, my passion, and the confident sounding out of my name in the classroom when he felt discouraged by the stubborn refusal of one of my classmates to learn the difference between the Latin verbs "**cécidi**, casum, cadere" (with the short **i**) from "cado, cadis," and "**caecìdi**, caesum, caedere" (with the long **i**) from "caedo, caedis". What a feeling of triumph two Latin verbs can give you!

In the morning he would arrive like a rocket in his spanking new red Spider - adapted to be driven with hands - in a brief interlude of exuberant escape from his disability. He was then seen struggling up the stairs, supported by his powerful Valkyrie-like wife. I'll never forget that kindly gruff face of his, with his coal-black eyes sunk under his black bushy eyebrows. Nor would I ever forget the world of values and ideals to which he introduced us, patiently holding our hand.

"Oodo, tell me about Donatéelo", was instead the invitation of the professor of Art History, who was from the region of Veneto. She expected from me the inevitable comment about what we called the "*movement of the left big toe*" of Donatello's David, which in fact comes out prehensile-like over the base of the statue with "*a naturalistic vigour,*" as the professor expected to hear, and we naturally would say. Her name was Bordon and, together with Cavallini for Science and Ferro for Italian, - known also as "Fevvo" according to her own pronunciation - made up the characters of the *"opera buffa"* that took place every day on the stage of our school.

The Science period was for us even better than a break. A real bedlam would break out. Comfortably seated at our desks, we kept up our conversations all across the classroom, defying poor Cavallini, completely incapable of imposing her authority. Suddenly, the exasperated scream, "*Oddooo! To the john!*"- her not so professional words to kick me out of class. But often, in her outburst of rage, she'd rattle her teeth, and out would drop her dentures, promptly put back in place with a masterful tap of the right thumb against the palate. Nevertheless, she had a soft spot for me because she had been one of my father's students. But what a disappointment in not finding in me a genius for chemistry! In vain she appealed to my name, convinced I would have the answer the rest of the class didn't. I was totally hopeless.

"*I am the Moon, and this is the Earth, and I turn, turn, turn...*" Seeing is believing… was the virtual representation that Cavallini created of the simultaneous rotation of the Moon on its own axis and revolution around the Earth. She was the Moon and the desk was the Earth and… she turned, turned, turned. In the gusto of her various revolutions, her hairpiece took on its own rotation on her forehead. Without interrupting the movement of the celestial bodies, it too was nimbly placed back to its original position.

And then there was *"Fevvo"*, wife of professor Apollonio, famous hermetic literary critic, so hermetic even his own wife couldn't understand him. Just imagine us! She basked in his reflected glory, and forced us to use his texts without being able to give her understanding of them. We'd end up memorizing entire phrases which Ferro would listen to quite pleased. Her literary sensibility had, after all, some glaring limitations if we recall that one of the questions she asked in an exam on Manzoni's "The Betrothed," which went down in history, was "*What colour were the stockings of Lucia?*"

She'd come into class teetering like a tired housewife - lumbering steps on low shoes, a huge bag which dragged her down. She then settled at her desk, placing the bag on the floor and her generous bosom over the edge of the desk, where it rested for the entire lesson. Time enough for Mattioli to do a sketch of "*Fevvo and her melons.*"

Mattioli was a merciless caricaturist, and we were at that age in which we all were guilty of guileless irreverence.

There's Always the Sea...

The sketches in which Mattioli's pen caught the various professors in their typical poses would make the rounds of the class surreptitiously, to liven up the most boring lessons.

Among her masterpieces was, unavoidably, good old Cavallini, who taught Mendel's Law of Heredity. Basing herself on "green peas and dry peas," Mattioli indulged her boundless imagination to conceive various possible crossbreeding, starting with the descendants of Cavallini herself, and ending up with the most surreal hybrids. In the middle of a lesson, we would catch the passing drawing of a strange tall being, with enormous droopy ears, and beneath it the comment: *"Cross between a lamp post and a jackrabbit. What will the dominant characters be?"* Mattioli didn't even spare our beloved *Cesarino*. Well, he was after all only a skeleton, though nicely polished, which was dangling in the Science lab. He would always welcome us with his smile, all teeth. Mattioli expanded as well, with a macabre sense of humour, on his possible offspring. We were at that age when we would laugh for no reason at all, simply because we felt like laughing.

And yet, as soon as I returned home, everything would die down. I felt the weight of nonna's resentments, because I seemed to prefer the company of my classmates. I had been her companion my entire life, filling the emptiness of her existence. Ironically, it was she herself now who pushed me away and trampled my fragile cheerfulness, which she needed so much. With a sad smile, I see again the dark catlike woman of the *"Ferrochina Bisleri"* advertisement facing the tiger with her bright smile, bursting with health. It was the famous publicity lithograph which nonna had hanging in the kitchen - symbol of the exuberance she so loved. Full of life, smiling, that's how she would have wanted to see me, re-living in me her own carefree youth.

But my life was marked by voids and melancholies. The more she pressed me, the more I closed myself in a shell, trusting that one day my loneliness would be *"invited* - as the poet Tagore would say - *there, where the festival of life is celebrated."*

CHAPTER TWENTY-TWO

We were at that age when one *"is in love with love,"* as good old Ferro would warn us – *"Be careful young buds!"* – when she noticed our recurring lapses and wistfulness. And sure enough like Merlin the Magician, Love deceived me by appearing in many disguises. A shock of Titian-red hair, a Raphael-like face, and I was ready to swear I would marry no one but a man with red hair, while I adored from afar my Renaissance page from Section III-B.

But during my summers in Cunardo, he would appear in the new disguise of the town's rascal who captivated me from the terrace below our apartment with his blonde exuberance. He had all the elements for the ideal man: an athletic body, a cheeky self-confidence, and he even played the guitar. I wrote love poems in Greek for him, but he wasn't a Texan and he was not moved. And so I would descend into the circle of my longing and heartache, the dark inner flight of stairs which joined our two apartments. Drawn by the bewitching sounds of my Orpheus, I would perch myself on the landing lost in raptures. At sunset, I'd follow him in his regular walk to the *Caffé* to be with his friends, just to see him, just to feel in his wake, ready to disappear like Eurydice as soon as he turned around.

Lightning could strike me even by looking at the intense stare from a portrait of the playwright Sem Benelli, my other long secret passion. Abstract forms, I avoided anything concrete, I chased only the impossible. The possible turned me off. Wooing, declarations of love all annoyed me, bothered me like an affront. No one in fact came close to my ideal, which was itself unattainable. As a result, I could live love in an indefinite and deferred dimension.

Now Cunardo and Ganna were the settings of my marvellous summers, so appealing as to even refuse my brother's invitations to accompany him in some of his travels. It was where comradely alliances were forged, where the game of flirting was beginning to test me, in narcissistic rounds of conquest and evasion.

At times the game could turn dangerous, as when my unwitting gifts of ... enchantress lured the seminarian of Vigevano to abandon his calling!

Every time I went to see zia Mariuccia, he managed to be around. He obviously had a crush on me, which he conveyed by looking at me with his meek and dreamy eyes, while with passion he played *Andalusia* on the piano. How could I not respond but to look at him with equally dreamy eyes? It's not easy at sixteen to remain insensitive to the suggestive notes of *Andalusia* and to a pair of gentle eyes. Later, though, for a long time I felt the guilt of having denied a soul to the Church.

"No doubt at all," zia had informed me, suppressing a smile, *"he left the seminary for you."*

I saw him again one day in a soldier uniform; he was leaving for his military service, the price to pay for having left the protection of the Church!

Was I still conditioned by that enduring state of orphan? Having always to gain the love of others, in the absence of the spontaneous and unconditioned love of my own parents, incited me to the insatiable relish of the conquest, discovering the gamesmanship of enticing glances with which to conquer and then leave. The delight resided entirely in that, in confirming my power, oblivious and carefree. Or was it perhaps that famous "little devil" hidden in the mirror, about which mamma had warned me against as a little girl?

"For a servant girl, honestly no ... quite honestly she's not bad indeed...." I would now sing before the mirror, imitating the maid pleased with her comely forms in the movie *Fra Diavolo*. A perturbing movie for my adolescent naïveté, which seemed to emanate a perfume of boudoir face powder, subtly inebriating and sensual, like the protagonist, that white prissy cavalier with a wig of silky curls, who had generated an equally sweet emotional turmoil in me.

Summer was drawing near, and we had to make the apartment in Milano ready in view of our long absence. The task was quite labour intensive. The armchairs in the living room had to be covered with their white dust sheets. The Persian carpets, after having been duly cleaned with the carpet beater from the kitchen balcony, were then covered with newspapers and mothballs, and finally rolled up and pushed against a wall. We'd close the shutters and the louvres, and everything was left in semi-darkness, in a quiet sleepiness, like an enchanted castle where everyone has been set by a magic wand in lifeless diaphanous forms, and everything would remain suspended until the next reawakening.

Cunardo was waiting for me. The heavy bolted door of the abandoned house was opened and I would take in that pungent odour of humidity, dense with memories of so many years. I would find again my friends, and now there was also Ganna and Antonia, and a whole new dimension.

The meeting place was the drinking fountain under the large horse chestnut. I could see it from my window in the small space formed by the crossroad of the roads coming into the town: the Bulgheroni downhill, the road to the station, and the one to the cemetery. It was the fresh spring water fountain which had supplied us with water during the war, and even now when the town was drought-stricken during the summer. Whoever went there would sit on the low wall next to it.

They had been part of my young war years; now they were *I ragazzi di Cunardo* ("the Cunardo kids") in part locals, in part vacationers, especially from Milano. I can still see them, all sitting on the wall waiting for the group to form in order to organize something, which usually ended up jumping on our bikes and ride out to invade Antonia's house in Ganna. I would look at them from the window to see when it was time to join them. Very soon, in fact, I would hear our arranged call-up whistle.

Gigetto, the pharmacist's son who lived nearby, would be the first to show up together with his cousin Sandro, the "long-legs" from Torino. Gigetto hid a pathological shyness behind his cat eyes and the sly smile; he was everyone's pet, especially mothers'. I would always pair up with Sandro for the final sprint in our excursions in the mountains, when just before the summit we all raced to see who'd get there first. That's when we'd partner up. Sandro would grab my hand and would pull me while I began jumping like a goat to keep up with his giant stride. We were always first.

Mariano Grimaldi, the son of a dentist of Swiss origins - a pioneering profession for a woman in those days - and of the Italian "attaché" at our embassy in Genève. He smugly flaunted the charm of his family background, his nice looks and his French inflection inherited from his mother. Hardly impressed by his diplomatic "attachment," we patronized him with good-humour.

Even good Nino Martelli was the object of the general innocent teasing - chubby and childish, he became the inevitable target. I would join in a bit reluctantly because he had been my constant and faithful beau since the first year of elementary school. The horrible clay figurines which he offered me as a little boy were now replaced with rich baskets of flowers, handed without fail to our concierge in Milano at every birthday and saint's day. Nonna was delighted and would display them on the kitchen balcony which looked onto the internal courtyard of the building to give them fresh air and... so they could be seen by the neighbours. But in spite of all her urging to consider this - *"a good match"*, *"son of the president of the Pharmacists Association!"*, *"owner of dozens of pharmacies in Milano,"* as she kept reminding me - I refused to "consider" the importance of that chubby boy.

We had the biggest laugh one evening after a dancing party at his home. We had just started to walk away all in a group down the road, enjoying the stroll in the bright light of the full moon, when someone discovered he had forgotten his cigarettes, the only ones we had among us. We went back to Villa Martelli, and after much ringing, the irritated voice of the caretaker answered. When we asked to speak to Nino, he replied,

"El tuset l'è già endurmenzà. L'è inscì ch'el dorme in mez a nu."

To imagine Nino Martelli as a little boy - *"tuset"*- sleeping like an angel, safely between the couple of caretakers, destroyed in laughter the last shred of regard we could possibly have for him. It didn't help to find out that, on that particular day, his parents had been absent. Was he normally sleeping between papà and mamma?

Nino Martelli's cousin Carletto was completely different: dark, lean, lively, Arab-like. He was my "big brother." We had in fact adopted each other as brother and sister because we were the craziest of the bunch, and we teamed up in playing practical jokes and pranks on the others.

Famous was the hoax inflicted on Maurizio Pollini, who was in those days only beginning the career which would have made him the famous pianist. *Enfant prodige* with all the characteristics: spoiled, capricious and egocentric. That particular summer he was the guest of Luisa Vanvitelli, his patron, in Cunardo.

Signora Vanvitelli, the old friend of my mother during the years at Villa Quies, had convinced herself that I was a rich heiress; and having discovered the young talented Maurizio and the need of a strong financial backing for his career, she had set her sights on me with the idea of "arranging the marriage" or better yet "the deal." The thing was so preposterous that it took nonna a while to grasp it. Among other things, the so-called suitor was a lot younger than I. In the meantime, I was enjoying myself, flattered to be invited to dinners and dances in the lavish Casa Vanvitelli in Corso Venezia in Milano. At last, the game was uncovered, and nonna appalled told me the truth. I was outraged and began to plot my vengeance.

When poor Maurizio was set on my trail even in Cunardo, he became an easy prey. Carletto declared himself game and so also the rest of the group. Maurizio had by now imposed himself on the group for too many days, and he had rankled everyone with his prima donna whims, demanding constant attention. It was then during a picnic in the woods that we prepared our trap.

Carletto took on the role of my jealous suitor, and maybe he played the part with excessive zeal. During the whole day he did all he could to provoke Maurizio into a fight. Finally, just when Maurizio had come very close to me, Carletto suddenly fell upon us from behind a tree, and flicked open a switchblade right under the nose of the poor startled victim. The hapless boy blanched. Maybe we were a bit too cruel, but we finally had the satisfaction of having clipped the wings of one who had until then treated us so haughtily.

Maurizio Pollini went out of my life, and I probably also from his memory. Clearly, he did not need my support to become the great concert pianist he is! In the years that followed, I thought with a self-satisfied smile at the brief passage of such a bright comet in my life. I wondered how it would have been if…?

Not excessively tall, with kind gentle eyes, a shyness ably curbed by a smile, which revealed it and belied it at the same time, this was Renato Terzi, the "philosopher" of the crowd, quiet, reserved, reflective. He didn't join in all our activities, but when he did, he was always with me or with Antonia; and since Antonia and I were inseparable, it was difficult to say whom he preferred, so much so that at one point each of us was convinced he had a crush on her.

He smoked a pipe, and Antonia and I had also taken a liking to puff on it now and then. We thought it looked so *osé* and cool. After all, it had been Antonia herself who had introduced me to my first cigarette in the washroom at the *Liceo*. Smoking in those days was very sophisticated. We identified with Humphrey Bogart and Lauren Bacall in that famous scene in which he lights up two cigarettes at once, and then excruciatingly slowly he places one of them between her lips. We also added the pipe, much less sexy but so much more fun. We passed each other the pipe as kids now pass each other a joint.

There we were, studying at the table in the small drawing room at the villa in Ganna. We were doing assignments for the summer in preparation for the coming year - unending Greek and Latin translations. Buried under books and dictionaries, what could have been more relaxing than to peacefully smoke the pipe Renato had given us? Suddenly, we hear Mamma Carlotta's footsteps drawing near, and the pipe disappears among the books. The problem was that a moment later little clouds of smoke started rising from the piles of books to the horrified face of Mamma Carlotta.

Renato was the most mature among the boys, the most emancipated; in fact he already had his own Vespa, a rare luxury in those days.

That hand which on the armrest of the seat at the cinema would inch close to mine, and with its fingers would graze mine, relieving minutes of suspense, that was my first romantic story. It was the "flight" with Renato Terzi.

One day he arrived suddenly, while we all were as usual at Lake Ghirla. He proudly showed off his brand new Vespa, and secretly he invited me to go with him on his motor scooter to a cinema at the nearby city of Varese. Leaving everyone, leaping on his Vespa and going on the sly just the two of us to the city was a matter of an instant, which immediately took on the taste of the forbidden fruit, of a transgression. We could have told the others, let Mamma Carlotta know. But we were afraid it would have been a letdown for them, maybe even arise some sniggers. Permission would have been easily given, but maybe that was precisely what stopped us from asking - it would have taken away the pleasure of the adventure. So the thing turned into an exhilarating ride with the wind in my hair, in a daring flight which seemed almost an abduction.

What I have left is the memory of that searching for each other's hand with an aching tenderness, that grazing and squeezing of our hands in the dark. A taste of a love that never was. Old-fashion innocence. And yet a scandal exploded. The daring knight had to present himself repentant to my grandmother and admit the guilt of his rash actions. His excuses were also presented to Mamma Carlotta and to the friends in Ganna. A story of other times.

Who were the girls of Cunardo? I remember the two sisters, Pieretta and Luisella, with completely opposite personalities. Luisella was pretty, shy and reserved, she seemed more like a novice from a convent. The daring and shameless Pieretta was the object of our disdain, due probably more to jealousy than indignation, since she openly made out with the boys; and so the more uninhibited boys would concentrate more on her, breaking the esprit de corps of our group. The crystal ball would reveal that Renato, after having made me his great unhappy love, which he hopelessly indulged in for years, ended up marrying sweet Luisella.

Then there were "the kids of Ganna," starting with the large family of Antonia: the second daughter Giovanna, flighty and rebellious, nicknamed "Giovanna the mad", and Lauretta, the "baby," some five or six years younger than us, sweet and chubby, our darling. Vittorino was the eldest, tall and strong, with the classic profile of an ancient Greek, he was the "hunk," but without ever putting on airs, and always so kind. Among the many others, the closest friends were: Beppe Mapelli and Lino Moretti, part of the love game which entrapped the Romagnoli sisters during our "Midsummer Night's Dream."

Antonia was in love with the bespectacled Beppe, a boring accountant but with the look of an intellectual. In turn she was adored and admired for her intellectual capacity by the rough but sturdy bully of Ganna, the blond Lino, who had become a reckless motorcyclist in order to overcome and hide the handicap suffered from a bout with polio. After many years of unrequited courting, Lino came to his senses, and discovered his true love in Giovanna, joining her in an unlucky marriage.

I also remember the bright blue eyes of Giampiero Santoro, and his smile while I'd spin with him in the endurance waltz contests, from which we'd come out breathless but winners, so young and full of life. And who knows how many other fleeting faces and smiles now darkened by the folds of time! For me the film ends there, when unconsciously we were weaving the first stiches of our future, from which I was still trying to escape in the spins of a waltz.

Every summer Antonia and I expected *"a new man,"* some different vacationer to renew our group; and in effect often a new addition ended up complicating the plots and sub-plots in the innocent game of our interweaving stories. New villas would open up for parties, and days and nights passed to the rhythm of sambas and rumbas. One year we gained five "new men" in one fell swoop, all from the flourishing Sartoro family - all of ten children between boys and girls, with the characteristic of having been born to alternate colours - literally, one red and one black, one red and one black. How could I not see it as a sign of fate when the red-haired Alberto began to court me? Yet there, seated on that green field, in spite of the colourful effect, I was gripped by a deep melancholy in front of how it all seemed forced, and I was instantly cured of my chromatic illusion; but not without a bit of existential malaise for these first tastes of the contrast between dreams and reality, for what might have been and never was.

We would get up at dawn and be on the road with the moist coolness of the morning. These were our excursions on the mountains of the Valganna and of Lago Maggiore. When we didn't know the way, we'd follow at the beginning the sections of the railway, jumping on the track ties among the acacias. Singing up the mountain paths, we'd reach the top by lunch time. We'd then spread the tablecloths and pull out of our backpacks the white loaves stuffed with prosciutto, salami, cheese, or the breaded veal cutlets so tasty when cold. Nonna would get up at dawn as well to cook me the herb omelettes. Those flavours, those fragrances, the pleasure of those tuck-ins with the hunger of youth after hours of climbing are the memory of a unique, one-in-a-life-time experience.

Sometimes we'd stop at a farmer's house to drink milk just drawn from a cow, brimming with warm froth. And we'd happen to find polenta still steaming in the pot hanging from the hook in the fireplace. We'd eat it with fresh milk. Then, after a rollicking rest on the haystacks with their heady scented warmth, we'd cheerfully set off again.

There were still vestiges of war. We'd explore with dismay the thrilling discovery of World War I trenches that would suddenly appear in the thick greenery. Or caught by a sudden downpour, we'd casually take shelter in German bunkers, which still opened their grim eyes on a lakeside landscape. But when we were in the mood for a real adventure, we'd head for the *Orrido of Cunardo*, a frightful gorge. Speleologists came from everywhere to explore it. The caves were many, deep and dark, opening one within the other to form a labyrinth. You had to be quite experienced to venture into them, but the boys from Cunardo knew most of them inside out. There wasn't a one who hadn't taken a stab at it to prove his courage and be accepted by right in the consortium of "men." So we were assured some good guides, but there still were risks, and the test of initiation was applied to the girls as well, to separate "the sissies" from the women, and make us part of the "group" with all honours.

Our destination was the Bats Cave; to cut the mustard you had to reach it. We entered it with torches, slipping on rocks wet from the water that ran along the floor and the walls, and which covered them with a slimy mould. Each girl was led by a boy. When the cave was reached, the torches were often snuffed out by strong drafts. We began to suspect that the boys knew exactly where to hold the torches to achieve that effect. The bats fluttered and squeaked above our heads, luckily keeping to the higher and darker chambers of the cave. But as soon as the torches went out, the flight patterns tended to drop a lot lower. I remember those moments suspended in the darkness, at that age when terror becomes an exhilarating thrill.

It was the era of Rolando and Marcello Del Bello, famous tennis players. They had a villa in Ganna, and one day, having met them on the bus, we got to know them and ended up playing on their tennis courts. Something to tell our friends in Milano. It was also the era of Coppi and Bartali. During the *Giro d'Italia*, they'd pass through Cunardo in the route of the *Tre Valli Varesine*, and we'd rush to the *stradone* to cheer them on; and of course everyone was rooting for the veteran Bartali.

The s*tradone*, that is "the Provincial road" in the days when the highway was still a dream, was a real protagonist in our summers - a place to go for a stroll at sunset, or to sit by the roadside looking at heat lightning and smoking a forbidden cigarette in the moonlight. A radiant moon as it's no longer seen, not yet defeated by the lights of the modern world, would turn the night to day when we came home from dances on our bikes. To the chirping of crickets, we'd glide in the night velvet, when the bike seems to roll without any effort from our legs that press down seemingly recharging with renewed energy at every turn of the pedal.

I can still see that vast breezy field that wandered up the hill to fold at the horizon and disappear down the other side, as if to discover the range of my life, of my future. We were at the border with Switzerland, on an excursion with Mamma Carlotta. We wanted to put our foot on the other side of the frontier, in order to be able to say we'd been in Switzerland, but I didn't have my passport on me. Mamma Carlotta remembered she still had the name of Giovanna registered on her passport, even though Giovanna had her own by this time. So I passed for the daughter shown on Mamma Carlotta's passport, who boldly went through flaunting two daughters bearing the name Giovanna. We created such a confusion of words that the poor customs officer, an inexperienced young Swiss, fell for it, and we went through laughing and singing *"La Svizzera... la Svizzera...."*

Someone should have told me that that was happiness. Instead, I was waiting for the future happy fullness of life.

"The fountain of life, while it gushes amid hardships, it plashes froth of tears and joy", sings the Indian poet Tagore.

In Cunardo the days of games and youthful good times followed one another. In the end, the inevitable sense of melancholy. Summer would draw to an end. The first autumn fogs began to hang over the Lake of Ghirla. It meant our departure

In the evening, silent in the mist and the rheumy green, the lake was waiting for our final farewell. Antonia and I would go down there alone, it was our secret ritual. We went to discover the magic of that scenery which showed itself only to us. The soft blanket of fog had almost settled on the water, beneath the dark crowns of the trees which emerged as if to breathe. A Leonardesque landscape. My very soul was there, in that fog, in that mist, in the sensuous humours of the woodland, in those rocks lapped by the water. Their melancholy had deep roots in my very being.

CHAPTER TWENTY-THREE

Back in Milano, we were caught up in the vortex of our school, whose joys and pains were shared by Antonia and me. We always came back from school together, getting off the streetcar in Piazza della Stazione, and from there on foot, until we parted to reach our own home: each on either side of the station tunnel, the tunnel of Via Ferrante Aporti, so familiar, so fixed in my memory with the sound of that name.

Often we did not go our way immediately, finding ourselves in the grip of discussions of history or philosophy. Up and down along that tunnel, Antonia would walk me home, then I would walk her home, while we tried to decide whether Caesar or Napoleon had been great men or the scourge of mankind; or we'd rack our brains trying to strip a tree of all its "accidents" in order to reach the Aristotelian "substance" of things.

Then in the afternoon we'd be again together for the home assignments, while Mamma Carlotta would serve us all sorts of goodies for snack. I remember the first time I was introduced to American crackers. They were the mellow golden "Ritz crackers" that melted in your mouth. At Antonia's we were free to go through a whole box of them. We'd fill our mouth with a whole cracker, one after another - an unheard of luxury for me.

I remember the day when a refrigerator was added to Antonia's household - an expensive modern novelty – and the two of us started experimenting, freezing everything we could think of. We went crazy for milk ice cubes. One afternoon, having finished all the milk with our brilliant idea, we had to go and buy it at the store on the other side of the *naviglio*. In those days, the legendary *navigli* of ancient Milano still flowed through the city. With our bottle of milk in hand we went back on the bridge over the *naviglio,* and we stopped to meditate leaning on the parapet and watching the dark water flowing under us. Suddenly, struck by the same idea, we started the dare.

"What if we dropped the bottle in the naviglio?"
"I bet you wouldn't dare!"
"What would we tell Mamma Carlotta?"

We burst out laughing at the thought, then we looked at each other, and in a flash we understood each other. The milk bottle started its incongruous fall toward the black water of the canal and disappeared in its depth with a "plop." We felt exhilarated because we had dared to cross over into the absurd, into the gratuitous, with that sense of release felt when you break the laws of rationality.

Light-hearted, we returned to the weighty Greek translation awaiting us. I remember how my eyes sometimes strayed to my friend's cleavage already revealing the curves of her beautiful bosom. How I envied it when compared with my still adolescent flat chest. Well, I was a late bloomer, and Antonia was one year older. Soon I caught up to her, as was clear by the nicknames I was gaining among friends and occasional admirers: "Big Eyes", "Miss Hips", "The Mermaid on the Lake." How far were the years when I was simply known as "Little miss braids"! And yet....

At sixteen I was wearing my first high heels, I slept nights with a clothespin on my nose to make it thinner, I'd wrap myself in the green cape with black fringes inherited from Lalla Baldoni, and felt ready to conquer the world.

I'd climb in the *Citroën DS*, which to me seemed really "divine," belonging to the *"new man"* of that summer, "the Frenchman." And I thought I had reached the height of sophistication when he'd move in closer to light my cigarette with the electric lighter prodigiously pulled out red-hot from the dashboard of the car. But I continued to live love within myself. I put up with, rather than lived, my "first loves," having the disappointing sense of the almost-real, a mere approximation to what I aspired to, what I imagined. On the other hand, all I needed were two stars in the sky to arouse such a longing in me; or a patch of road to who knows where, when I'd see the last curve open up to the sea. I was fascinated by the unknown rather than the concrete.

There's Always the Sea...

I liked travelling in the backseat of the car when zio Marco would take nonna and me for a ride to Torino to visit relatives. The Milano-Torino in those days was still without any centre or border white lines, and it disappeared dangerously in the autumn fogs, a constant adventure, a mad journey into the unknown. My gaze wandered in the tendrils of fog curling among the rows of silver birches in the gentle Lombard landscape. Delicate silver hints in the dark green of the evening. In the peace and silence of my nook, I breathed in deeply the magic spell of the woods I went through as they scuttled off behind me, until my soul was saturated with their mystery. It was like going through one secret door after another, sensing the infinite and complex potential of my life, tasting the promise of what I would become. For an instant I could almost touch the future I held within me, a beehive full of sweetness. I reached out my soul to where something or someone was waiting to breach my solitude.

It was that time in life when feelings have the poignancy of the ineffable, the anguish of the unresolved and when, as the Indian poet says, *"The deeply buried "I" struggles to emerge into the conscious, to free itself of its complexities and come out into the light."*

To this day, I love travelling in the rear seat of a car, alone, gathering my thoughts, losing myself in them without distractions. But now life's mystery is diminishing, and space and time are losing the wonder of when it was I who filled their unrevealed with my imagination. Now that I have seen and now that I know, the tedious has filled all the mystery. Even the world has shrunk, and I travel with the impossibility of seeing things for the first time. The experiences and the wealth of information in the modern world give us the sense of knowing everything already, of having seen already everything. We are no longer able "to see," to anticipate, to be taken by surprise.

Those were the years when post-war Milano had a full revival of its intellectual life. Years of the happy marriage of "Piccolo Teatro" and Giorgio Strehler, with his famous production of Brecht and Goldoni. We lived it with such enthusiasm, we felt, we absorbed all that cultural fervour! The Shakespeare theatre seasons with Gassman and Albertazzi; Vittorio Gassman and Salvo Randone who took turns in the role of Othello and Jago; the famous pair of Anna Proclemer and Giorgio Albertazzi and their interpretation of Hamlet; The unforgettable Oedipus of Gassman.

And then there was the light-hearted mundane Milano of the musicals by Garinei and Giovannini at "Teatro Lirico," the "Massimo Dapporto Company" with the famous "Blue Belles" corps de ballet. Nino would take me to see them. You could sense in the air the need to come out of the rubble, to rebuild, to start living again. It was the time of Renato Rascel, with his blurred comic balderdash, and of Walter Chiari, with that adorable blend of the touching, naïve and sentimental - the anti-hero a bit battered and hesitant on the threshold of the new world. I remember him in a two-bit scene in which he starts telling enthusiastically the story of a film he likes. As the story unfolds, Walter Chiari becomes more and more emotional, and his voice breaks until he bursts out sobbing. At that point the long monologue comes to an end with *"Ma come mi sono divertito!"* (Oh, but I enjoyed myself so much*!)*- tears pouring down his face.

The greats of jazz were coming from America and we'd go and hear Duke Ellington, Benny Goodman, Louis Armstrong, Count Basie and Lionel Hampton with his magic xylophone. Louis Armstrong drew the crowd at the "Teatro Nuovo," with its young public gone wild and standing on the seats at the end singing as one, swept away by the excitement of his music and of his personality, flowing with him going down the aisles like a swollen river.

It became fashionable to collect jazz records, and those who had the most interesting ones or the latest would invite friends for musical matinées. Nino and I were not part of this group, with our hand-cranked music box, the stylus that constantly needed new needles, and a measly twenty "Seventy-eight" records, with a mixed repertoire of classic and popular music. A bit difficult to become knowledgeable in music. Then one day I heard about the latest arrival from the United States, the "long-playing." Religiously I took in this information and learned the sound of that word, insignificant to me, ready to show it off one day if I should decide to make an impression on a boy. *"Do you like the long-playing?"* convinced that it was a new kind of American music. My friend looked at me puzzled and muttered something embarrassed. A long time after I understood the blunder, but it was already too late to put it right. The friend had already vanished from the horizon.

Television was also making its appearance in the more well-to-do homes, and in the evenings the hapless possessor of a television set found the entire neighbourhood knocking at his door to watch the unusual spectacle and share the privilege. Naturally, Nino Martelli had one, which became an excuse to routinely invite me to his home. For that, I confess I didn't mind taking advantage of my sway over him. The treatment I received was indeed first class.

At the cinema we'd be moved by the great neo-realistic films of Vittorio De Sica, Rossellini, Risi and Lattuada. Nino had also subscribed us to the retrospective series given by the "Istituto Gonzaga," where they were showing the great American masterpieces: a season on Hitchcock or Frank Capra, the series with Ingrid Bergman and Elizabeth Taylor. I never tired of seeing *Notorious, Spellbound, A Place in the Sun*, or *Suddenly Last Summer*, where Elizabeth Taylor played with Montgomery Clift and the fabulous Katharine Hepburn.

I also had "afternoon at the movies" with Mamma Carlotta, and those were altogether different. Mamma Carlotta was a movie buff, and every once in a while she'd take Antonia, Giovanna and me, and herald, *"Should we do a movie marathon?"* Naturally, our reaction was always enthusiastic. During the entire afternoon we'd leave one cinema and go inside another, doing a binge of films echoing the style of Carolina Invernizio: *Buried Alive, The Deaf of Portici,* etc., the worst kind of Gothic fiction.

Then there was the phase "zia Mariuccia's style," with her own cinema tastes to which I had to submit whenever I went to visit with her in Vigevano. Although I had never wanted anyone to substitute my mother, zia came the closest to being a vice-mother, as I was for her the daughter she did not have. She called me her *cita*, her *masnà,* in Piedmontese dialect. We'd go out posing as mother and daughter. She'd link arms with me all proud and happy as well for the chance I gave her to step outside the monotony of her life. She could be herself with me, and she'd tell me about her gay youth, about the "elegant times" long gone. She was full of piquant tales, and she could bring to life for me the fascinating world of long ago, in which she wallowed with nostalgia.

Our sorties included the movies, in which she sought the equivalent of that brilliant and sentimental *glamour* of her past. She apparently found it in the films of Sonia Haney and Esther Williams, which she preferred because they enabled her to dream, to carry her into a world where she could forget the provincial dullness of the crass and vulgar Vigevano that she loathed. *"All of them such highfaluting pipsqueaks!"* she would comment ironically.

She had married making virtue out of social necessity, suffering the intolerable and unhappy lot in that era of being still nubile at the age of thirty. It was an arranged marriage with a "provincial" man, zio Piero, too good not to grow fond of, but who repressed the verve of zia Mariù in a life of dull monotony. He was the quintessential stay-at-home man, calm, quiet, whose exasperating patience roused even more the vexed and unfulfilled exuberance of my rebellious *zietta*. There were constant fireworks, with her needling him and his putting up with it, raising his patient bulging eyes to heaven.

"Never a trip, never a vacation!" complained zia. But whining did not suit her character, and she quickly cut it off with a sharp one-liner thrown out with a flash of her laughing eyes, ready to make fun of herself before anyone else. Self-directed irony resulted from knowing herself not very attractive with that excessively beaked nose on a lively gregarious face.

"A great viveur, your zio!" - she would tell me bitterly amused - *"As they say, you can tell the day by the morning. The first evening of our honeymoon, having just arrived at our hotel, can you imagine what is the first thing he orders before the ...'Ah, finally alone!'...a camomile tea!"*

Then she'd start humming: *"Per far l'amor ci vuol giudizio e le donne lo fan per vizio di ingannare la gioventù."*

There's Always the Sea...

(To make love you need good sense, and women do it for the fun to dupe the youth.)

When zio Piero died, zia also went into a decline, though she survived him by ten years. In spite of everything, they had loved each other during their long and troubled life. He left asking her to forgive him for not having given her the life she would have deserved. Now she was missing the best challenge for her mordant wit. It was as if that conflict, that constant clash with her companion had been a way to retain conscience of herself, to feel alive. With him gone, she had lost the counterpart in the dialectic of her own existence.

With the same tone half serious and half ironic, zia Mariuccia would also joke about her own poverty and her faded class. One day, taking out from the china cabinet an ancient coffee set from her great grandmother, she held in her hand a small cup all chipped. And almost to hide her embarrassment, she turned toward me and quipped,

"*I keep this one for when I offer coffee to the maid.*" I can still see the mischievous flicker of her eyes, veiled by a touch of bitter irony.

Hers was a brilliant Gozzano-style self-irony, the "*Twilight*" poet, whom she loved so much. She loved him precisely for the way he had to colour his own sentimentalism with a tinge of bitter irony, romanticizing the banality of everyday life. She liked to recite *La Signorina Felicita,* with whom she identified herself:

> *Signorina Felicita a quest'ora*
> *scende la sera nel giardino antico*
> *della tua casa. Nel mio cuore amico*
> *scende il ricordo ...*
> *A quest'ora che fai? Tosti il caffè,*
> *o cuci i lini e canti e pensi a me,*
> *all'avvocato che non fa ritorno?*
> *E l'avvocato è qui che pensa a te....*

(Signorina Felicita, night descends at this moment on the ancient garden of your house. Memories descend on my loving heart. What are you doing at this moment? Grinding coffee, or sewing laces, singing and thinking of me, of your lawyer who is not coming back? And your lawyer is here thinking of you.)

Like Signorina Felicita, like Gozzano, zia Mariù knew she was living an incurable romanticism in the daily grey dullness of her bleak provincial town. And she knew she was dreaming the impossible dream. In the mirror of her bright intelligence she could in fact perceive the commonplace of her own face and of her own fate, and she'd smile with her sad awareness of her own innocent Bovarysm. And so the lively flash of her eyes languished in the "twilight "of her life.

We got together also in Milano, when zia would come to replenish her wardrobe. Very rarely could she afford the boutiques. On those rare occasions, however, she'd beam like a young girl when the shop assistants would praise her about how shapely and young looking she still was. But I'd also catch a gleam of sadness in her eyes.   For her suits we'd go to *"Peppino il sarto"(* the tailor), as we called him. Peppino was a distant cousin of mine who had moved from Sicily looking for a better life, having to support two grown sisters destined to spinsterhood, and his old mother. He worked from dawn to dusk to support himself and *"the three witches of Windsor,"* as zia Mariù called them, one more tiresome and shrewish than the other. With that heavy burden, he certainly couldn't dream of taking a wife, though he was a handsome man with beautiful black eyes under bushy eyebrows.

"Peppino-the tailor" had become an innocent evasion for my Flaubertian *zietta*. I would watch the meeting of those two solitudes, of those two frustrated lives in a sad corner on the outskirts of Milano, in a squalid though clean apartment. I still see the cloud from the chain-smoking Peppino, which was to take him to an early grave; his back curved over the worktable covered with fabrics and chalks, his thin and hard-working fingers, stained by the nicotine, pushing to and fro the iron that seemed to hold the weight of a lifetime of bondage. And yet zia didn't seem to notice the smoke or the chatter of the witches, not even the greyness of it all. For those few hours her exuberant personality appeared to dissolve the world around her, and to find herself in a joyful understanding with Peppino through jokes and repartees and the breath of free spirits.

One day zia decided to find him a wife. She had her eye on an elderly single woman in Vigevano. The fateful day for the arranged meeting was set in the shiny salon of my home. Zia thought it was quite appropriate and romantic given that she was a piano teacher. But in the scene I recall, she is a moustached Valkyrie wresting from the piano Wagnerian outbursts to the consternation of poor Peppino lost in the armchair, who seemed to want to concoct with his cigarette, like with Aladdin's lamp, clouds of smoke in which to disappear. I don't know which had the greater effect, her whiskers on him, or his hefty three witches for her; all I know is that the marriage was not to be.

For me Vigevano meant also the bicycle races with zii and cousins down towards the Ticino River, picnics on its banks, and swimming in the river. In Vigevano, one was born and lived on the bicycle, and zia and the bicycle were as one. She would tell me about the rides in the countryside during the war, looking for food in some farm and coming under machine-gun fire from low-flying fighter planes; and the chilling encounter with a German column while she had three-year old Marco with her. But it was thanks to Marcolino that they were safe because the German officer was moved in seeing that beautiful child with his blond curls who, as he observed, *"semprare tetesco"("looket Cherman")*.

"Spring is here!" was the praise reserved for Antonia and me when we went out all dressed up for the new season. *"Spring is here!"* we'd exclaim when we noticed the change in the air that enwrapped us like a silken shawl. In Milano the sign of spring was also the kiosks of flowers all over the city now filled with colours. The woman at the kiosk would invite us to *"buy a patch of spring!"* as we passed. And for nonna and Mamma Carlotta we'd buy those nosegays of fresh spring colours called in fact "spring," or a bouquet of violets nestled in green leaves. It was the season of daffodils, of the *narcisate* at the Buco del Piombo - the traditional outing with zia Ida and Pinuccio, "going for daffodils." We'd pick armful of

them and come back to Milano with baskets spilling over. Will I ever see again those endless fields of daffodils, in swells of perfume, those hills embroidered up to the horizon with ivory-coloured corollas? I carry them in my mind's eye, my very own privilege.

That spring marked prelude to the end of *Liceo,* and the terrifying *Esami di Maturità:* "Baccalaureate Examinations." The exams covered the last three years of *Liceo Classico.* Our dining room was turned into my battlefield, with the table large enough to spread the mountains of books and dictionaries. That same table with its fringed shadows that had been with me since I was little, that had witnessed so many stages in my life: from the remote dinners with all my family, served by the maid with her white starched cap and the organza apron, to the unforgettable argument between mamma and papà; the miserable post-war meals; the Christmas festivities; the table games with nonna and Nino; the evenings listening to the radio; the readings in the black leather armchair. And now it was to provide a space while preparing myself to achieve the *"maturity"* of my eighteen years.

The mirror of the china cabinet beside the table is reflecting a pale doe-like face, which I deceive myself into thinking that it resembles that of my adored Audrey Hepburn. I was delighted by it, and I was bursting with life as I danced around that table, sliding over it to the rhythm of a jazz tune as I had seen her doing in a movie. Out of all that, what I have left now is a red Murano Venetian glass which I'm clasping in my hand, a shipwreck from the treasures of the china cabinet. I am clasping it, and it is as if I could grasp again all that which once surrounded it. The ring-a-ring-o'roses which would start up again on those quiet summer evenings. I can still hear rising from the street the singing voices of children,

"Oh quante belle figlie, Madama Doré, oh quante belle figlie...Son sette meraviglie, Madama Doré, son sette meraviglie..."

And the sound of the organ grinder that would then call me to the balcony to throw down some coins.

There's Always the Sea...

It's summer, the *III Liceo* is finally finished, and I am lost in my books in a scorching heat. I am now facing the famous terrible *"Esami di Maturità."* From my open windows, I'm kept company by Neapolitan songs coming from the neighbouring houses, or by the popular Florentine lyrics of Odoardo Spadaro.

"Firenze stanotte sei bella in un manto di stelle... Dorme Firenze sotto il manto della luna, ma dietro ad un balcone veglia una Madonna bruna..."

The voices of Milano, the voices of the courtyards: the noise of dishes at noon, the sound of a piano, the voice of Nicolò Carosio doing the play-by-play of a soccer game on the radio, the call of a mother - *"Maria!... come and take your zabaione."* Maybe another girl studying for the exams. At sunset, the shrill of the swallows.

The dark fascination of the tale of *Malombra* delivered by episodes on the radio - a prelude to the modern soap operas - would bring me the eagerly awaited break between "Oedipus Rex" and the monads of Leibniz. Then night would come, and I would still be up with my books with a huge coffee pot at my elbow. During the warmest days of that torrid July, when the high heels would sink into the soft tarmac of the streets, I kept the bathtub full of cool water, and every once in a while I would immerse myself in it seeking relief together with …Oedipus Rex.

The *"Maturità"* marked the end of my daily contact with Antonia. At university we took different paths, but our friendship did not end. We saw each other regularly for our endless chats to bring us up to date on each other's life, or to go over our memories of *Liceo.*

"Do you remember that day we played hooky?" We had mustered up the courage and had decided that we could not end our school career without knowing the thrill of skipping school. And so there we were exulting at the fairgrounds surrounded by couples of soldiers on leave and servant girls; I could not truly tell if more intoxicated by the terrifying falls with the roller coaster or by that feeling of complete freedom conquered with the courage of our transgression, of our rebellion against the rules.

If we were feeling low, we'd meet to go and get ourselves a *tiramisù*, our magic potion, guaranteed to pull us out of any and all doldrums and restore courage - a small glass of *Marsala all'uovo*. If things were really serious, all we had to do was call with the password "*I need to have a good cry,*" and the other was ready to offer her shoulder.

That time I was the one who launched the appeal, and Antonia came running. I poured out all the despair for my bitter disappointment in love. We were soothed by the voice of Pierre Brasseur coming from the record player, *"Bédélia avec ses long cheveux..."* Suddenly, we heard a loud explosion coming from the kitchen, at the other end of the apartment. We ran, scared at the thought of a gas explosion. Instead we found four hard boiled eggs exploded in the middle of the kitchen. In the heat of our conversation we had forgotten them on the stove. They were going to be our lunch.

I never went back to Cunardo in the summer. During the university years I would spend periods abroad to learn languages. The old group of friends broke up, each one going their own way, making other friends. Cunardo remained only in my mind, in my heart, in my memories, and in the brief autumn visits to my nonna.

What I still have of that period is the flavour of the best friendships, the ones of the adolescence, and the tolling of the church bells, slow, in the valley.

CHAPTER TWENTY-FOUR

I was attending university. Antonella Dallara and I had made the same choice, and so we both ended up dismayed among the impeccable hallways of the modern "Università Bocconi." A private university, it projected that tone of a well-off environment certainly missing in the run-down State universities. We would soon be moving about happily in the comfort of the luxurious student mess hall and the ease of a well-stocked and equipped library - inconceivable luxuries anywhere else.

The envy of "La Statale" (the State university) was understandable, and often "blood was spilled" in the best medieval goliardic tradition. One morning, in fact, we discovered that the statue of our founder, Luigi Bocconi, towering in the entrance, had overnight been covered in green paint by our rivals. We too turned green.

The prestige of the "Bocconi" rested primarily on Economics, but it also offered a department of Foreign Languages for the students of Commerce planning to work abroad. Typical of those years, while the Faculty of Economics had only boys enrolled, "Languages" ended up being filled by only girls. I can remember Eugenio Zanetti, one of the rare males enrolled in Languages because he wanted to be a journalist. He looked like a plucked rooster lost in a henhouse. Besides, he was also particularly ugly. Certainly our faculty was not like Architecture or Law, where it was common knowledge that the few girls enrolled in them did so in the hope of finding a husband, and none of them ever graduated.

My real calling would have been History and Philosophy, but due to my shyness, the idea of eventually teaching had scared me, and I had fallen back to Foreign Languages, though that was considered a step down after having done Classical Studies. That choice stayed with me as a blot on my record, as a stigma. Imagine, after being covered in the glory at "Parini," I did not choose Classics, but Languages! Only the fact that Dallara, one of the top students in class in the *Liceo,* had made the same choice made me feel better. And so, even if we had never been very close till then, Antonella and I became great friends.

I had chosen languages because of my love for travels. I could just see myself working on a big ocean liner going around the world.... Antonella, on the other hand, went for a less prestigious degree because her fiancé was urging her to get married. Her future was clear. It was useless to study for an important profession. Like any proper young bride in the 1950s, she could only aspire to be a wife and mother. And sure enough, in no time at all she was pregnant, and started spawning one baby after another, until having reached number four, the husband flew away to greener pastures.

They had known each other since she was fifteen years old. Ironically, she had been the object of the envy of all her classmates when Luca, a handsome young *Liceo* student, would come to meet her already in grade ten, when she came out of school; while the rest of us, especially I, were only ugly ducklings. She did try to complete her studies before getting married, but then, giving in to her fiancé's pressures, she got married before finishing her thesis. Almost immediately pregnant, she spent the nine months at her desk. As a result, she had a difficult delivery, almost losing her life in the process.

It was a typical drama of that period. She had sacrificed a great intellectual potential, every professional ambition, every possibility to fulfill herself as a person for the only man she ever loved her entire life. In the end, she found herself with no career and no husband, remaining alone to raise four children, without the possibility of starting a new life. He had set his sights on her because she was "a marriageable girl," "the girl next door," so different from those with whom he continued to have fun. He saw her as the innocent adolescent he would be able to mould into a devoted little wife and good mother of his children. He then found himself with a very smart woman, intellectually his superior, sure of herself and able to form her own independent opinions, and he couldn't forgive her for that. So he left her for a dumb but adoring bimbo.

"*Come, come, young ladies!*" our good janitor Alcide would urge us, always ready to give us a hand with our famous "university attendance record book," which had to have the professors' signature to indicate we had attended their lessons. It wasn't always possible to be present everywhere, and it wasn't always worth it to undergo such torture. In exchange for a smile or perhaps a small tip, Alcide collected the books and provided us with the professors' signatures.

I was beginning to learn to fend for myself. Studying four languages and their relative literatures all at the same time was not as easy as we had thought. In addition both Antonella and I had a household to manage, she with her husband and I with my brother. And so we came up with a clever form of cooperation. For the exams of the less important courses, the optional ones, one of us read the books necessary and underlined the essential parts, and the other studied by reading only those parts instead of the whole text.

I was slowly breaking out of the cocoon in which my brother and nonna were trying to keep me protected. Now I was a frightened first-year university student in the hands of the seniors of the Faculty of Economics, who took advantage of the goliardic tradition to show off their male chauvinism in front of the "newbies" from Languages, teasing and embarrassing them with vulgar practical pranks. But I had my "contacts," a suitor in Economics, and I made full use of my sway over him!

Claudio was perhaps the last knight from bygone days, and he came full tilt in my defense. As an "elder," he intervened with his authority to save me from undergoing the unpleasant rituals, and thanks to his prestige among the "elders," he managed to have me draw up a screed properly revised, purged of all the goliardic obscenities. Maybe I missed a piquant kind of fun, but my "innocence" was safe. In any event, the scurrility of the world at large was already at the gates. All too soon I would come to know many other forms of malice.

Those bug-eyes staring me from behind the desk during the Italian lessons gave me the creeps. It was Professor Gallardo, short and chubby like a little pig. I didn't know where to look, but sometimes I was so mad and outraged that I enjoyed returning the stare just to see him drool. My academic marks seemed to improve, and so I soon learned to use these secret weapons. But not everyone was harmless and easy to control as poor Gallardo, and at that time we girls were really defenseless and without recourse, far from being able to accuse those in authority of sexual harassment, as became possible in the feminist period.

There was a rumour around that the professor of geography was an old satyr. The girls would come out of the exam hall horrified. They told of how that spry little old man would end up literally under the table, and would touch them. We couldn't even conceive to report him! It was disconcerting though to see that most of the examinees would end up with top marks in the exam. Antonella and I escaped the danger by gamely deciding to enroll in the course of another professor considered the holy terror of the Faculty. Therefore, the geography exam that should have been easy, in a subject I had always loved for my curiosity to know the world, became a nightmare. The professor's hobby horse was unfortunately economic geography, and he was surly and hard. We ended up having to study the agricultural, mineral, handicraft and industrial resources of every single country, and the top mark slipped through our fingers. We saved our dignity, but our grade-point average dropped in the record book.

How distant seemed the times when our beloved professor Canesi would save us with his muttering from the obscenities of Plautus and Aristophanes now that our exuberant professor of French enjoyed embarrassing his feminine public wallowing in the picaresque realism of Rabelais, and gloating in calling our attention to the "*loud pissing*" of Gargantua. It was the Fifties, and we found ourselves still vulnerable in the hands of a male chauvinist society. Naturally, the professors were all males.

There's Always the Sea...

When I enrolled at "Bocconi University," I had barely the time to have an inkling of what had been the "old guard." I heard of the death of the legendary professor Castiglioni, a leading light in Classical Studies. He had been my mother's professor at "Liceo Parini." I remember, however, that I too had a brush with the big names of our times. Antonella and I would go out of our way to ensure ourselves a front-row seat in the large auditorium where professors like Mario Fubini and Francesco Flora came to give a series of lectures over the course of a few weeks. Fubini held the chair at the University of Torino, and Flora at the University of Bologna, but for a brief period they'd come to Milano to spill their "pearls of wisdom" for us at the "Bocconi." It was a big event and we were all excited.

What a letdown however the first time we saw the small and rickety figure of Fubini enter the lecture hall! We literally saw him disappear behind the high desk. All curled up, with glasses perched on his nose buried in a book, he was talking to himself. We couldn't relax and enjoy the lesson also because his voice flowed flat and droning, inducing us to sleep. We could barely manage to concentrate and catch all his words, while desperately writing them in our notebook. It was a course on "the Divine Comedy." When we re-read our notes at home, however, we were spellbound by the intensity and the beauty of what he had said, and the world of Dante was magically opened to our eyes. Professor Flora was just the opposite, and the usually heavy "Promessi Sposi" became a fascinating novel through a powerful flow of words whose tone was colourful and resonant. Terse and polished just like the city of Torino the first, exuberant and passionate like the city of Bologna the second.

We also studied American literature, and everything which represented the Old World was set jarringly against the new and shocking face of the New World. The face was that of Charles Haines, "Professor Haines." Stocky, exuberant, unpredictable, rebellious, he brought a rush of colourful originality in the stale machinery of our academic traditions. He quickly became our hero. At ease with students and a womanizer, you could spot him standing surrounded constantly by clusters of female students, like a ruffled rooster, his red bushy hair around an open and bright ruddy Scottish face, not indifferent to the pleasures of a whiskey.

More than for his academic merits, as incredible as it may sound, professor Haines went down in history for his success in *Lascia o Raddoppia,* the popular TV quiz show at the end of the Fifties, led by the very popular Mike Bongiorno, just arrived from America with his exotic Americanized name. It was the first of a long series of similar games which became a great success, lasting till nowadays.

As if the fact of participating in a TV show of that kind wasn't enough to *épater le bourgeois,* during the questioning the bizarre professor used to appear inside the glass-enclosed kiosk with a showy multi-coloured parrot perched on his right shoulder. He cleaned up the game pot showing off his formidable memory. For days and days we followed the escalation of questions and answers, and of the money risked in the wager. Then, the grand finale, the last question, which was to become famous: the year, the day, the hour and the minute of the San Francisco earthquake. Like the great showman he was, though he must have known very well the answer, he doled it out with the eyedropper to create greater suspense. He started by giving the exact year, then silence followed as the seconds ticked away ... We all, his female students and admirers were following this with bated breath ... Then he gave the day, followed by the scream of the public ... *"Now the hour?!"* - *"How can he possibly know?"* And the seconds were passing ... Even the parrot seemed to be twitching with excitement ... Finally, the hour and the minutes were stated in a dead silence. A pandemonium exploded in the theatre, while millions of *Lire* rained down on him. Professor Haines had won *Lascia o Raddoppia.*

I don't know how I ended up being invited to his home at the end of the academic year. I had indeed a crush on him, but it was just a mere intellectual infatuation. I went with Antonella for propriety sake. Of that occasion I still have a reminder: two records of Ives Nat, a phenomenal French pianist who had died very young and not much renowned, whom Professor Haines, a lover of classical music, introduced to me, and then wanted me to keep the records. The two handsome green covers are still visible in my old collection of LPs, elegant case to an exceptional interpretation of Beethoven's sonatas, and token to an exceptional encounter which otherwise would have disappeared in the fogs of oblivion.

On the threshold of my twenties, my interest for the opposite sex still floated blindly in an abstract sphere. I was becoming gradually more aware of the attention of men, and it pleased me. Now and then I allowed myself a soft spot for someone, but always in the realm of the unattainable, as if I didn't want anything to become real. I loved my freedom and independence, and I was very hard to please. In those years it was still possible to find museum pieces like me, romantically waiting for "the great ideal," the man who would have fulfilled all my dreams, the one man who would have shared them. I knew that as soon as I saw him I would have recognized him, because it would have been quite different from the lukewarm reactions my admirers had provoked in me till then. I wasn't ready to compromise. At times it was hard to wait, difficult to refuse, as with that journalist at Antonella's wedding - immediate liking, intense wooing by him. He was married.

"Today I'll make bread, tomorrow I'll make wine, and the day after my little princess I'll find."

I would sing to myself while I slaved to shine the floor of the salon, trying to calm down and resign myself. It was my magic formula. It assured me that my hopeful biding my time would be rewarded just like for the leprechaun waiting for his princess in the fairy tale. And so, like him I sang and slaved... and still lived in the world of nursery rhymes.

The game was quickening, the moths were circling around the flame. Who was the flame and who was the moth? I watched and noticed, and was watched and noticed. The moths kept circling. Who would burn first? They were Nino's friends: ex *Liceo* classmates, and now all attending university at Industrial Chemistry. A whole bevy of them would come to see my brother. They'd spend whole afternoons discussing social, political or philosophical questions. And it was as if suddenly the floodlights had been turned on the stage, and I had passed from being invisible to being centre stage. For them, I had always been an insignificant little girl, yet now from the advantage of their greater age, they looked at me with respect. And I was enjoying myself.

I enjoyed seeing Serra bang his head against the dining room chandelier when he'd jump up as soon as I came in with the coffee tray. I'd laugh seeing Matteotti arrive on roller skates from across the city. I'd laugh seeing Giberto Capriotti, with a passion for mountain climbing, always dressed as if he had to climb a mountain then and there. He'd get out of his Land Rover with heavy "tanks," those hobnail boots, and move in his typical forced march, all doubled over, with a mountaineer stride even along my hallway. I loved hearing about the adventures of *"Gigi the dandy,"* as his friends called him, the less frequent visitor and certainly not my brother's favourite. He would drive around in his spanking new red *Giulietta*. We had just recently seen a preview of it in the Alfa Romeo showroom at the Galleria of via Manzoni, and my brother and I left our hearts there.

Gigi must have had a lot of money and he showed it with his voluble attitude. But he did it with self-irony, and so made it easy for us to forgive him. If he happened to spot a beautiful girl while dashing in his red racing car along the streets of Milano, he would make a dramatic screeching stop next to her and declaim,

"I am Apollo, the god of Love. If you climb in my chariot of fire, I'll take you to the kingdom of the Sun."

I'd never had the privilege of seeing him in his "chariot of fire" on a street, but I doubt he would have deemed me worthy of such an offer. Nor would I have fallen for it.

I was far more intrigued by our childhood friend, Mirko Baldoni, having now turned into a vigorous young man who in the warm Milanese summers would arrive on his roaring motor scooter, with the sleeves of his immaculate white shirt rolled over his sun-tanned arms. That sight melted my youthful sensitivity. But Mirko could only see me as a little sister and he was always very paternal and condescending with me. At most I was able to have him take me to the movies … in the parish film hall in *via San Gregorio!* In vain I tried to find some sentimental suggestions in the retrospective of old movies like *Brute Force,* in which Harry Morgan, still some years from his seasoned interpretation of the good-natured Colonel Potter in *M.A.S.H.,* played the Nazi who tortured his victims to the sound of Wagner; or *The Big Knife,* in which Jack Palance is slowly pushed to commit suicide. Oh, such fun! Meanwhile, in vain I pined away in silence.

Finally, discouraged by my useless longing, I turned my attentions to the dusky Pietro Sormani. After all, hadn't I vowed back in my *Liceo* days that I was destined for a "red"? Noble features, well-born, proud, how could he not strike my fancy? I looked forward to his coming, I'd run to open the door, I displayed all the charm I possessed. But in terms of results, I felt to be no more than a small fly alighted on his sleeve.

After attending Journalism School, he became the special correspondent in London for the *Corriere della Sera.* Three cheers, hurrah! I had to go to England as well for my studies, and, as I expected, he gallantly offered to escort me around London. "*This is it.*" I thought in a transport of joy. "*This is the moment.*"

I got to know London as I could never have done by myself, from the most prestigious locales to the most dubious corners in Soho. But Sormani, ever the gentleman, not once did he fail in his role of proper escort of his friend's younger sister. How frustrating! But I had fun. I remember the feeling of the "forbidden" when we went around the city's more colourful and typical pubs. I'll never forget the "Old Owl," covered with its grim layer of dust and spider webs, real ones, allowed to gather naturally over the years following the criteria of the most original British black humour, or rather Gothic taste. Everything was definitely shocking and meant to be, and made me sing the praises of the originality and nonconformist spirit, clearly highly eccentric, of the British.

Sormani took on a more human dimension in my eyes when he pulled the biggest gaffe of his career. I don't remember for what reason he decided not to attend a concert by the famous opera singer Maria Callas, of which he was to send a review. Nonetheless, he did send his review on time the following morning to the office of *Il Corriere* in Milano, remarking on the great success of the concert. The problem was that Callas had not been able to give the concert because of a sore throat!

It was Franco Faveri who restored the balance to the ups and downs in my sentimental life. His persistent wooing provided me with a season of sparkling social high life, with concerts, theatre and balls. I was on cloud nine when he invited me to the most sought after event of the season in Milano: the Press Club Ball. We had to go in costume and "La Scala" had even offered the use of its theatrical wardrobe. I went to the ball in the dress worn by Callas in *La Traviata*!

One scene stands out vividly in my memory, the amazing sight of the gangly Franco Faveri wavering across a room like a flamingo. He was coming awkwardly all askew, waving a sock in one hand, the bow tie dangling from his neck, as he called for his mother to help. He was getting ready while Nino and I were already waiting for him in the living room of his house, where we had this unexpected apparition. Son of an English woman, he had inherited the attractive Mediterranean features of the father and the Anglo-Saxon spastic movements of the mother. He looked as if he were constantly sliding on slippery ground, his arms and legs swimming in the air, in a desperate plea for help in his perennial state of confusion. How did he manage to carry out his duties as a judge, following in his father's footsteps? At a certain point I let him slide in another direction, unable to take him seriously. I never found out where he finally landed.

I had conquered then my place in the sun, entering once again in my brother's life. He took me with him in his many trips to France, Germany and Switzerland. He could afford it because by then he was doing laboratory research for the renowned Montecatini Company. He was working on polymers with the future Nobel Prize winner Giulio Natta, with whom he later co-signed some patents. I sadly remember him when, during his health decline, he'd ask himself whether his discoveries would have damaged the world, polluting it with the spread of plastic. He was never to see it, his illness having interrupted his young life and an outstanding brilliant career.

I had just the time to savour the life full of adventure and interesting experiences that he wanted to give me. We'd go to Switzerland to purchase gasoline, chocolate and cigarettes, braving some funny situations with the frontier customs officers if, as usual, we had gone over the limit allowed. Nino banked on my feminine charm. We would go to Germany in search of the latest blond beauty to have caught Nino's fancy. I recall that white soft swollen mound of the quilt on which Nino and I collapsed dead tired after a long marathon drive from Milano. It was the typical German eiderdown forty centimeters deep. We woke up after a long sleep on a quilt as flat as a pancake. Dismayed and worried, we tried in vain to bring it back to its original condition before it fell into the hands of the terrible Frau who had welcomed us to the guesthouse with the manners of a Vercingetorice. Kussnacht, "Night of the Kiss," we were not to remember that German hamlet for its gothic charm and its romantic allure, but rather for the bellyfuls of *Wurst und Sauerkraut* at the "Krokodil," where the locals drained liters of beer in the wide open maws.

We'd make quick trips to the *Côte d'Azur,* the French Riviera. It was the period of Juliette Greco and Sidney Bechet, and of the existentialist *caves.* How alive I felt in those smoky dens! My every cell seemed to vibrate to the sound of that voice and that sax. We were in unison with all the youth of that generation... intensely conscious of the "existential question." We adored Sartre and Kierkegaard. We fed on Françoise Sagan and her scandals, and ... "we loved Brahms."

We christened our new Austin Morris, bought by my brother around Christmas, by going to Nice to spend New Year's Eve. For ages we had daydreamed about that elegant white silhouette with a daring red interior in the large showroom under the porticos in Piazza San Babila, until we felt it ours. The money put aside bit by bit from Nino's salary was just enough. Our car had to be English of course, not an ordinary Italian one. And so it was. To put it to a real test, we refused to pass into France using a normal tunnel. No, Nino decided we would defy the San Bernardo Pass.

The year's end, with 20° below, found us climbing for kilometers up a mountain, sliding on ice in a narrow passage between walls of packed snow. Not another soul on the road. Only the two of us and the white of the snow as far as the eye could see. At a certain point we began to think that perhaps we had taken the wrong road. Not a road indication or a sign of life anywhere. At the umpteenth turn, finally we thought we might have reached the top of the pass. There it was: a big road sign, showing in the middle of a red triangle… a huge black exclamation mark! - *"Boh!"* it seemed to be the indication given, the right comment on our folly. And there we were, up there in the middle of nowhere, laughing our heads off like two fools.

But the New Year's Eve dance was a great success. A unique experience for me to spend that special evening in a public place, never to happen again. I remember the euphoria in sharing the excitement of celebrating the end of the year with a crowd of perfect strangers, for us even foreigners. We were welcomed in a warm embrace of effervescent French in the middle of noisy firecrackers, noisemakers and a whirlwind of streamers, which gave us a sense of friendly exuberance. We made friends with the great mime Marcel Marçeau, who had enchanted us with his magic during the evening.

And there were the bright lights of the casinos to which Nino introduced me. I got to know them all: San Remo, Campione, Cannes, Montecarlo. I delighted watching the ability and the elegant moves of the croupiers; I reveled in the refined atmosphere, heightened by the sound of the French language which I loved. I felt like a grand lady as I glided on the green carpets between the exciting glimmers of the roulettes. That piling up of coloured chips, the cabalistic mystery of the numbers, their fickle chance which I dared fascinated me. The little ball darted, *"Rouge, Pair et Passe."* And I would win. I was very lucky and the thing exhilarated me. I didn't know just then that for my brother it would be the start of a dangerous slippery slope that would drag him toward an abyss in which the family jewellery and silverware would disappear... *"Rien ne va plus"*....

On the occasion of the *Fiera di Milano* every April, my cousin Antonino would arrive from Palermo. This way I had another escort who would vie with my brother to entertain me. In fact, a degree of rivalry arose between the two, a bit of jealousy towards me. But for me, this meant other interesting experiences. My cousin would take me to "La Scala," but I couldn't quite accept lyric opera when I'd see a prosperous Renata Tebaldi balancing on the walls of Castel Sant'Angelo while singing out the love of Tosca for the handsome Cavaradossi, he too played by a stout Giuseppe Di Stefano. I preferred to go to the opening nights in the most luxurious cinemas. I saw for the first time the famous movies in 3 D. As we entered the cinema, we were given a pair of special dark glasses, through which the screen took on depth and highlight. In other words, we'd see the scenes in three dimensions. The public, however, turned into a funny bunch of racoons watching the show. Maybe that's why the novelty wore off.

That year my cousin arrived just in time for the great event of the 1960 movie season: *La dolce vita* of Fellini. My brother had refused to take me because "not suitable" for me. My cousin, scandalized by such *pruderie,* dug in his heels, and with the authority of his ten years seniority luckily he won out. I don't recall having had my innocence troubled. What I remember is that I was enthusiastic, and that I understood the drastic decision of that intellectual father who kills his children and then himself in his desperate refusal to raise them in a corrupted world, which he sees without hope. When we are young, I think we all go through a certain moment in which, whether our life is happy or not, on an abstract level we feel compelled to view it through the philosophical filter of a Schopenhauer type existential pessimism.

And then there were always the Baldonis, staunch and stable Baldonis, the protective wall in my life. I was now old enough to be accepted by Lalla as a friend and confidant. I would share in her romantic flings, like the strong infatuation for a young engineer building dams in Egypt, who dragged her in a series of adventures while she followed his footsteps on the African continent. And after that doomed "great love," the inevitable lapse into a compromise - the nice quiet young man, the ideal suitor, who brought her to the threshold of the wedding.

Everything was already bought and the house was ready, but some guardian angel saved her with a tube of toothpaste. When Lalla noticed that her future husband meticulously emptied the tube of toothpaste starting methodically from the bottom and rolling it with absolute precision, she recoiled, thought it over, and ran away. The hapless young man was left in the lurch with toothbrush in hand, but Lalla wisely escaped a marriage of pernickety greyness and boredom. Lucky her that she read in time the signals! Because it's a fact that one can foresee how it's going to be, the signals are clearly there. The problem is that often we see them as things of little consequence, which we may even change by the force of love. Instead, later, they grow into unbearable defects. But by then, it's too late.

After an unhappy love and one happily avoided, Lalla spent the rest of her life calm and serene together with her mother whom she adored, and with whom she forged a perfect symbiosis until the death of the old lady.

The decline of signora Baldoni was slow. Gently, bit by bit, she vanished in a world of her own. She would sit in her wicker armchair on the green patch of grass in front of their old villa in Valsassina. The soft plaid on her knees. The devoted daughter at her side.

During one of my visits from Canada, I went to see her. With her usual maternal warmth she asked about my life. The usual ritual between me and signora Baldoni. I was her *Dudi*. But since my marriage, Lalla had tried to tell her that I was no longer *Dudi*, that now my name was Giusy. And so now I was laying at her feet all about the life of Giusy in Canada. And she'd listen and ask me,

"*Are you happy, Giusy?*" And I would talk... "*And how is Giusy?*" And I would tell... "*And how is Dudi?*"

Smiling I would tell her… *"And how is Giusy?"…"And Dudi, how is she?"….*

In her vague understanding of things had she perhaps sensed a deeply hidden truth? Two independent moments of my life which could not merge; two persons within me that could not co-exist. Giusy began to exist at the expense of Dudi, who moved away from me. She had not been able to withstand the difficult years to come, the emotionless Canadian world. I had had to leave her behind together with my memories, in a world that no longer belonged to me. She had remained there, next to signora Baldoni, who was now crying. And I was crying as I left.

"The wise man is only a child who regrets having grown up," tells us the poet Cardarelli.

CHAPTER TWENTY-FIVE

How gently into the very depth of my soul settles that elm-reflecting pool of water I now gaze at. A drop falls, it forms a circle which slowly expands, overlapping other circles that expand and die, like an echo of distant images. A glimmer of things seen already, of moments already lived surfaces from my unconscious, and I'm whelmed with the pathos of days long gone.

It was the summer of 1956, first year university. Lalla had suggested I go to Cannes.

"If you want to spend a summer in France to learn the language, I suggest the College of Cannes."

"Cannes?!"

I responded, astounded by the absurdity of the proposal of a study holiday in such an expensive locality; it brought to mind the fashionable *Côte d'Azur*, the expensive resorts on the glamorous French Riviera, the casino; and I couldn't believe it. But Lalla insisted that it was an economically affordable place and that she had spent there a marvellous summer. And it turned out to be so for me as well. In that small building, beyond the railings, in the thick vegetation of the walled-in park, I felt a great sensation of freedom and adventure. For the first time, I had gone by myself beyond the borders of my country and beyond the metaphorical boundaries of my domestic cocoon between nonna and my brother. I discovered other realities and saw the world from new perspectives.

I remember how astounded I was to hear someone speak of Proust's homosexuality and of the ambiguous lives of the *Poètes maudits* - things which my professors in Italy had never dared mention. I'd follow somewhat hesitantly my classmates in their nightly outings, and one night I found myself in a dance club where to my shock I gawked at all the women dancing with each other. I struggled to filter and dignify the thing through my classical knowledge of Lesbo and the poetry of Sappho. I took it all in, I registered, and all of a sudden I felt emancipated; but I chose as a steady friend Amedea, outgoing and lively, but who, in spite of any free-association with her name, was a well behaved girl from a "good Milanese family" with whom I felt at home.

Cannes, the promenade on the *Croisette*, chancing upon famous actors like Jean Marais, Danielle Derrieux, Michèle Morgan. I considered myself in the centre of the "real world." We mingled with young men from other countries, which gave us the sensation of having new worlds opening to us. With the look of young school girls who had skipped class, Amedea and I moved deftly between one date and another, trying to behave like girls sure of themselves without losing our "feathers." Those days, the relationship between a boy and a girl began with a long and discreet period of courting, which allowed a few days of pleasant company before the inevitable moment when, as we said then, we'd begin to *limonare*, or with the more elegant anglicized term, *flirtare,* which for me was the moment to make …a strategic retreat.

Days, I still remember, when I felt I was living my life to the fullest. Impalpable moments in which, being young, the most insignificant experiences are perfused with incredible vitality. Looking back, they just reflect a luminous innocence.

Swept by the wind on the Red Rocks, as I say goodbye to Mat, the blonde Swede; or as I daringly follow the dangerous curves along the French Riviera with my hands on the steering wheel of a car for the first time in my life. It was the convertible of the cocky American who was having fun daring me while he controlled the pedals. I felt alive like the wind in my hair. The bold Philip lost me, however, when he shocked me at the door of the College by grabbing me for the American custom - as he defined it - of the "goodnight kiss." Or the moment of the self-conscious good-bye with the shy Belgian, Gerard, who had been helping me prepare for the French literature exam. He had finally found the courage to declare himself, and he left me as a keepsake of his love the book which had failed to be our go-between. I was living my artless, liberated "salad days."

The foreign boys were particularly considerate and careful with us, maybe because they felt intimidated by their ignorance of our "code." The Italians, on the contrary, encouraged by the fact they were far from home, felt free to ignore the code which was well known to them, and which advocated a certain behaviour with the girls of good upbringing.

Amedea and I chanced upon a couple of these, with whom we ended up spending an unusual evening. Rich "daddy's boys" showing off a tasteless arrogance. Perhaps to establish right away a mood in keeping with their intentions, they took us to a smoky and shady night club. The ambiance was thick and heavy in every sense. Amedea and I looked at each other appalled and we got ready to be on our guard. Before our unbelieving eyes, the evening show began: a daring striptease. It was the first such experience in my life. Amedea and I didn't know where to look. We couldn't bear it very long. In common accord we got up together and together we moved toward the exit. Our escorts followed us rather surprised and put out. Then suddenly, on our way home, as we were crossing Juan-les-Pins, something gave us the best idea of how to liven up and save the evening, while at the same time make fun of them. In a nice park along the sea, we saw the pavilions and the amusement rides of a wonderful fairground. A look between me and my friend was enough, and we let the boys know that we wanted to go there. The two cocky Don Juans ended their evening on bumper cars. And Amedea and I had a world of fun at their expense.

The shrewish Madame Fleury was the headmistress of the college. Unheralded, her screech of disapproval would reach us, *"Mais non, non, mes jeunes-filles, non, non, non ...Faut pas...Faut pas!"*

In keeping with her name, her figure emanated a scent of violets. Her frivolity was, however, only apparent, because in effect it covered a core of intransigence and harshness which seemed to concentrate on her pointy nose. *"Faut pas... Faut pas!"* But she was hardly able to discourage our exuberance, and in the college a playful mood of intrigue and subterfuge reigned supreme.

The height of this mood was reached when the *Montecuccoli*, one of the training ships for officers of the Italian Navy docked, with on board the cadets of the Naval Academy of Livorno. A swarm of white uniforms invaded the city, and the female college became like honey for the bees. Cannes was transformed into a huge reception room where to arrange encounters. They were everywhere. We'd meet them at the beach or on the streets, and we'd arrange to go dancing or to an open-air cinema in the evening - naturally, always in groups.

While we were still finishing our dinner in the college dining hall with the great glass wall which looked on to the park, we could see appearing in the dark, like moths attracted by the lights, the white silhouettes peering through the glass in search of their evening date. And of course we had to show surprise and righteous indignation, stifling our laughter to avoid the rage of the headmistress who would have jeopardized our evening.

One evening, when we were late for our agreed meeting time, the famous potatoes croquettes, my favourites, ended deftly in my open bag under the table... *"Il ne faut pas!"*

The croquettes, for me in any case, never ran out because I had my connections in the kitchen. His name was Ardil, the Algerian gofer boy, the colour of honey, the first non-white I had seen in my entire life, all legs and arms, and huge eyes under his curly hair. The whole kitchen crew would poke fun at him because they knew he had a soft spot for me. He'd pinch the *frites* for my sake, while in the morning he'd have waiting for me a double portion of my favourite yogurt. But since he was the mascot of the college, he was forgiven all. He called me "Ginà," convinced that I looked like Lollobrigida. Those were the years when *Lollo* was still number one internationally, before Sofia Loren would replace her. Lollomania was all the rage in France as well, and everybody sang the praises of Ginà.

We were on tour in Avignon when at the entrance to the Papal Palace I heard the milling crowd begin to grumble noisily. Someone began to yell *"Ginà! Ginà!"* and the people began to crowd around me. A few curls had been enough to fool them.

I recall that glaring white in the sequence of sundrenched halls, leading into the garden through the open French doors; that glaring white under the sun-filtered pergola. I ambled blinded in the swarming of white uniforms, held back by my shyness. It was the official welcoming party offered by the Italian Consul General to the sailors of the *Montecuccoli*. A number of girls from our college had been invited. I was moving around searching. I was sure he had to be there in that display of masculine elegance. I was sure that all at once I would have recognized "him." But I did not see him. Destiny, however, was waiting for me just around the corner.

That evening a classmate asked me to take her place. She had promised to go out for a night swim in a group, but she didn't feel up to it anymore. And I saw him. It was as if he had stayed there waiting just for me. We stayed together the entire evening as if no one else existed around us. We'd glide and played in the dense and dark water like two dolphins. We'd chase each other on the still warm sand. We were happy. Time slipped through our fingers. Midnight struck as in the fairy tale, but this time the fateful hour was for the prince who had to be back on the ship. Eight of us piled in one taxi to accompany our young naval officers to the port. The guards were waiting for them and came to the car urging them in no uncertain terms. But no one dared to budge. Impeccably dressed in their snow-white uniforms, they were hiding behind their back the *corpus delicti*, the wet underwear they had used to go swimming, for lack of swimsuits. The day after, they were all on picket duty onboard, all leaves revoked.

It was the last day. The *Montecuccoli* would have resumed its voyage, taking my dream away. I had only one last chance to see Achille. What better name to match my adolescent tastes?! It carried the echoes and the fascination of the classical tale read in "the Iliad." I could already see myself as a new Briseide, Achille's sweet and faithful slave. That day the ship was open to tourists, and the college had also programmed a visit. But Amedea and I were not included in the group; it was the turn of those girls who had not gone to the party given by the Consulate. Wasted were all my pleas to the inflexible Madame Fleury. But I didn't give up. Together with Amedea, we rented a pedal boat and we reached the ship at anchor. Achille saw me from the bridge and we said our goodbyes. I left sick at heart.

The excursion to Provence was the grand finale of our stay in Cannes, and I threw myself into it heart and soul. Arles, Les Baux, Aix-en-Provence, that unique concentration of colours, aromas, sensations - the landscape that I would have later recognized in the paintings of Matisse, Van Gogh, Cézanne. Aix was for me a place of strong emotions, for there was where my French origins had their roots; it was Aix that my noble great-great grandmother had left to go as a young bride in Italy. I wandered amid the magnificent palaces of the '600s, along the ancient Cours Mirabeau, where perhaps Maman Cécile, "la Baronne," had her promenades in her horse-drawn carriage. In those solitary untroubled corners, among fountains and monuments, up those impervious uphill climbs, along the majestic tree-lined boulevards, it seemed that time had stopped in a distant past which emanated the mysterious charm of my own secret story.

The sleepy provincial stillness of Arles was shattered by our arrival in shorts. *"Les shorts! Les shorts!"* the boys would cry out, seeing us walking on the streets in our shorts. *"Les shorts! Les shorts!"* cried out the men following us up a spiral staircase which Amedea and I had climbed on as we explored the inn where we were staying. We had been drawn by some dance music coming from above our rooms, and we had discovered this hidden staircase which led us to a large hall where they were celebrating a wedding with singing and dancing. As soon as we appeared, more amused than embarrassed and followed by our pursuers, among that happy country-style feast, the clamour increased, and to the shout of *"Les shorts! Les shorts!"* we were promptly dragged in a whirlwind of dances. I have no idea where Madame Fleury was at that moment.

I returned from that summer in France with a palette full of colours and perfumes, of memories and fascination.

"Da la cintola in su tutto 'l vedrai" (Him upwards from the waist thou mayest behold") could sum up my relationship with sex in those years. Dante's Farinata degli Uberti and I would have made a perfect couple. Hands, face, manly shoulders, eyes more than satisfied my imagination. For me there was nothing more erotic or suggestive than the scene of the glance between Gregory Peck and Ingrid Bergman in *Spellbound* - those eyes framed in a close-up, with all the intensity of the anticipation (but anticipating what exactly?) losing themselves in each other. Sexuality was for me represented by the powerful sensuality of Jennifer Jones in *Duel in the Sun,* and in Gregory Peck's intense passion. I conceived attraction on a sensual level, passionate, not really erotic. And there I was, unwitting and unprepared, head over heels in my love story. It marked the end of a carefree age. As the poet says, I experienced *"all the nuances of joy and pain."*

Ah, the complete unconditioned happiness which can be experienced only at that age, when everything explodes at once within you. After, we'll know other happy moments, perhaps even more real, deeper, but never will they encompass all our being. We will have seen too much by then, suffered too much. Never again will we obtain the primal condition, that total freedom of heart and mind, that unconditioned availability of the self which wanes with each passing year.

I savoured the purest and most intact of joys when I managed to find the address of Achille and we reconnected. He would come from Livorno, I from Milano, and we'd meet in Genova. We were happy everywhere, strolling along the sea, up on the hills, along the city streets. We didn't need anything else. We walked in one single dimension, in one single unit of intensity, in our own unique seclusion, that of our happiness.

Between meetings, those airmail letters with the tricoloured borders which peeked out of my mail box next to the concierge's lodge were sufficient nourishment. I'd be on the lookout for them from the kitchen balcony. I'd see them sticking out of the slit, and I'd rush down. The concierge began to share cheerfully in the game, and make a personal delivery at my door, celebrating the event and announcing it to me by an extended ringing of my door bell. He would hand me the letter with a smile and not a single word. Ineffable moments which still touch me from that far off past. Like that coming home on the train, where the happiness radiating from me must have been so visible that people were looking at me aware of something extraordinary, and men approached me as if to ferret out the secret.

Many months went by. Then, the long awaited vacation in Santa Margherita came with such unbelievable anticipation, and yet it found me unprepared. The days spent at the beach, the strolls, the long evening hours dancing would end, as he said, in a "guerrilla," in which I struggled to defend myself from his unexpected assaults. It marked the end of the long romance. Brainwashed by my catholic upbringing, I was rebelling. The meetings became less frequent. After a long silence on his part, I called his hotel. I heard laughter of women in the background. The following time I was told he had left that very morning. I had been "abandoned," but not …"seduced." I should have been proud of myself. I had duly "saved" myself for the required bridal chastity. But the tearing of my heart was devastating. Resignation and compromises changed my life from then on, certain that I would never find my "true" love again.

The following year it was Paris. My Paris of the summer of 1957. If only I could recapture that atmosphere, that feeling in the air, but especially that vibrating of every fibre in my being. It was the Paris of the '50s, the "real" Paris, the one that no longer exists, but most especially, it was the Paris of my 20 years of age. If only I were allowed to dive once again in the Paris of my 20's! Never will I see her like that again.

That glimpse of the "Sacre Coeur" that would appear unexpectedly in the night, a scar of white light at the end of a dark alley, caught my breath every time; a spellbinding vision for me. The multi-coloured whirlpool of Place du Tertre, the teeming bustle of artists, the moment of my portrait, the meeting with the artist who would give me those glimpses of Paris to take with me, the honour of being invited to his atelier, all this gave me the illusion to capture a last breath of the *Montmartre "d'antan,"* with the great poets and painters still wafting in the air. I saw all of their works later, and it was a *coup de foudre*. I drank them in with my eyes and with my soul in obsessive visits to "Jeu de Paume," where modern art was then on display, and which was the temple of the *Impressionists*. With a thirst for beauty, I basked immersing myself in the flowery fields of Seurat, barely suggested by the light and by the flecks of colour, or in the glowing forms of Van Gogh. All the charm of Provence was brought to life in the shadows of the rows of trees of Cézanne, in that quest for the sun, in those large clouds, in the evening's melancholy.

Together with my classmates from "Bocconi" I was staying at the "Cité Universitaire." Between lessons we'd go strolling along Boulevard Jourdan, alive with cafés full of foreign students from the *Cité*. For me it was an exotic world. The feeling of having gone beyond my narrow horizon was exhilarating. It felt as if I were embracing the whole world being in contact with such a variety of races and facial traits. It was the first time that I saw and approached people of different ethnic origins.
I had made friends with two Vietnamese brothers; but Kim, the more pleasant of the two, who reminded me of the "Jungle Book," had taken a liking for my friend Luisa. For my part, I was pressed by the shy but intense courting of the young Jean, who looked at me with adoring eyes and played the violin for me. He dreamed of becoming a great violinist. He lived with his brother in a richly appointed apartment, a mixture of French and Oriental taste. I have kept the card he gave me when we went away, with the exotic multi-coloured bird spreading its large silk wings. Who knows where the diminutive Jean flew when the storm overwhelmed his country? Was he able to escape? Is he still playing the violin? At the bottom of the card only four words in his small handwriting, *"Jusy, ne m'oublie pas!"*

Even the experience of the Self-Serve was for me a new and exciting thing then. Having to move in that exotic international crowd heightened the sense of freedom I felt, and of total estrangement from my small provincial world. I'd sit at a table with my classmates and already I'd feel his eyes on me from the table next to ours. Or was it I who was seeking him, excited by a mixture of attraction and fear, of the risk and of the forbidden. He looked like Henry Belafonte, my youthful passion, and it would have been so easy to lose myself in him. But my self-defence prevailed.

In the evenings we'd go to the small cine club in "Saint-Germain," where they gave avant-guard films like *Un chien andalou, L'harpe birmane,* which made us feel very *engagées*; or we'd end up "smoked" in some existentialist *cave* with women all dressed in black like Juliette Greco, while the sax player played out the notes of *Petite fleur.* My intellectual cravings would impel me to raid *les bouquinistes de la Rive Gauche,* where I'd load up on old leather-bound editions of the classics.

But there was also the more bourgeois social life, more touristy, which we were discovering by running around in the *Metro* – a new experience which gave me the sense of being able to move deftly in the labyrinths of this world – or on the *Bateau Mouche*. It was the Paris with the aroma of *baguettes,* whenever the baker boy would pass on the bicycle with his basket full of fresh bread; and of the *café-au-lait* of the daily breakfast, with its taste of tar, in which to dunk the buttery fragrant *croissants*; or the Paris with the taste of a *croque-monsieur* at the "Champs Elisés."

The effect of Versailles was that of opening the doors on a stage as vast as all of history itself, and I was dazzled by its grand scenography. It brought to mind the tragic events which until that moment had only taken place in the pages of school texts. It stirred my imagination with the secluded spots in its woods, which hid private abodes and temples of love of kings, queens and favorites. The magic effects of water plays of its fountains still come through in the old black and white photos of the album of back then - the vine leaves on its leather cover now worn, the images faded.

Milano became greyer and smaller in my mind's eye as I took in the vast space of Place de la Concorde, of the bridges cast over the Seine, the broad perspective of the buildings following the curves of the river. *Ciels de Paris* ... how much space for the clouds to romp in! At Fontainebleau we stopped one evening to admire the play of *sons et lumières*. In the darkness of the night, the castle burst into light and history.

When dawn broke at the "Moulin Rouge" or at the "Crazy Horse," as we dragged ourselves tired and starving, someone would suggest *la soup à l'oignon* at "Les Halles" market place - the very soul of Paris, now gone; the working Paris that came alive with its teeming activity at five in the morning among the damp scents of the market; while the social life of Paris went home for the night, and Place Pigalle put out its lights. You don't know the real Paris if you have not tasted the steaming heat of that bowl of onion soup in a pearly frosted dawn, while all around you smells of vital stirrings are wafting.

From "Les Halles" to "La Tour d'Argent," guests of the Indian prince who had taken a fancy for my friend Luisa's blond hair. Flattered, she had accepted the invitation to lunch quite happy that, as a courtesy, the invitation had been extended to me as well. The appointment was for *"les treize."* Quite at ease, we showed up around three in the afternoon! We had confused *treize* with *trois*! But well-practiced by an Oriental philosophical patience, our noble gallant gentleman welcomed us impassively. My role as a chaperone earned me the most extraordinary culinary experience of my life, in a luxury worthy of an Oriental nabob.

"Dix francs! Dix francs!" was the piercing shout of the little old hag who appeared out of nowhere like a fairy tale evil witch in the Tuileries Gardens, the very moment we rested our weary bones on one of the many metal seats. The exacting payment to rest in a park, and all those couples of young and old openly kissing in every corner of the city were "French" things that filled us with indignation.

Luisa and I also made a picaresque excursion to Normandy thanks to my knowing Michel, alias "the Norman." The excitement for the trip was dampened somewhat when, the morning of our departure, my unbelieving eyes saw "the blond man from the North" arriving in a battered *Deux Chevaux*, with a huge prelate sitting at the steering wheel, screaming and spilling over, who was introduced to us as *"mon oncle l'Abbé,"* that is the uncle of my "Norman*."*

We crossed all of northern France in the footsteps of the Maid of Orléans, with stops at Reims and Rouen, with the broken down *Citroën* that had the small problem of a door which wouldn't stay closed. It was all tied with ropes, but for safety sake, it had to be held shut by hand. So we went through the entire trip with us three young ones taking turns in grabbing the door, charged also with warning the driver of every bump on the road which could alter the precarious position of the door. Being the abbot a bit on the blind side, we had to continually yell in panic "*Les champignons! Les champignons!*" as the car narrowly escaped the road bumps with a scary swerve.

Then the moment of the historic vengeance arrived. During our stay in Paris, the guide for my group students was our French professor's assistant at the "Bocconi." He was the classic *bullo dritto*, conceited and arrogant. With the advantage of being abroad in charge of a group of almost exclusively girls, he literally felt like the rooster in the henhouse, with the right to get away with anything. But we also were abroad and far from any source of real authority, and the situation could easily be reversed. In fact, he found himself alone in the hands of Erinys. We decided to french sheet his bed. We easily bribed the chamber maid, who was already our ally, and we snuck in enemy territory, after which it was child's play: by folding in half the top sheet, the bed of our victim was turned into …a sack. We were delighted to imagine the chagrin and pique of "dott. Galluzzo," forced to re-make his bed just when he was going to turn in. But laughs best he who laughs last… because the moment of my nemesis came as well. Fate had it that at the French exam, at the end of summer, I found as member of the examining committee…dott. Galluzzo himself! The embarrassment made me suffer, and the mark… suffered as well..

The day before our departure, I went back there to bid my last goodbye. It had been the most intense love affair during my stay. For two weeks I had gone there every day. I crossed the Luxembourg Gardens and went all alone for my very private appointment - my visit to the Louvres. Two weeks of intense esthetic and cultural joy. All those images, those forms lovingly studied in books were now leaping before my eyes in all their tangible beauty and magnificence. I see myself entering the large foyer as if in slow motion; then … an apparition. Etched against a luminous red background was flight in its pure essence caught in a marble whiteness: the Nike of Samothrace, all breezy veils and wings majestically spread in flight. It was as if all the wonder of the classical world absorbed in years of enthusiastic study had materialized. I stood there dreamy.

And then I saw *la Gioconda (Mona Lisa)*. I saw her in the best possible way, a way in which no one can enjoy her any longer. I was there alone, no tourists, no protective obstruction between me and her. I could stare in those eyes, mysteriously looking at me as in a magic apparition, a myth which had come down to me through the centuries. It was difficult to believe. It was as if her smile was for me alone, mocking, wonderfully enigmatic; and I lost myself in it, deeply touched by the emotion of Beauty itself. It was the last image of Paris I took away with me.

CHAPTER TWENTY-SIX

The train was bound for England, in the first of the two summers I was to spend in London. I had with me the address supplied by my university of the school where I would attend English courses. There I would be given the names of families willing to have foreign students stay with them. I was exchanging this information while travelling with my classmates from "Bocconi," when someone asked me, *"But where will you stay tonight when we get there?"* Suddenly I was panic stricken by my complete failure to think ahead. I certainly could not solve the problem of accommodations the night of my arrival in London, and certainly not if it depended on a school most probably closed at that hour.

That night, I ended up in the cell of a convent, a kind of youth hostel whose address I had miraculously gotten from a classmate travelling with me. Lying on that small penitential cot in a cubicle slightly bigger than the bed, between bare cement walls, I was staring at the ceiling barely grazed by a vague glow filtering through the window behind me, high and deep-set like in a prison, and I felt lost and orphan in the wide world.

But when daylight came, my first encounter with the English and their exhilarating eccentricity swept away every trace of loneliness and melancholy. I spent the morning familiarizing myself with the surroundings, and in the early afternoon, I finally managed to start my search for "David's School," relying on some vague notion, and on the eternal belief at that age that everything will sort out in the end.

Conclusion, with dusk upon me, I found myself totally lost in a desolate residential area, no one in sight, in front of me a huge, thick, dark park. Wary, I started venturing among the trees, panic rising as the sun was rapidly setting, and the potential dangers becoming clear. And then, there he was - the comforting figure of a London bobby taking shape in my path.

It was the good old times when the English bobby represented something familiar and good-natured who, like in the black and white movies, strolled the streets cheerfully twirling his rubber baton, the only weapon then allowed him.

My bobby smiled at me. He must have noticed I looked lost. With relief I reviewed the address on the slip of paper I had in my hand to ask him about it, but when I raised my head, the policeman was nowhere to be seen. I looked around me in dismay, thinking I was having hallucinations. While my eyes searched bewildered, all of a sudden in the silence I heard *"Peekaboo!"* and the large smiling face of the bobby under his hard black helmet sprung out from behind a tree. The zany policeman just wanted to have a little fun at my expense; then, without another word, without the least loss of dignity, he proceeded to get me out of trouble and led me to my destination. This would be one of a series of experiences worthy of *Helzapoppin'*.

In fact, after the playful bobby came the spry little old lady, the retired teacher to whom I went for some help with my written English.

All white from the silvery neatness of her hair to the lace and the starched blouse, she opened the door with a chirping bird sound, whose vulnerable frailty she seemed to share. She introduced me into an environment equally neat with flowered sofas and armchairs, soft cream coloured carpets, Victorian consoles, the whole embraced by a wide and bright bay window which filtered the thick green of the garden. After the tea ceremony in charming porcelain cups and the exchange of personal information which created an intimate and cordial atmosphere, we set to work over a small table in peaceful silence... suddenly broken by the buzzing of a fly, more annoying by the minute. In a single leap, Miss Jones was flying through the air. Napkin in hand, she was furiously chasing the fly. Lightly as a butterfly, I saw her literally flying in spurts from armchair to armchair, while the fly seemed to go wild together with her hunter. I kept looking bewildered and unbelieving. Her mission a failure, she gracefully came down to earth disappointed and defeated, muttering *"I can't bear flies!"* and she handed over to me the weapon. I found myself with the napkin in hand and the urgent request to kill the enemy. Luckily I managed it simply waiting for the exhausted fly to land on the window pane, and I won Miss Jones's heart.

It was, however, Gilda Buckmaster and family that defined the rhythm of my life in London. I had finally managed to get their address: Nevern Mansions, Nevern Square. The Metro stop was Earl's Court. I tramped around for the longest time looking for a residence that had no street number. As usual, the solitary passerby rescued me at last, and I found myself at the front door of what would be my sanctuary for the next two months.

I was welcomed by Gilda: blond, short, sturdy, bursting with a nervous and suppressed energy… Neapolitan! A war marriage had brought her to London. She had married John, the tall and phlegmatic English officer. A frustrated artist, she regretted having interrupted her studies at the Conservatory of Naples, a career as concert pianist gone up in smoke. She poured her failed artistic ambitions in a repressed rancour and in her children. Paul, the oldest at ten, studied the cello. Beth at eight was doing classical ballet. Then came the three year-old Andrew.

The atmosphere in the house was a mixture of Mediterranean emotionalism shared by the mother and the son, countered by the phlegmatic calm of father and daughter. Everything seasoned with a touch of Anglo-Saxon eccentricity and artistic flair. In the most unlikely moments, the living room was filled with the furious echoes of Gilda at the piano, followed by the son on the cello, while Beth in her tutu twirled on her toes around the room. In a corner, unruffled, the father immersed in the pages of the *Times*. All the ingredients for a Frank Capra movie.

The keenest recollection I have of John Buckmaster is when he appeared before me on a Sunday morning to pick us up after Mass. He was wearing only a heavy tweed jacket, he was decidedly without trousers. The long naked hairy legs, which I examined dumbfounded, ended in a pair of socks which showed disgustingly through a pair of Franciscan sandals. I was speechless. I looked over to Gilda to see her reaction. Nothing. Was it possible that no one noticed that he had forgotten to put on his trousers? The mystery was revealed when, having taken off the jacket, I realized that underneath he was wearing a pair of summer shorts!

Nothing is funky or unconventional for the English. They have an absolute respect for one another's most complete freedom. In other words, they simply ignore each other. From this come perhaps the contradiction they express in their dogged search for the most unusual eccentricity. In other words, a desire to be noticed, to stand out, like the famous episode of the man who crossed the stage naked during a ceremony. And when no one notices you... even murder might be a remedy.

Paul got his first childhood crush for me. He'd follow me like my own shadow. He'd ask me to wait for him for ten years so he could marry me. He loved taking me around the city, as a guide, but out of his mouth came only horror stories. At every street corner, every building he'd dig up stories of bloody scenes, horrible crimes of the past. It seemed we were on the footsteps of Jack the Ripper. That little kid seemed to enjoy wallowing in the gory to the point of making me sick. But I realized that he wasn't a mocking Tancredi who in "Il Gattopardo" had fun at the expense of a naïve stranger. Paul instead wallowed in those dark waters for his own pleasure. What emerged in him was the Gothic aspect of the English character, the taste for the macabre, a gloomy morbidity which struck me in various ways. The whole summer I was haunted by a horrible monster, half man and half fly, displayed on an enormous poster covering the entire façade of a building in Piccadilly Circus. It was the publicity for a famous movie of that year, *The Fly*. But the English did not seem to be bothered by that obscene defacement of one of the most pleasant squares in London.

I preferred their myriad ghost stories, and I loved it when they crossed into their unrivalled sense of humour. One evening I was invited to dinner by some friends of the Buckmasters, and while we were pleasantly chatting around the table, we were all struck by the sound of persistent running water coming from the floor above. Someone finally made a comment about a probable tap left open. *"Oh, no bother!"* replied unflappable the petulant hostess, who proceeded to inform us that it was simply Archibold taking his bath. Asked who Archibald was, her husband explained with great aplomb that it was the resident ghost. Everyone calmly proceeded with the dinner as if nothing was amiss. I was greatly disappointed, and I never did understand if they were joking or talking seriously.

Everything seemed accepted by the unflappable eccentricity of the English; and nothing was refused by their uninhibited nonconformity - not even placing Church promotion on milk cartons. Of course, since there were so many different Christian sects, there must have been a lot of competition! Coming out for the first time from the restricted outlook imposed on me by the Catholic religion, I was flabbergasted by the possibility for each individual to have his own…custom-made religion.

The face of England was also the image of Queen Elizabeth on horseback that filled the screen at the end of every movie, while everyone stood at attention and listened to *God Save the Queen*. To me it appeared ridiculous. I'd remain seated, surrounded by the incensed stares of those nearby. My rebellious nature refused to spring up like a puppet in front of that cliché image, which after all meant nothing to me, forgetting however good manners at someone else's home.

England was the students who streamed from the portals of Eaton College like a flock of black swallows, as I passed on the train which was going to take me to Brighton. I never saw Brighton. Instead I found myself among the smoky industrial fogs of Manchester! I had taken the wrong train.

England meant for me the intense experience of Stratford-on-Avon, with my German friends Trudie and Helga. I had met them at a park; they were also there for a study holiday. They'd receive from home packages of delicious *sauer brot,* very dark, heavy as a brick. They'd always share it with me during our snacks on the Serpentine.

England was also the slow gliding of boats on the waters of the Cam, under the weeping willows in Cambridge, as in the movies based on the novels by E.M. Forster. And it was meandering alone in the peaceful English countryside which I loved, learning to live alone; almost a foreboding of the emigration which would have then taught me the price to be paid in terms of solitude, when being abroad would have become my normal status.

England for me had the flavour of the steaming porridge at morning breakfast, and the incomparable taste of fresh fruit preserves. It was the comfort of a cup of tea which kept me company throughout the day: as soon as I was up in the morning, at lunch of course, at five in the afternoon, for dinner, and for a snack before going to bed. It ended up creating not a few problems for me as I went around the city. But how could you refuse a cup of tea in England? Easy, as soon as they took their eyes off me, my tea contributed to watering the house plants.

The London of the '50s was also the *beatniks*. They gave the city an original nonconformist tone. I was fascinated by their way of dressing and behaving. Their stance of defiance against everything spoke to my rebellious nature, still undefined, still undeclared... until I found myself face to face with a group of them. I was going to the local library on a bicycle Gilda had lent to me. I was having a lot of fun adapting to the challenge of keeping to the left, though I tried to avoid the roads with heavy traffic. And so I turned into a narrow, rather deserted alley, when I found my way suddenly blocked by a group of strangely dressed boys rakishly approaching me. I had never seen their type so up close and personal, and I wasn't at all thrilled. Rather than intriguing rebels, they looked like neighbourhood hooligans. I felt trapped. I had no other way out. I lowered my head, pushed on the pedals with all my strength and dove headlong. Maybe surprised by my impetus and by my nerve (though my heart was beating like mad), they let me through with only a few sardonic comments. I had an adventure to tell.

The London I loved was the London poetically transformed by Turner's painter's eye, all lights and colours filtered through its fogs, through its rains. I'd spend hours in the "Tate Gallery," losing myself in the mysterious depth of those misty landscapes, in their intensely suggestive skies. I never got enough.

London was Hyde Park Corner, the "Speakers' Corner." An area of the park where anyone could make a speech freely saying anything he wished, including speaking against the Queen. The place looked like a meeting of lunatics waving their arms to the stare - either convinced or shocked - of the people listening to them, railing against someone or something, standing on empty fruit crates to emerge in the crowd. Not far from there, from the rich hotels around Marble Arch, you could see caped and masked gentlemen come out furtively at dawn like in a Venetian Carnival. Protagonists of secret trysts, this was their way of protecting their identity.

The English were perfect gentlemen. They never bothered a girl with indiscreet stares. But how often I sensed being spied from behind a newspaper! The trusty *Times* behind which they barricaded themselves even in their Clubs, protecting their privacy in their all-male establishments. I preferred the up-front gallant homage of the Italian men, who without offending, gave me pride in my femininity and inspired a sunny joy for life.

London was also the cheerfulness of simple people that made me feel extremely welcome when they greeted me in the shops with a *"Hi, honey!"* It seemed as if everyone knew me. If you then happened to have with you an animal, the people just melted, while they could easily ignore a baby, who was often left in the carriage outside the store without any passerby bothering to cast a glance.

1958, was a London of long ago, when an unattended child did not run any risk; when I could safely go to study in an isolated and deserted park, without feeling threatened by anything or anyone; when meeting strangers was still based on trust in your fellow human beings.

Parks were places in which people met. They were the very soul of London. Green and luxuriant thanks to the abundant rainfall, at the first ray of sun they teemed with colourful people: gentlemen with umbrella and bowler strolling during a work pause in the City; nannies with children; young people lying on the lawns, that indestructible grass you could enjoy like a carpet; foreign students from every part of the globe; but, especially, so many pairs of elegant little old ladies, sitting on park benches, neat and smiling, always ready to have a word with you.

Single women made up a large part of the English population due to the plurality of women over men. These were the jovial little ladies who in English films were always seen preparing fragrant muffins and choice blackberry jams; or who, with the same smile and the same gracefulness, moved around *"arsenic and old lace,"* burying corpses in the garden.

Holland Park, close to where I lived, was my favourite retreat. I'd spread my books on the grass and buried myself in English literature. In October I would have my third-year English exam. That's where I met Rudolf Kandaràuroff. His appearance was not as imposing as his name; nonetheless he was a pleasant German boy, whose Germanic stiffness was softened by his Russian origins. He worked for Trans World Airlines. He was a real born traveller.

I got to know London as I never could have all by myself. We covered London far and near from the top of the double-deckers, and then even farther afield on the above-ground Metro, on buses and trains: Hampton Court, Windsor Castle, where in the armoury I was astonished to bump into the suit of armour of a certain Earl Oddo, and fascinated, I imagined the historical paths of my name.

We'd spend whole days exploring the English countryside with its typical Tudor villages, the small Gothic churches next to ancient cemeteries. I had fun looking at the century-old tombstones. I saw the magic of Cathedral Lake in Surrey, so called because at certain hours of the day the effects of the light give way to a mirage at the bottom of the lake - a submerged cathedral. And at that instant the remote stretch of water beneath weeping willows and birch trees becomes a world of fairy tale. *La Cathédrale engloutie* of Debussy?

Rudolf introduced me to the Rhine wines and I understood the meaning of *"the wine that cuts the legs from under you."* With a perfectly clear head, I got up from the table at the restaurant that night and... my legs gave way.

Quickly Rudolf held me up and ushered me outside with great poise. It was one of the most embarrassing moments in my life, and the first and last time I ever was inebriated. When he'd take me to the theatre, he'd always show up with a box of "Black Magic." In those days the most successful musical was *Salad Days,* the "green" days of our youth, as defined by Shakespeare. It had been running for seven years, as was the norm in London. Of course every few years they had to change the young protagonists. How small and provincial appeared Milano to my eyes! And so was I!

The day came when Rudolf invited me to his apartment and unconcerned I accepted, and… I had to use all my tact to avoid the moment of reckoning. He desisted as the gentleman that he was, though astonished that I had reached the age of twenty-two without wanting to have that experience. I saved the evening by seducing his taste buds instead. I took him to the kitchen, had him sit on a small refrigerator hoping he might…"cool off," and I began preparing the most sophisticated Italian dinner. He remained my friend. He even came to see me one day in Milano. What remained of him were two red travel bags of TWA, which he brought one day for me and my brother. That's how I had walked in the world, unaware and unprepared. I had thought myself level-headed… until that revealing moment.

It was the great event of the season: the concert of Harry Belafonte at Covent Garden, with Odetta, and the launch of the soon to be famous South African singer Miriam Makeba, with her characteristic *click* song. The same programme which would cause a world-wide sensation when Belafonte returned in concert at New York's Carnegie Hall in 1960.

I spent all my savings, but I couldn't forgo a similar occasion: seeing Belafonte live. I was rewarded by an electrifying show, overwhelmed by the exuberant charm of my favourite, no less than the rest of the public, which Belafonte swept along with the most intense emotions, making us laugh and sing along with him to the rhythm of *Waltzing Matilda.*

I was with a girlfriend, and at the end of the show we decided to try to catch him at the exit and manage to get his autograph. But after the longest lying in wait in a crowd of young people which pressed and moved hysterically, we were forced to give up. Suddenly, perhaps as a reaction to the crescendo of my emotions and the tension of the wait, I got a lump in my throat and tears in my eyes. The cat-like sensuality of Harry Belafonte, his breathtaking vitality were for me in that moment the object of my unconscious turmoil, of my faceless, incoherent desires. They represented the unreachable, they were the mystery. And the wrenching and the scars deep within me were opened once again.

Books have always been in my life the interposing element between me and reality, which became more significant in my eyes because illuminated and filtered by books. I saw reality in books and books in reality. And one day a revelation surfaced from the very pages of a book. I was wandering among the tables filled with second-hand books in an old bookstore in London, when my eye was caught by a title. It was a text on sexual education. Only a moment's hesitation, then I overcame all embarrassment. I was abroad, and I felt protected by two degrees of anonymity. I rushed home and retreated in my room. I read for hours from cover to cover that very serious, scientific, illustrated text. Repressed intuitions came to the surface, other revelations were made. I was shaken so much that when Mrs. Goldberg, where I was then living, called me for dinner, she looked at me worried that I had a fever. I was twenty-two years old and only then did I finally know! It was still not enough, however, to prepare me for the reality that awaited me. Brutally it would come on my wedding night.

Like a magnifying glass, distance has a way of enhancing events. Irrelevant things seem to swell in our memory because of the emotions that issue from them. Emotional ripples, suggestions, interactions with things and people come together to form the supporting structure of our present. It's not the quality of what I have lived, but rather that which I have really felt that gives importance to my memories, to make me what I am now.

Paul Buckmaster remained part of my life for a long time. I can see him getting off the train at the station in Milano, a thin, lean, nervous boy, concealed by his enormous cello, bigger than him. Carrying his instrument and suitcase, I took him home with me like a shaggy little bird tired of the flight, to rest a couple of days before resuming his trip. Gilda had achieved her dream of having him study at the Conservatory in Naples, and she took advantage of me to have him rest in his long trip. This took place twice a year, coming and going. But with all her ambitions and by continuously exalting him, she had turned him into an unbearable *enfant prodige*, full of foibles, demands and whims. I always looked forward to his leaving, and from then on I decided that in London I would avoid the Buckmasters. The Goldbergs took their place.

It was ten years later, in Canada, that I bought that record of Elton John of 1969. On the back cover, among the members of his band, I saw in block capitals the name Paul Buckmaster. Beneath the name, a nice face, jaunty and incisive, a goatee, sardonic eyes under the wide brim of a Texan hat. In the caption, Paul Buckmaster appeared as "*arranger*." I'm speechless, a lump in my throat. My Paul…the cello player. From the Conservatory of Naples to the entourage of Elton John! I think of Gilda and of her dreams for her son. Or was she flattered perhaps by that popular success? Ten years had gone by, the ten years I should have waited for him to grow up…and now there was his face, staring at me mockingly. Past and present enfolded me in a whirlwind of emotions.

I would find myself in London again more than thirty years later since those Buckmasters times. "*London revisited*"…what a disappointment! The views of my beloved old London ruined by the horrible geometric shapes of modern buildings, resulting in a monstrous hybrid which suffocated the squares, wiping out perspectives, blocking the stage of the skies above.

We are now at the airport, about to leave. A sudden impulse - I get into a telephone booth, all modern with shiny buttons…all grey. Those red booths, so familiar, so..."London," come back to my mind. They had saved me so many times suddenly appearing among the grey cement of the city... provided I had in my purse the required nine pennies, as large as slices of cucumber! I smiled. I look through the telephone book all excited, and I find the name, Paul Buckmaster. What will I say to him? What kind of a man can he be in his late forties? Will he also have a wry smile for *"les neiges d'antan?"* I dial the number. No one answers. I go on my way, which will pull me away forever.

Richmond, a suburb of London. Its huge park a forest of giant trees. Rain is falling in large drops on the grass. It was pleasant walking there in the warm summer rain. In the emerald-green clearing, a troop of fawns are grazing peacefully. Then they flee inside the woods ... I wonder if they are still there. And Dr. and Mrs. Goldberg? I lived with them in the summer of '59.

He was a surgeon and they had come from South Africa. They had to leave everything and emigrate because they were persecuted and ostracized by the community, which would not tolerate him treating coloured people. He was no longer able to exercise his profession.

I remember his large ruddy cordial face under a mass of bushy white hair, a large and heavy set man with an exuberant personality, which revealed his Russian Jewish origins. She was typically Anglo-Saxon in her gaunt figure and her awkward and uncoordinated movements. Her prominent teeth completed her look of a permanently smiling seal. And yet, she too must have aroused passion in her man. They had a ten-month old boy that resembled the mother, even in his neurotic behaviour. He literally spent hours holding on to the rail of his crib, shaking it furiously. I'd study in the next-door room with this strange rhythmic background accompaniment. It didn't seem to surprise anyone. Eight-year-old David, the oldest, was a fattish and outgoing blond boy like his father. He'd come home from school calling his mother, impatient to tell her about his day. He was immediately silenced because his excessively exuberant and emotional behaviour was not considered appropriate according to the Anglo-Saxon code. He would shut himself away, mortified. He was already victim of neurotic tics. I felt sorry for him. I treated him with kindness and he grew attached to me. In a short time, when returning home from school, instead of looking for his mother, he'd run to me and throw himself in my arms. It was rather embarrassing, to say the least.

This rather original quartet was joined now and then by the powerful Russian grandmother, coming to visit, and completely upsetting my days. Luck would have it that she did not live very close. She looked like a grenadier, always on the war path. She'd reproach her daughter-in-law for letting the apples rot in the garden, and she'd spend afternoons cooking huge pots of apple jam, drafting me by force to peel the apples. She'd also drag me in very long strolls, forced marches would be a better word for it. She was fixed on shortening the way to our destination by crossing the golf fields of the nearby Kew Gardens. She'd pass unflinching amid the yells of the golfers, ignoring the golf balls flying by us like bullets. She'd wave to them cheerily as she moved on. The only advantage for me was the intense exercise of English conversation which her chattiness imposed on me.

Thanks to the Goldbergs I came to know Devon. They brought me with them on their summer vacations in Bideford, on the Atlantic coast. We'd cross England even then along the ancient Roman roads, for lack of highways. The route was between two tall bulwarks covered by bushes which curtailed the view. Every once in a while, I'd ask Dr. Goldberg to stop the old Morris and let me climb up the bulwark to see what was concealed on the other side. And both of them would laugh at my enthusiasm emphatically expressed with "W*hat a beautiful panorama!"*

They seemed to amuse themselves a lot at my efforts with the English language. Even when I praised the lady's cooking, she would say I spoke like Shakespeare. But I got my own back when in the evening we'd watch some quiz show on television. We had to guess the meaning of unusual words. For them the difficult words were those of Greek and Latin origin, while I understood them all, winning and leaving them open-mouthed. I remember also during our trips, how amused I was to see the lorries stopped along the side of the road with the tough drivers enjoying their five o'clock tea! That was England as well.

Long gone experiences, slashes in the fog of the past, from which everything resurfaces with the appeal of the lost moments of our youth. I can still see the magic spell of the moors, at sunset. The gentle undulating silhouette of the heath fading in the hush of its vastness, the path vanishing in the horizon between hillocks brushed by the purple heather. No other human presence. Suddenly, a galloping herd of wild ponies is etched against the heather violet sky.

Bideford, neat and demure village with flowered balconies. The sun-kissed English coast, fruit-growing land. We'd walk down medieval streets between the colourful display of the season's first products at farmers' stalls, and the curios in the artisans' shops. Here and there some ponies that had come into the village would freely chomp on pinched fruits.

I remember the high dangerous bluffs on the ocean, the deep-set beaches in small coves, from which you had to run away at a certain hour, when without warning the coves would be suddenly invaded by the rushing tide, and there was no way out.

But my favourite moments were when I walked along those free paths in the countryside, intoxicated by so much open space. I felt elated by my solitary conquest of the world.

I was often passing through the streets of Dartmoor, and I'd see the old jail in the distance. The fields teeming with prisoners working in the typical black and white striped overalls seemed a playful parody. They'd pause in their work to stare at me and send me their effusive compliments. I'd reply with joy, happy and pleased. Even the convicts were cheerful and jovial in England! The whole world seemed to be smiling, and I felt myself bursting with verve and youth. I had the whole world in the palm of my hand.

EPILOGUE

I don't know if or when I ever held the world in my hand, but I certainly did let it slip away. It didn't seem to me that there were many choices still open to me as I found myself day after day standing over that corroded grey granite sink in the apartment in Milano, washing dishes. I was choking back tears whenever I thought of the unfair lot I seem to have been destined for. A heavy heart for something vague which seemed not to have happened or to be happening to me. Perhaps the vanished dream of travelling free around the world. But I was realist enough not to believe in that anymore. My responsibilities were here now, and I had made my choices. Every choice made reduces your horizon.

Following my university degree, I had accepted a job in the *Segreteria Esteri* of a large bank in Piazza della Scala. Of my dreams to travel only the irony of that name was left. The contacts with foreign countries were in fact limited to communication by letter and teletype, the technological marvel of the time, precursor of the email. This machine during the night cranked out a long paper serpent that uncoiled along the floor all the way to our desks. We'd find it in the morning, with its series of repetitive messages, which were separated by me and my co-workers, - all from "Bocconi,"- according to the language in which they had to be replied. Nevertheless, during the day, we welcomed that clicking sound which interrupted our monotonous work at the typewriter. We could reply immediately, establishing a tit for tat written exchange.

The biggest distraction from the daily monotony, however, was Mr. Monti. Mainstay of the office, he did everything, knew everything, solved every problem, and trained all of us girls. Gruff but kind, with the looks of a large wheezing walrus, he was in perfect symbiosis with his powerful typewriter - a giant Olivetti, which under his jackhammer fingers, worked at unbelievable speeds. Every two seconds we'd jump at the ring of the bell, followed by the loud bang of the carriage being violently slammed back to the start of its run. His furious pounding did not admit any hesitation or pause: it was continuous, unbroken, relentless…except…except when suddenly it was replaced by an equally loud snoring. Monti had fallen in a deep sleep right over his typewriter! It all would be repeated regularly in a continuous counterpoint of sound instruments. A long time after, I found out that it was caused by a rare illness.

Although the situation was disconcerting, Mr. Monti was too good and efficient in his work to be replaced; but it was also very hard for us girls, new to that state of affairs, to keep a straight face. Just as suddenly, the poor devil would then re-emerge from his brief comatose state and resume his work in progress like a flash, as if nothing had happened, with the utmost poise, picking up exactly where he had left off. The situation comedy would reach its peak whenever Mr. Monti's awakening took too long. Then, the office manager, Mr. Olindo Umiltà, timid and humble as his name, ventured to intervene from the vantage of his higher desk, from which he kept an eye on us and, vexed, would begin to open and slam shut one drawer after another. The result was immediate. The typewriter's carriage took off like a rocket.

There were other unforgettable moments in this drab banking experience of mine, such as the kind invitation extended by the Director General of the bank to us girls of the "prestigious" *Segreteria Esteri* to share the balcony of his richly appointed office, which looked on Piazza della Scala, on the occasion of two extraordinary public events: the solar eclipse and the appearance of Queen Elizabeth (or was it vice versa?) and her consort, Prince Philip. The two most important members of the British Royal Family had appeared to greet the crowd from the balcony of the "Teatro alla Scala," directly opposite ours. Notably effusive was the smiling glance cast in our direction by the Prince, unclear if to nod his respects to our important financial institution or, as we preferred to think, as homage to us girls.

In spite of these highlights, it was still one of the dullest jobs in a most colourless atmosphere. What good had it been to study Shelley and Baudelaire to end up translating bills of lading? I had accepted it because its hours and location allowed me to handle my responsibilities in living with my brother. In fact, I had to perform all the duties of a woman in a home with a man; in short the woman had to cook, wash, iron, manage the entire household, and take care of the poor helpless man, as she has been properly taught since she was a little girl. The fact that I also had a job outside the house was my problem, which I had to work out along with these other responsibilities.

And so I found myself more alone than ever - home and work, work and home. My friends had all scattered, almost all of them married, and as I, absorbed by their family responsibilities, with the obvious advantages which I did not have. And that's why the sudden lump in my throat, facing those dirty dishes every night in the greasy kitchen sink. Or maybe it was because of the clock ticking away. My friends had children already, and strong was the social pressure to conform, which made me feel emarginated. I was a "single" woman, not married as I should have been. We were at the beginning of the '60s.

The revelation came one day, going up the escalator in the shiny new surroundings of "La Rinascente," the first department store in Italy, which had elegantly blended its touch of frivolity with the gravity of the Milano's downtown style. In fact, even in the ever spreading crass American materialism, "La Rinascente" has always kept a nuance of flair thanks to its historical origins and to its literary baptism. It was the unfailing decadent poet D'Annunzio who coined its name back in 1917. But its history goes back to that little shop of ready-made clothing, first of its kind in Italy, which had been conceived toward the end of the 19th century by the industrialist Ferdinando Bocconi, brother of "my" Luigi, in whose shadow I had been moulded. That small enterprise on Via Redegonda would later become the glory of the porticos of Piazza Duomo.

Afro was born, Antonia's eldest, and I was delighted to go exploring in the children's department of "La Rinascente." With a smile, I picked up a small yellow overall. Dreamily, I held that soft thing so full of promise in my hands. My whole being was filled at that moment with a maternal instinct, and all of a sudden I was whelmed by the anguish of having been left behind. The standards in those days made me feel that at the worrying age of twenty-four, my biological clock was running out of time, and I was missing the most important experience in my life. No one on the horizon. The man I loved vanished.

Was it really free choice, then? When around that table in the large conference room at the bank I was being interviewed for a job, and he continued to stare at me, the only woman among ten men; was that the moment when the choice was made? But by whom? Someone esle had caught my attention. I had looked forward to that evening when we all arranged to meet and celebrate the long day we had gone through. But I found only him there. He had "persuaded" the others to stay away, counting on their complicity as men. Already then he had considered me "his" against everything and everyone. At the moment, I was naively flattered, without seeing the arrogant despotism in which I would soon be trapped. I had taken the first fatal steps along the inescapable road opened for me, which, against my will, would take me all the way to Vancouver, on the Pacific Coast of Canada.

The *"Ultima Tule."* From that coast, I thought, we could only plummet into the void.

Deserted streets passing among dilapidated houses, none higher than one storey. The contorted figure of a staggering Indian, dragging himself along a wall. In a doorway, the withered face of another, in a drunken stupor. Squamish - our first Sunday excursion outside Vancouver. Beyond that, nothing for miles and miles, not even a road. Standing in the middle of "Main Street" - saloons, pubs, general stores, gas stations - I looked at my husband as a surge of resentment and tears rose in me: *"Where did you bring me!?"* I cried out in a voice broken by desperation. It was the Far West. The Canada of the '60s. On Sundays, even

Vancouver was deserted - all public places closed, even movie houses. It was the Lord's Day.

I had cried even during the endless flight which had brought me over an ocean and a continent, from Rome to Vancouver. I was travelling alone towards the unknown. My husband was to follow me three months later. In September I was supposed to start teaching at the University of British Columbia. For two solid hours I flew over the vastness of the Rocky Mountains. I thought of the epic feat of the pioneers who had crossed them in their wagons. Deaths, and certainly cannibalism had been needed to survive. Yet I didn't feel any more fortunate. I thought about the twenty-minute flight over my Alps, of more human dimensions, though still majestic. I had always been naturally drawn toward the South, the sun, the warm countries, *il mal d'Africa, il mal di Sicilia....* I had always abhorred the North. I viewed with horror the vast frozen lands, the deep fjords, the endless forests. I had objected, I had raged, I had wept. *"The wife must follow the husband."*

And now, there they were, the cold fjords where Vancouver was laid out, creeping dark and silent in the gloomy bowels of the mountains at our back. And the mountains, the stunning Rockies, beautiful and impressive enough to take your breath away, with their virgin secrets untouched from the very beginning of creation... alienating. No man had ever put his foot there. Not a church steeple, not a hamlet to humanize them.

Vancouver was a flat city in those days, spread out over the green fields and woodland, with her small houses like in *Seven Brides for Seven Brothers,* made out of the timber from her forests. Every now and then one of these houses would be moved from one part of the city to another, literally lifting it from its foundations and moving it on a trailer pulled by a powerful truck. Flabbergasted, I'd watch it pass with surreal slow motion in front of my window. Downtown, one lonely building rose some ten storeys high, which thrilled me because its shape reminded me of my *Pirellone* in Milano.

I'd wake up to the harsh cries of the seagulls, to the deep hoarse "uuuh-uhm…uuuh-uhm" sounds of ship horns, almost a distant lament of dantesque souls lost in the fog. I'd quiver, as years before at the shout of Giorgio Albertazzi, amid the cries of the seagulls: *"Mamma, I need the sun!"* in Ibsen's "Ghosts." But here the curtains did not fall. And the cawing flocks of crows landing on the roofs and on fir trees took me back to the dark Nordic fairy tales like *Die sieben Raben* of the Grimm brothers.

The human scene did not help to lessen the impact. I felt crushed in a Pirandellian way by the mask others imposed on me. The Anglo-Saxon patronizing ways made us feel like immigrants of an inferior race in their colony. The most desirable residences on the hills overlooking the city could be bought only by British citizens, and were appropriately named "British Properties."

"What kind of a name is that?" I was often asked with disdainful curiosity in shops, when seeing my name on the credit card. *"Where do you come from?"* was the standard question. It felt as if I had to constantly justify myself. In the higher social circles, my *italianità* found a more refined but equally condescending reaction: *"Oh, I **love** Italy!", "I **love** Florence!"* Places so…"exotic" and "quaint." If we were at a party, the enthusiasm was emphatically expressed by a spastic jerk of the hand that held the inevitable drink.

Discrimination against women was no less than in Italy, but it wasn't even compensated by that charming Italian gallantry, with its flattering attention to the female gendre, the lack of which was a big blow to my spoiled vanity. All at once I found myself erased both as a social person and as a woman. No better treatment was reserved for me in the academic circles, where I was immediately penalized for being a woman, for being Italian, and for having only an Italian university degree and not a Ph.D. Graduate students coming from Great Britain had priority. I was considered unfit to teach Italian literature, and relegated to teach language courses.

This was my first contact with Canada. But I remember as well the glorious scenes of Canadian autumns, vast palettes of flaming colours, avenues and forests where I'd walk full of joy, reliving the autumns of my Valganna.

More than just an ocean separated me from that beginning, from that long corridor where the story of my life had started - an abyss of culture, of history, of social setting and social values. Now I found myself in a world with echoes of Jack London, of the land of gold diggers, of the Klondike…

But maybe another tear had been made before this one. I was coming from far away, from the glittering lights of that salon in Milano, from the evenings of mamma in our box at "la Scala." The rift had already been provoked by the war. My parents had remained on the other side, and the scenes which include them are drawing farther away and slowly dissolving. An old black and white film. It was nonna who had ferried me to the other shore. She had set me on a new path; she, who had come from even farther back in history, and who had been forced to lock away "Flanders and Limoges" in the closet, and roll up her sleeves. On a different stage, the character's core is being put to the test again. But nonna had passed on to me the value of my roots, on which to stand and gather myself, and know who I was. I was alone in my voyage of emigration, but I was leaving with the baggage she had prepared for me.

My last travelling companions, my brother and my grandmother were remaining behind. The former facing soon the illness that was to break his splendidly promising career, and drag his life in a melancholic prolonged decline; the latter rapidly fading away in her old age. In the last pages of my album, nonna is caught by the camera looking like a frail tiny bird, with her head folded on her chest, betrayed by sleep in a warm afternoon. On her lap the needles have slipped from her gnarled fingers, carrying the beginning of a piece of knitting for her Canadian great granddaughter, whom she would never know.

Their disappearance seemed to coincide with the end of something which for a long time had been suffering from a death foretold. As my father and my mother, they too would not have been able to survive. Something very dreadful had swept away the sense of propriety, of what is right, that need for what is refined, for beauty and gentleness... the values of my father.... That world was being thrust aside by a wave of violence, of ego, of the most ruthless materialism; my parents' world was bending under a tidal wave of crass vulgarity.

"I am the body that has travelled around the world; you are my soul which remained there, where I forged my identity...." Where did I read these words? Even my personal world was changing. Did I realize that, or was I changing as well in order to survive? No, you never really change, you adapt yourself. The sea which once used to speak to me of faraway adventures as exciting as a race along the foreshore, now had a voice which stirred only melancholy.

This perhaps had been the biggest tear in my life. This, between my family's aura of an ancient print and the brutality of a present to which I felt I did not belong, but that from now on would belong to me. I replay the scene of the cup hurled against the wall, the long dark streak of coffee scrawled the wall: the first sign of my new private life. And yet, there had been warning signs. My joyful desire to share with him the magic moments of my childhood - Cunardo, my first childhood attachments, the friends of my youth - had met only with irritations and jealousy. Why do we see this only in hindsight?

Places flash back in my mind, moments are superimposed. I'm still an adolescent, there, in Milano, at the Giardinetti della Stazione: carefree afternoons, playful pirouettes on roller skates in the beds of dry fountains. Then, a cold February day, ten years later, in the same place. I can still hear the explosion of profanities. I recall the swear words vented brutally at me, the desecration of my memories, which blurred my eyes with tears. The personal insult was in time followed by a social one, when the *"giardinetti"* became the reign of syringes and of drifters, just like the area of my elementary school, "Il Collegio del Sacro Cuore," became the stage set for prostitutes.

I turn my eyes back to that morning...I can still feel my daze on that day, in the most enchanting setting in the world: Siena, the hotel on the hills, piazza del Battistero. I move toward the altar on my brother's arm, as if following a plot destined by an unseen director, moved by an inescapable force, ..."*like a lamb to the slaughter,*" my cousin, who had acted as witness, would tell me years later.

Nonna had foreseen everything. Spread on my bed were all the "purchases" I had been collecting in the beautiful boutiques of Milano. Amid finery and laces, the white frothy *parure.* For "*my wedding night,*" I say with a mixture of embarrassment and pride. Nonna then looks at the worn-out pajama showing under the pillow, and with her wry wisdom, quips, *"And this is for the day after..."* In fact, the impact with reality was to happen even before. The white virginal veils, protecting me in their provisional cocoon, were to prolong my naïve illusions by only a few minutes.

I had reverently prepared those "veils" singing to myself, "*Oh dolci baci, oh languide carezze / mentr'io fremente le belle forme discioglieva dai veli.*". (Oh sweetest kisses, oh languorous caresses / while feverishly I stripped the beautiful forms off their veils) As Pavarotti sang from Verdi's *Tosca.* I should have thought instead of...*The Lombards at the First Crusade* ..

I tried to love him, to give myself to him, but he would not "see" me. He thought he loved me, he merely possessed me. He continued to blindly live his delusion, forcing it on me as well. I tried to speak to him from the other side of the abyss - misleading moments of understanding. I'd give voice to my soul, only to have it bounce off a wall of insensitivity, making me withdraw into silence and loneliness. Until any last attempt was shattered by abuse and humiliation.

It comes back to me as if it were today, and always will come back, the intensity of those dark blue eyes staring into mine in a deep understanding, an intangible secret which will be always mine and mine alone. It was I who had given life to those eyes only a few moments before, and only a few moments before they had opened upon this world, and they seemed to see only me.

I was being brought on the gurney from the delivery room to my hospital room, and she, (*"It's a girl!"* I kept hearing, happy) all bundled up like a Russian doll in the arms of the nurse, was going toward the nursery. For an instant, I literally drowned in those unbelievably blue eyes. I held them within my closed eyes, inebriated by the powerful mystery they held, and which had brought her to me. She was to be the light in my darkest years.

Scraping together *"the golden wisps of my moments of happiness,"* as they are called by the Prince of Lampedusa in "Il Gattopardo," I hold the simple acts of love of my beloved girl, her tenderness, her successes. Then I could add the moment when "my other creation," my book of literary criticism, had been accepted for publication. This marked the start of the reclaiming of my profession, followed by promotions. From my profession as a teacher, which I did with passion, and love for my students, I drew intellectual and emotional satisfactions. The leitmotiv of the other side of my existence was mostly defilement and lack of communication.

I had just passed fifty, when I reclaimed my freedom. A new split between what went on before and what I have lived after. But this leap into the void was meant to follow a backward path, leading me to rediscover my true identity and my roots. I went deep within the heart of Sicily, among those houses clustered upon layers of century-old history. There, in the shadow of that Rocca, where in the clash of arms my ancestors had taken shelter, where my father had been born. For years I swam in those waters, in the sea of Sicily; I drank in the sun among Norman stones and Saracen olive trees. And I was no longer alone.

It's a calm wintery afternoon. As I'm writing, a slow symphony of snow drifts down to silence the world. The silence seems to hold life itself deferred, and it reflects my own inner peace. In the other room, I sense the presence of my partner immersed in a book, the assured comfort of having him near me. He's been sharing my life for these last fifteen

There's Always the Sea...

years. Around me I only hear the echo of the girls' voices, who will be here again tomorrow, my little granddaughters.

     Vancouver, a splendid city laid out between fjords and mountains. Now, we both have chosen to live here.

ABOUT THE AUTHOR

Giusy Oddo was born in Milan, Italy, where she obtained her degree from Bocconi University. She moved to Canada in 1965, and until 1990 she was a professor of Italian literature at the University of British Columbia in Vancouver. Following her retirement, she resided in Sicily for six important years, rediscovering the deep roots in the land of her father. The experience moved her to write this book of memoirs, of a period straddling the war years and the rise of the modern European society and beyond.

Her other numerous publications are of an academic nature. She currently lives in Burnaby, B.C. with her husband.

Made in the USA
Charleston, SC
24 November 2014